# China Insights

This book series collects and presents cutting-edge studies on various issues that have emerged during the process of China's social and economic transformation, and promotes a comprehensive understanding of the economic, political, cultural and religious aspects of contemporary China. It brings together academic endeavors by contemporary Chinese researchers in various social science and related fields that record, interpret and analyze social phenomena that are unique to Chinese society, its reforms and rapid transition. This series offers a key English-language resource for researchers and students in China studies and related subjects, as well as for general interest readers looking to better grasp today's China.

The book series is a cooperation project between Springer and China Social Science Press of China.

More information about this series at http://www.springer.com/series/13591

Xiaojing Zhang • Xin Chang

# The Logic of Economic Reform in China

中国社会科学出版社
CHINA SOCIAL SCIENCES PRESS

Springer

Xiaojing Zhang
Chinese Academy of Social Sciences
Beijing, China

Xin Chang
Chinese Academy of Social Sciences
Beijing, China

ISSN 2363-7579 ISSN 2363-7587 (electronic)
China Insights
ISBN 978-3-662-47403-7 ISBN 978-3-662-47404-4 (eBook)
DOI 10.1007/978-3-662-47404-4

Library of Congress Control Number: 2015957215

Springer Heidelberg New York Dordrecht London


Printed on acid-free paper

Springer-Verlag GmbH Berlin Heidelberg is part of Springer Science+Business Media (www.springer.com)

# Preface

Modern China, since the Opium War, has dropped far behind and suffered from attacks and bullies. "Inferior technologies, systems and culture" becomes a prevailing cultural psychology among most Chinese. Changing the pattern that "China is comparatively weaker than western countries" and reinvigorating China start from cultural criticism and innovation. Since then the Chinese have begun to "open their eyes to see the whole world around" and learnt from Japan, Europe, America, and Soviet Russia. We are in tension and anxiety for long, dying to get over from being behind and bullied, poor and weak, and surpass Western powers. As it were, in the pursuit of dream of power nation and national rejuvenation for the last century, we focus on understanding and learning but do little, even nothing, to get understood. It has no significant changes even in the modernization evolvement after China's reform and opening up in 1978. Such a phenomenon is well demonstrated by a great amount of translation of western writings in the 1980s and 1990s. This is how Chinese perceives the relation between China and the world in modern times.

At the same time when the Chinese are pursuing for the dream of power nation and national rejuvenation in modern times, they are also trying to seek for DAO to rescue from national subjugation and get wealthy and powerful by "material (technology) criticism," "institutional criticism," and "cultural criticism." DAO is firstly a philosophy, of course, as well as a flag and a soul. What philosophy, what flag, and what soul are critical to resist national destruction and get wealthy and powerful? For over a century, Chinese people keep exploring and attempting in disgrace, failure, and anxiety and have undergone the phase of "western learning for practical application while Chinese learning as basis," the failure of constitutional monarchy practice, the bankruptcy of western capitalist politics, and the major frustrations of world socialist movement in the early 1990s but finally harvest Chinese revolution success, national independence, and liberation, especially combining scientific socialist theoretical logic with Chinese social development history logic together and find out a Chinese socialism modernization path—a path of socialism with Chinese characteristics. After the reform and opening up in the recent 30 years, China's socialism market economy has seen rapid development; economic, political, cultural, and social constructions have made tremendous achievements;

comprehensive national strength, cultural soft strength, and international influence have substantially improved; the socialism with Chinese characteristics has had huge success; although not perfect, the institutional systems are generally established. China, a dream catcher for the last century, is rising among the world nationalities with more confidence in unswerving path, theory, and institution.

Meanwhile, we should be aware of the long-developed perception and the cultural mental habit of learning from the West constrain Chinese from showing "historical China" and "contemporary real China" to the world, although China has risen to be one of the current world powers. Western people and nationalities, influenced by the habitual history pattern that "China is comparatively weaker than western countries," rooted in Chinese and western cultural exchange, have little knowledge of China's history and contemporary development, let alone China's development path, as well as cognition and understanding of philosophical issues such as scientificity and effectiveness of "China theory" and "China institution" on China, and their unique values and contributions to human civilization. The omission of "self-recognition display" leaves much room for malicious politicians to widespread "China collapse," "China threat," and "China national capitalism."

During the development process of "crossing a river by feeling the way over the stones," we concentrate more energy on learning from the West and understanding the world, and get used to recognize ourselves by western experience and words, but ignore "self-recognition" and "being understood." We blend ourselves into the world more forgiving and friendly but are not objectively or actually understood. Hence, justice and responsible academic and cultural researchers should undertake the important assumptions to summarize DAO of successful socialism with Chinese characteristics, narrate China stories, illustrate China experience, use international expressions, tell the world of the real China, and let the world acknowledge that western modern pattern is not the end of human history and the socialism with Chinese characteristics is also a valuable treasure of human thoughts.

Chinese Academy of Social Sciences organizes leading experts and scholars and some outside experts to write series of *China Insights*. These books introduce and summarize China path, China theories, and China institutions and contain objective description and interpretation to modern development in aspects of political system, human right, law governance, economic system, economics, finance, social administration, social security, population policy, value, religious faith, nationality policy, rural issue, urbanization, industrialization, ecology and ancient civilization, literature, and art.

These published books are expected to let Chinese readers have better understanding of China's modernization process in the last century and more rational concepts on current troubles; intensify the overall reform and national confidence; agglomerate consensus and strength for reform and development; improve foreign readers' understanding of China; and create more favorable international environment for China's development.

# Contents

# List of Figures

# List of Tables

# Introduction

China's economic reform was launched in the year 1978. Over the past 30-plus years, it has created an internationally remarkable miracle of growth. In 2013, the new Chinese government led by Xi Jinping and Li Keqiang announced to the world an outline for a new round of reform through the Decision of the CPC Central Committee on Some Major Issues Concerning Comprehensively Deepening the Reform approved at the Third Plenary Session of the 18th Central Committee of the Communist Party of China (CPC).

China's economic reform has always been forging ahead in a mass of controversies. It is still too early to provide a comprehensive description of this process. Nevertheless, more than three decades of reform have accumulated very rich experiences, from which we can glimpse the approach and the underlying grand logic of this reform.

To begin with, the reform follows a cyclical pattern. Reform usually takes place when there are no alternatives. Inertia is found inevitable in any system and institution, both in China and the world. China's reform in the late 1970s emerged when the society and economy nearly fell apart. Reform and change were desired by the whole society. It was the excitement and passion felt after one narrowly escaped death that provided the impetus for reform, which was rather incomparable. However, the impetus and bonus of reform have almost been exhausted over the 30-plus years. Nowadays, reform is at low ebb; it is the most difficult time. This is why a new round of reform needs to be initiated and a consensus of reform to be reconstructed.

Secondly, economic reform is inseparable from reform in other fields. Reform is a systemic program, which requires mutually supplementary and coordinated measures in all fields. If only economic reform is advanced, it may finally fail for the lack of support from other fields. Furthermore, partial and fragmented reforms are often in conflict and even cause institutional frictions. By its very nature, institutional reform should be promoted as a whole; otherwise it will result in huge cost for institutional operation. Therefore, China's economic reform needs to be advanced together with reforms in politics, culture, society, and ecology and hence starts a new phase of comprehensive reform.

Thirdly, the relations between reform, development, and stability should be well addressed. China's transformation and development is in fact a process in which reform, development, and stability are all guaranteed. This may have caused some sacrifice of efficiency (e.g., the slow pace of reform because of concerns over stability) but has achieved long-term and sustainable growth. Only with social stability can reform and development be continuously promoted, which in turn will lay a solid foundation for social stability. Without stability, it is impossible for reform and development to advance smoothly, and what has already been achieved may also be lost. This is why China will choose an approach of progressive reform, allow the existence of a dual system, and tolerate the resultant arbitrage and efficiency loss. These problems are frequently criticized. Such an incomplete reform is in particular blamed for the solidification of interests of some groups. Compared with the shock therapy, however, it can be found that the long-lasting stable growth of China is exactly attributable in large to this unification of reform, development, and stability so as to implement reform effectively. This three-dimensional unification is quite different from the unidimensional emphasis on efficiency in the western mainstream economics.

Fourthly, the practical logic and theoretical logic of the reform are well matched. China's reform has not followed the western mainstream theory but instead guided by the principle that practice is the sole criteria for testing truth. The practice of reform often surpasses and even revises theory. This of course does not imply that there is no theoretical logic in China's reform. The whole process has shown that it is not "by chance" that China has succeeded. Wisdom is underlying the practices of rural reform, township enterprise development, state-owned enterprise (SOE) reform, market system establishment, gradual and orderly opening up, the implementation of the high-standard Trans-Pacific Partnership (TPP) through free trade areas, and things alike. A theoretical logic goes through these practices, and these practices can be theoretically explained. This theoretical logic is that being based on China's reality and the unique initial conditions for reform, and at the same time embracing globalization and actively adapting to and keeping pace with the world trend of development. Reform advanced in this logic in various domains actually transcends the debates between the progressive approach and the radical approach.

Fifthly, top-level designs are combined with the approach of "wading across a river by feeling for stones." The dominant approach in the early period of the reform was "wading across a river by feeling for stones," because there was neither a legible blueprint nor enough experiences for reform and hence it was less feasible for top-level designing. Top-level designs have become increasingly important as the reform advances, especially when it enters "deep waters." Grassroots experiments, though locally suitable, are not systemic or nationally coordinated and therefore likely to cause fragmentation of reform. Therefore, top-level designs are necessary to comprehensively coordinate local efforts, in which theoretical preparation, overall arrangement, mechanism design, and things alike are involved. However, it is not to abandon the approach of "wading across a river by feeling for stones." The situation is very complicated at this stage of reform, therefore this approach is needed to explore new ways and accumulate experiences (e.g., for mixed ownership and

SOE reform). For major reforms that have to be accelerated but to which there are no definite solutions, it is right to encourage and support some qualified places to make experiments and hence control risks and influence within local areas.

Lastly, reform should be implemented continuously and in global competitions. There is no end to reform. This is not only applicable to China, a country without mature and fixed institutions. Reform is continuously on the way even for mature market economies such as the USA. Institutional competition and reform competition for obtaining institutional superiority will become a global normalcy. From the perspective of institutional economics, what contributes to the evolution of internal and external institutions includes not only reactive responses to international trade and flow of factors but also proactive institutional adjustments for better competing for market shares and mobilizing factors of production. Globalization has resulted in "competition of institutions (or systems)."[1] It is especially noteworthy that since the 2008 global financial crisis, rebalancing, structural readjustment, and reform have become the main theme of global development. The third and fourth plenary sessions of the 18th CPC Central Committee have set out an overall plan for China's reform; structural reform plans and long-term growth strategies have also been put forward in the USA, Europe, and Japan. A competition of reforms has been quietly started.

Whether reform can be advanced continuously is a manifestation of state capability. In *Reflections on the Revolution in France*, Edmund Burke (1970) argued that a state without the means of some change is without the means of its conservation; and without such means, it will inevitably risk losing the part it wants most to preserve in the system. This reveals at the fundamental level the impetus for reform: China's constant reform is exactly made to "preserve" the nature of socialism.

The most important logic, it can be said, is to continue China's self-reform persistently against the background of global institutional and reform competitions. Deng Xiaoping once commented in the 1980s that the meaning of China's reform is to lay a foundation for the sustainable and smooth development in the next decade and the first half of the next century. Without reform, sustainable development will be impossible. Reform shall be viewed not in terms of 3–5 years but in terms of 20 years, and the first 50 years of the next century. It must be firmly carried on.[2]

## References

Burk E (1970) Reflections on the revolution in France. Penguin Classics (1986), Harmondsworth

Deng Xiaoping (1993) Selected works of Deng Xiaoping, vol 3. China People's Publishing House, Beijing

Kasper W, Streit ME (2000) Institutional economics: social order and public policy (trans: Han Zhaohua). The Commercial Press, Beijing

---

[1] Kasper and Streit (2000).

[2] Deng Xiaoping (1993), p. 118.

# Chapter 1
# The Beginning of Reform

At the very outset, when the Third Plenary Session of the 11th Central Committee of the CPC was sounding the clarion call for reform, the Chinese government did not have a clear blueprint as to which way to go. And the chief architect of reform Deng Xiaoping had not yet finished his "top-tier design." Like Wong Kar Wai's style of filmmaking, there was no written script for China to follow in its reform. Nonetheless, "crossing the river by feeling the stones" has yielded promising results to the Chinese people.

Looking back on the inauguration of reform, we find that China's reform took off precisely at a time between the end of Cultural Revolution and the eve of social and economic collapse, and at a time when the developed economies had just experienced a decade of stagflation before Ronald Reagan and Margaret Thatcher resorted to liberalization reforms as a rescue. Meanwhile, the wave of globalization was also beginning to gather momentum, which was about to sweep the world in the coming two decades. This time, finally, China got on the train of globalization and kept up with the wave of reforms. The reform initiated in the 1970s has since changed China in a dramatic and unprecedented way.

## 1.1 China and the World in 1980

In the late 1970s and early 1980s, reform was an important keyword in the international arena. In the East, China was launching a round of marketization reforms that would bring fundamental changes to its thousands of years' history; in the West, the liberalization reforms proposed by Reagan and Thatcher were getting well underway. In fact, similar reforms were also undertaken in a number of other countries. As Martin Feldstein (2000) put it, the 1980s was a decade of major changes in economic policy across the world. What was common in these changes was the governments' decreasing role in economy. Such changes took place in the United



X. Zhang, X. Chang, *The Logic of Economic Reform in China*, China Insights,
DOI 10.1007/978-3-662-47404-4_1

States, China, from southern Chile to Beijing, Mexico and Latin America, and to Margaret Thatcher's Britain and the whole Eastern Europe and the Soviet Union.

Looking back today, it becomes apparent that a global race for reform was at full steam at that time. On the one hand, due to the breakout of Oil Crisis, the Western countries saw an end to the Golden Age of growth after WWII and were suffering from a decade of stagflation before real structural reforms were taken to bail them out. On the other hand, after the decade-long Cultural Revolution, reform and opening up became the single alternative for China. Just what a historical coincidence! Today, 30 odd years later, under the great impact of the International Financial Crisis, these countries are again in a race to rebalance and readjust their economic structures. The curtain for a global competition for reform has just been raised!

However, compared to today, the earth-shaking reform of the late 1970s can be viewed as a movement that took place at a time when China was an outsider to globalization. It was only with the deepening of reform and opening up that China was gradually integrated into the wave of globalization and became a real part of the global division-of-labor system. In fact, it was not until the 1980s that China began to establish frequent economic and trade "exchanges" with the outside world and globalization really began to gain force, heralding the next two or three decades of "great moderation" and globalization boom. China is lucky enough to have got on the train of globalization. The world should feel lucky too, for China's participation has provided a steady and strong driving force for the train.

Obviously, China is closely linked with the world. This makes it easier for us to understand why China's reform is by no means an isolated or incidental event. As will be seen, although China's reform was essentially driven by domestic factors, it could also be attributed to international factors.

A widely-held belief is that after the 10-year devastation of Cultural Revolution, China had come to the brink of a socio-economic collapse. In other words, unless fundamental reforms were undertaken from economic foundation to superstructure, China would sink into real chaos, crisis and even collapse. Reform was no longer a mere slogan, but was widely hailed by the whole society as soon as it was put forward. What we saw the acclaim for reform was exactly the excitement stemming from a rebirth from the desperate situation! A consensus on reform might have been reached in rising social expectations.

The reform was hard at the beginning: stalemate must be broken, and ice-breaking measures must be taken to counter multifold resistance. After shutting its door for a long time, China decided to take a look at the outside world. Its rigid mind yearned to be aroused by external stimuli.

In 1978 alone, 13 Chinese Vice-ministerial officials were sent abroad to visit 50 countries. After that, hundreds of ministers, governors, first secretaries of the party committee and their staff quickly followed suit. At the end of the year, when summarizing the effect of study tours, Deng Xiaoping gleefully noted: "Recently, our comrades have made some visits to other countries. The more we see, the more we realize how backward we are." For Deng, acknowledging backwardness was crucial to gaining domestic support. On December 2, 1978, he told those drafting his speech that would launch his reform and opening policy that "The basic point is:

we must acknowledge that we are backward, that many of our ways of doing things are inappropriate, and that we need to change." Overseas study tours as such reinforced many high officials' conviction that Deng's perception was correct: change must be made in China. Of all the study tours in 1978, the most far-reaching one was led by Gu Mu to Western Europe from May 2 to June 6. It became one of the three major turning points, the other two being the 11th Party Congress of CPC held in November and the Third Plenum held in December, that had prompted China's reform and opening (Vogel 2013).

The study tours are reminiscent of the Iwakura Mission that set Japan onto the road to modernization. From December 1871 to September 1873, 51 Meiji government leaders traveled by ship and rail to 15 different countries. Led by court noble Iwakura Tomomi, a top leader of the Meiji government, the mission was composed of officials from all major sectors—industry, agriculture, mining, finance, culture, education, the military, and the police. When the mission left home, Japan was essentially a closed country, and the Japanese knew little about the outside world. But after visiting the factories, mines, museums, parks, stock exchanges, railways, farms and shipyards of other countries, the members came to realize that Japan must introduce both new technologies and new organizational strategies and ways of thinking to remodel itself. The mission not only brought its members to the awareness just how far behind Japan lagged from the advanced countries, but also stroke common ground among the members about how to make change. Rather than becoming discouraged by what they saw, the officials returned home energized, excited by future prospects for Japan and eager to send more teams abroad to study in more detail.

No single group of Chinese officials ever traveled for such a long time as the Iwakura Mission. However, many separate study tours undertaken by senior officials in 1977–1980 did produce a similar influence on the Chinese mind.

The study tours achieved at least two effects. First, China realized its own backwardness. During the years when China was closing itself to the world, other countries had made remarkable progress. Hence, the question arose: since socialism is superior to capitalism, why is a socialist country lagging behind the capitalist ones? This perplexion can be reflected in one of the study tour reports: "We are a socialist society. Our system is far more superior to capitalism. However, due to inexperience and some defects in socialism building, the superiority of socialism has not been brought into full play."[1]

Second, China realized that capitalism could offer some positive experience in science and technology, capital, management, etc. This helped lay an intellectual foundation for the upcoming establishment of special economic zones (SEZs), opening up of cities, and introduction of foreign direct investment (FDI). Deng said: "It will take a very long historical period to consolidate and develop the socialist system, and it will require the persistent struggle by many generations, a dozen or even several dozens." Dozens of generations! Just what a long span of time! After all, barely 70 generations have passed since Confucius. In the Third Plenary Session

[1] Deng et al. (1979).

of the 18th Central Committee of the CPC, Xi Jinping made an explanatory speech on the Decision to the session, pointing out that it was reform and opening up that had sustained the rapid development of Chinese society and economy and had secured a relative advantage over capitalism in the past 35 years.

This indicates that to build and improve socialism with Chinese characteristics, we should always keep in mind that capitalism is competing and racing with us. System and reform competition is both an inexhaustible source for China's socio-economic development and an inevitable course in humanity's advance toward a higher stage of development.

## 1.2 Initial Conditions and Reform Options

Both domestic pressure and international "stimuli" compelled China to reform. But how to reform? Where to make breakthroughs? And what sequence should the reform follow? These questions remained largely unanswered.

The selection of reform path was closely associated with the initial conditions. There were two distinctive initial conditions (or reform backgrounds) in China: the planned economic system and a poor backward agrarian country. These two conditions determined that China's reform must address the dual challenges of transformation and development. Whereas the former refers to an institutional change from planned economy to market economy, the latter indicates a transformation from an agrarian country to an industrial one.

First, the pre-reform Chinese economy was typically a planned economy. It had the following characteristics: (1) predominance of public sector in ownership structure. Essentially, building the planned economic system in socialist countries is a process of publicizing and nationalizing the means of production. Before the reform, the Chinese economic system was characteristically "large in size and collective in nature" (一大二公) in terms of ownership structure, and met the common standards of traditional planned economy. Within the public sector, urban industries were classified into three major categories depending on the degree of public ownership: "whole-people" owned, state owned, and collectively owned. In rural areas, state and collective ownerships of land were more dominant. However, the peasants did not have full collective ownership right, as they had to fulfill the mandatory unified purchasing and production plans of agricultural products designated by the state. Rural land was managed collectively on the basis of state ownership, and the peasants only had the right to use it. After the socialist transformation in 1956, the share of public sector in national income exceeded 90 %, while the share of individual and private sectors dropped to 7.1 % and less than 0.1 %, respectively. The completion of socialist transformation indicated that China shifted toward a full planned economy in both ownership structure and adjustment. (2) Direct mandatory administration over economic activities by the state. A major characteristic of centrally planned economy is that the state or government was a central agent in economic operations, while the enterprises, which only carried out given production plans, became an appendage to the government. The state mainly controlled and managed economic operations through economic development plans for a particular period of time. It established special economic planning departments to draft development plans, and exercised complete control over the enterprises through indices, planning parameters, practical assessments, etc. The performance of the enterprises was reflected in their implementation of the plans and the preferences of the authority. A highly planned and mandatory economy required a detailed planning of all aspects of economic operations. However, due to the insufficiency of information, the plans were mostly rigid and less flexible. (3) A highly centralized economic decision power. The state was not only responsible for the macro-level resource allocation, but also made micro-level plans for the income and expense of enterprises and individuals to achieve resource allocation among micro economic agents. This resulted in the fact that except the state or government, micro economic agents were practically non- existent. (4) Planned allocation of social resources. A core mechanism of planned resource allocation is to use administrative/mandatory means as a replacement of price mechanism. Under the centrally planned economic system, the market's role in resource allocation through price mechanism was minimized. (5) Non-price characteristics of transactions. In institutional economics, transaction is the most general and prevalent economic activity in mankind's economic behavior. Whereas transactions in market economy are typically achieved through the price mechanism, those in planned economy are replaced by administrative instructions, and the objects of transaction are deprived of their commodity attributes.

Second, China has a distinctively dual economic structure, as can be reflected in the dualisms between rural and urban areas, and between workers and peasants. Development economists believe that given the differences in productivity between agriculture and industry, rural industrialization should be followed to eliminate the biased development of dual economy. A review of the economic history of advanced countries reveals that rural industrialization constitutes an important part of modernization. Since industrialization is crucial to the transformation from traditional agrarian to industrial and even post-industrial societies, its degree is often regarded as an important measure for the modernization level of a country or region. So far as China is concerned, rural industrialization is also an inevitable course of development. Therefore, the reform and opening-up and the development of socialist market economy in China can, to some extent, be viewed as a transformation of its dual economic structure. On the one hand, a large number of rural surplus labor keep flowing into modern sectors (e.g. industrial sectors), significantly increasing the efficiency of resource allocation. On the other hand, rural industrialization also enables China to make new breakthroughs in the industrialization and urbanization levels.

Both the planned economic system and the dual economic structure determined that China was facing dual challenges in its reform: transformation and development. The precedence of rural reforms over urban ones and the emergence of rural enterprises tuned out to be viable options to meet those challenges. After all, Chinese rural economy was less planning than urban economy at that time, and developing township-village enterprises (TVEs) was the most "convenient" way of rural industrialization.

Of course, China's reform should also comply with the other principle: utilitarianism. Reform must be started in those areas where situation was getting imminent and might encounter the least resistance. At that time, the worst situation occurred in the rural sector, and the least resistance came from that area, too.

The shattering rural economy, particularly the stagnation of agricultural income over the past decades, was a main driving force of earlier policy making. As of the late 1970s, planned economy had not yet solved the persistent problem of grain supply. In the first half of the 1970s, the number of families with insufficient grain supply kept growing, while grain dependence and inter-provincial grain transportation was on the decline, both of which were indicative of the economic system that had been driven to the brink of a serious grain crisis. And there were no signs of improvement. In 1973–1980, China imported an annual average of over 6 million tons of grain, a large part of which was wheat. In the years of highest imports, grain accounted for a huge proportaion of national imports, such that when China wanted to introduce machinery and technologies to achieve leap-frog industrial development, the rural sector was unable to reduce its industrial population, imposing a serious restriction on the development of the country. Against this background, therefore, it would not come as a shock that China's reform should have started with the rural areas. In 1979, Chen Yun suggested giving top priority to agriculture while reducing the investment rate across the country in the national economic plan. This created a policy background for the shift of resource allocation to the rural sector. Thus, tolerating reform pilots in the rural areas became an inevitable choice for China.

Another important fact about China at the initial stage of reform was that China was a typical agrarian country, in which 80 % of its labor force was living in the rural areas. Due partly to the large population with limited arable land, and partly to the implementation of the purchasing plan of agricultural products and the price system in pursuit of industrialization in the past three decades, most peasants had a lower-level living standard and little access to certain social welfares provided by the country. This made it easier for them to shake off the yokes of the old system, engage in market- oriented economic activities, and develop new economic relations (Fan Gang 1996). This is a fundamental difference from the Soviet Union and other Eastern European countries, in which a large part of their population worked in state-owned sectors with full access to national benefits. Why did the reform start with the rural areas? And why was it more easily implemented in the rural areas? The reason lies in the smaller resistance.

Meanwhile, China encouraged the development of township-village enterprises. In particular, it allowed such enterprises to enter into profit-oriented industries. This helped ensure the deepening of rural reforms. Later, as things turned out, the development of township-village enterprises became the key to the success of China's reform throughout the 1980s. By 1989, the output value of township-village enterprises had made up 25 % of the total product of society. Of this, the total output value of village- township industries made up 30 % of the national industrial output value. On June 12, 1987, Deng remarked enthusiastically about the achievements made by the TVEs when interviewing Yugoslavian visitors. He said: "Our greatest success—and it is one we had by no means anticipated—has been the emergence of a large number of enterprises run by villages and townships. They were like a new force that just came into being spontaneously. These enterprises engage in the most diverse endeavors, including both manufacturing and trade." The international academic community is also positive about the role of township-village enterprises, believing that it underlies the innovativity of Chinese economic reform and the success of Chinese economic growth.

## 1.3 The Reform Path Reflects a Consistency between the Logic of Theory and the Logic of Practice

For many people today, the Chinese path to reform achieved an "accidental" success. But, in fact, as we will show below, the logic behind the reform practice is supported by theoretical explanations, and is thus consistent with the logic of theory. The Chinese success is by no means "accidental."

Regarding the great rural reforms, for instance, some scholars maintain that China only made some simple and micro-level adjustments in the shift toward the dual-track price system. However, the seemingly simple dual-track system, in which peasants could sell their agricultural crops at a market price after fulfilling the duty of selling quota at a state-fixed price, had greatly emancipated the productivity of the rural areas.

Huang Yasheng (2013) argues that Western economists praise the dual-track price system because its mechanics are straightforward, but they have ignored a precondition for the system to work: peasants had to be confident that the planned targets would not be ratcheted up later. But obtaining the peasants' confidence was not an easy thing, for the "ratcheting effect" prevailed in an unrestrained system. That is, the planners would ratchet up the planned targets in accordance with the previous performance. The success of the dual-track price system in China indicates that China had avoided the "ratcheting effect." As a matter of fact, the dual-track price system was neither novel nor Chinese. The Soviet Union tried for many times but failed. The Chinese and Soviet experiences suggest that the success of the dual-track system lies in exactly whether a political system can avoid the "ratcheting effect." And the dual-track system, for its simple or complicated technological mechanics, is a secondary or insignificant factor. The Chinese leadership in Deng's era committed itself to not ratcheting up the targets and did so credibly. This is the most fundamental difference between China and the Soviet Union in the reform of the dual-track system. Therefore, it was the politics of the Deng Xiaoping era, rather than the mechanics of the reform, that accounted for the Chinese success.

The other difference between the two countries rests on the economic structure. Chinese reforms started in the rural areas. And China was far more agrarian than the Soviet Union when that country began its own reform program. Other conditions being equal, rural China has always been more predisposed toward entrepreneurship and capitalism than urban China. Today, many of the best private manufacturing firms are not located in Beijing or Shanghai, but originated in then-agrarian provinces in the 1980s such as Zhejiang, Hunan, Anhui, and Sichuan. The institutional reason for this was that rural economy is susceptible to a number of arbitrary factors such as weather and soil, causing rural China to be less conducive to planning than urban China. Politically speaking, the Cultural Revolution was primarily a political shock that cleansed urban China of the vestiges of capitalism, but there were still some free market activities in rural China, which paved the way for the success of rural reforms in the Deng era. A good case in point here is the land-contracting system. However, for the land contracting reforms to work, economic agents need to have some knowledge of residual claims. That knowledge was still extant in rural China (probably because there were still some private plots in the rural areas), but absent in the urban areas. Functionally, the vestiges of free market activities in rural China acted as a policy multiplier that amplified the effects of economic reforms. This explains why many reforms that had elicited a huge supply response in China and Vietnam completely failed in the more industrialized Soviet Union.

It is thus evident that the success of China's reform did have something to do with its peculiar initial conditions. Such conditions include: the decentrality of Chinese economic plans, the support of growing rural entrepreneurship, the dispersion of massive manufacturing machinery, and the availability of commercial information, technical knowledge and funds raised by overseas Chinese. What is more, institutional changes, market competition, financial pressure, innovation and the ongoing reform also formed a positive cycle.

It is worth noting that in the early period of reform, there was not a mature theoretical preparation and top-tier design in place about where to reform, how to reform, and whether to adopt a gradual or radical attitude toward the reform. Plus, as China just opened its door, it had little access to information on the outside world and still less foreign experience to learn from. The newly acquainted foreign experts could only render their opinions for "reference" purposes and were far from playing a decisive role. Furthermore, the Chinese issue was far more complicated than what could be inferred from foreign experience or theoretical economic models. All these initial conditions made it particularly difficult for China to "design" the reform. In retrospect, however, we discern a high consistency between the logic of theory and the logic of practice of the reform. Such a consistency is not a simple coincidence, but the source of success of the Chinese attempt at crossing the river by feeling the stones in constant error trials and innovations. It is a combined result of the reform architect's wisdom and the people's initiative.

## 1.4 The Wisdom of Reform: "Playing the Edge Ball" and "Crossing the River by Feeling the Stones"

Turning back to China and tracing it back further, we find the Chinese effort to explore socialism and reform did not start overnight, but had gradually built up over a long period of time. From the 1950s, a number of reform proposals were introduced to address the issues with the centralized planned economy. The Soviet Union and other Eastern European countries also developed systematic theories based on their own reform experiences (e.g. the Polish economist Wlodzimierz Brus' decentralization theory and the Czech economist Ota Sik's model of planning and market). However, none of them really tackled the issue: Is socialism compatible with market economy? Or is there natural antagonism between the two? Deng Xiaoping answered the question. In 1979, he said: "Socialism can also have a market economy." And in his 1992 "Southern Tour" talks, he further explained that planning and market forces are not the essential difference between socialism and capitalism, and that planning and market forces are both ways of controlling economic activity. On October 12, 1992, the 14th Party Congress of the CPC officially announced in its report the new objective of developing a market economy under the socialist system.

Practice often precedes theory. Before the socialist theory of market economy was fully elucidated and officially recognized, practice had already started. But as the old Chinese saying goes, "If the name is not correct, the words will not ring true." This indicates that much of the reform practice was running the risk of "incorrect names" and was promoted in a way of "playing the edge ball" of the system.

There were three basic contexts for China's transition from planned economy to market economy: a centrally-controlled hierarchical constraint system, the Soviet Union serving as the only model that realized the ideal of socialism, and the primacy of policy over system in authority. Against these contexts, it would be extremely hard to make important and once-and-for-all system breakthroughs unless violent means were used, as in the case of the Soviet Union. However, history has proven the inefficiency of such means. The viable option now left for China was to take advantage of policy resiliency or flexibility. A typical example was the Regulations on Several Issues in Current Rural Economic Policy, also known as the "Provincial Six Articles", released by the Anhui provincial government. In the Regulations, terms of "developing different production responsibility systems in accordance with different kinds of farm work," "implementing the distribution system according to one's work," etc., could all be understood from different points of view. It was precisely from the positive point of view that the reformists interpreted and developed the policies, thereby promoting the reform. There were both rational and irrational elements in the existing systems and policies. In the process of "playing the edge ball," China was able to distinguish the rational from the irrational, and promoted the rational while abolishing the irrational. In 1979, the State Council issued the No. 74 document (State Release [1980]), calling for a major development of commune and brigade enterprises, and requiring that management bureaus be set up in all provinces, principalities and counties to manage the enterprises. But as the commune and brigade enterprises grew, they came into a severe conflict with the existing system. For example, Lushi County (Henan Province) built a tung oil plant to purchase the tung oil seeds produced by the commune peasants, which, however, ran into fierce conflicts with the local grain supply and marketing system. The lawsuit became so widely known that it aroused the attention of Deng Xiaoping. Since the peasants strongly supported the new policy, the State Council soon released the notice to cancel the Ministry of Food and the All-China Federation of Supply and

Marketing Cooperatives. But of course, there were also negative examples in the use of the skill. In the early period of the reform, due to the fuzziness of policies, smuggling was rampant in the development of export-oriented economy and the establishment of special economic zones. In response, the central government quickly took counter-measures to ensure economic development. The "playing-the-edge-ball" skill displayed its superiority in both positive and negative aspects. In 1983, when Liang Lingguang, governor of Guangdong Province, recalled the history of reforms in Guangdong, he said: "A flexible grasp and adoption of the special policies and flexible measures endowed by the central government, innovation and exploration, these are essential to Guangdong's one step further than other provinces in reform and opening up."

Similarly, "crossing the river by feeling the stones" was another skill used by China in the early period of reform.

At the beginning of the reform, the Chinese government did not have a macro blueprint or top-tier design in mind, but rather explored the way by trying the errors and "crossing the river by feeling the stones." In December 1980, Chen Yun spoke at a working conference of the Central Committee: "We need reform, but we must take steady steps…It is more crucial to begin reform with small-scale trials and constantly summarize the experience from these trials. That is to say, 'we cross the river by first feeling the stones underneath'" (*Collected Works of Chen Yun*, vol. 3, p. 279): Deng Xiaoping agreed readily with Chen's theory of "crossing the river by feeling the stones" and developed it by proposing ideas of "being bold to try and daring to break" and "having the guts to blaze a bloody new trail (of reform)". "Crossing the river by feeling the stones" is a metaphorical way of constantly summarizing experience in bold experiments. It played such an important guiding role in emancipating people's mind and promoting the reform that it has become a classic buzzword on the lips of Chinese.

In retrospect, China employed the skill of "crossing the river by feeling the stones" in the reforms of the dual-track system, the "crash through" of price system, as well as opening up. It has produced both positive and negative experiences. For instance, the dual-track system caused a massive speculation in quota and IOU issuance. The price "crash through" in the late 1980s also failed. Summarizing the experience from the reform, Deng regretted that Shanghai had not been included in the first batch of special economic zones. Examples as such show that when no established blueprint or prior experience was available at the beginning, "crossing the river by feeling the stones" was a wise and utilitarian choice. It was exactly in constant error trials that China started its reform and pushed it forward. But of course, when reform turned to a new stage of development and got more complicated, it required the coordination and support of concurrent reforms in various fields. At this time, an overall plan or top-tier design of the reform became necessary. Meanwhile, with the accumulation of reform practices, and with the clarification of the prospective reform blueprint, it seemed ripe time to work out a top-tier design. China needed to combine the grass-roots initiative of "crossing the river by feeling the stones" with full theoretical preparations and top-tier arrangements to avoid detours and promote the reform.

## References

Deng Liqun, Ma Hong, Sun Shangqing, Wu Jiajun (1979) Thinking after visiting Japan. China Social Sciences Press
Fan Gang (1996) Political economics of progressive reform. Shanghai Yuandong Press
Feldstein MS (eds) (2000) American economic policy in the 1980s. Economic Science Press
Huang Yasheng (2013) How does China's economy take off. Comp Econ Soc Syst 2
Vogel EF (2013) Deng Xiaoping and the transformation of China. SDX Joint Publishing Company

# Chapter 2
# Crossing the River by Feeling the Stones

The reform of China's economic system as a whole was in the early period largely featured by "destruction," supplemented by some "construction." At this stage, approaches such as "Crossing the river by feeling the stones," "stimulus-response," and try and error were adopted, in an order from the "outside" to the "inside," from the easy to the difficult. That is, places or fields subject to the strictest control of the planned economy were bypassed. Rather than addressing the most difficult parts first, the reform was advanced wherein breakthroughs could be most easily made. It extended gradually from where traditionally external to traditionally internal but peripheral to the system and then to the whole system, especially the center. Such an order and approaches were adopted out of the following considerations.

Firstly, China is a country with a large population, a vast territory and an unevenly developed economy. Great gaps in resilience and receptivity exist between urban and rural areas, coastal and inland regions, and state-owned and non-state-owned economies. It determines that it is impossible for reforms in all the fields to march forward together; instead, they need to forge ahead separately and progressively.

Secondly, China's reform involves all the fields. Such a complicated, large project determines that reform cannot be completed overnight in all the sub-systems. Rather, it needs to be implemented and deepened progressively, with carefully chosen parts in which to make breakthroughs.

Lastly, China's reform, with the establishment of a socialist market economy as the goal, often has few ready theories or specific experiences to refer to. Therefore, it is necessary to mobilize the endogenous or spontaneous driving forces for reform among the diverse socio-economic subjects, enlarge steadily and effectively the participation of the grassroots and the public, and facilitate bottom-up reforms through grassroots experiments in order to reduce reform risks.



X. Zhang, X. Chang, *The Logic of Economic Reform in China*, China Insights,
DOI 10.1007/978-3-662-47404-4_2

## 2.1 The Rural Reform Initiative

Agriculture is the foundation of national economy, especially in China. In the early reform period, the rural people accounted for 80 % of the whole Chinese population. It would be impossible for the national economy as a whole to develop rapidly without developing agriculture and mobilizing the initiative of such a large number of farmers. Meanwhile, collective economy was predominant in the rural areas. Compared with cities dominated by state-owned economy, they were a relatively weak link in the planned economy and the most easily broken part. As a result, the reform of China's economic system inevitably started from the countryside.

### *2.1.1 The Micro-level Management System Reform in Rural Areas*

The rural reform started from the management system reform arising from changes in the rural land relations. Put specifically, the collective management pattern, characterized by "three-level (people's communes, production brigades, and production teams) ownership, with production teams as the basis," was gradually broken, and established was the household management system of contracted responsibility linking remuneration to output.

At the turn of summer to autumn in 1978, the Anhui Province was hit by a very serious drought that had not been seen in a century, which devastated everyday life. The Anhui Provincial Party Committee then made a decision that farmers could borrow land that was unlikely to be collectively cultivated and harvest what they would cultivate, and the state would not monopolize the sale of grains. This policy of "borrowing land to cultivate" provided incentives to agricultural production, and triggered off the practice of contracting output quotas to production teams or households in some areas.

The Xiaogang Production Team in Fengyang County of Anhui was a leading role model of this contracting practice in China. In the summer of 1978, most of the 100-plus people in the 20 households had to beg for a living because of the drought. To get out of poverty, the farmers from 18 households in Xiaogang Village voluntarily took the risk of making such a written statement at the end of that year: "Here we divide the land to each household, with the signature of the head of every household. If this can be allowed in the future, we each promise to hand in grain tax of the whole year, and no more ask for money or food from the state. If this cannot be allowed, we carders are willing to take whatever punishment: being imprisoned or killed. The village members also promise to raise our children until they are 18 years old." In this statement were put down 18 red fingerprints, tragic and stirring. In that same year, the grain outputs of this village totaled 66 tons, equaling the sum of outputs during 1966–1970.

Xiaogang Village's contracting practice, which allowed farmers to "turn over what is required to the state and the collective and keep the remaining to themselves," broke the old system of the planned economy in rural areas, and started the process of establishing household responsibility system around China. In 1978, there were 1,200 production teams in Anhui adopting such a contract system; that number jumped to 38,000 in the following year, representing 10 % of the total in this province. And by the end of 1980, 70 % production teams had already adopted this system. In the meanwhile, this contract system was developed, overtly or covertly, in Sichuan, Guizhou, Gansu, Inner Mongolia and Henan. In the autumn of 1980, 20 % production teams in China had adopted this system; this percentage increased to 50 % at the end of 1981.

This contract system created and spontaneously spread by farmers interrupted traditional rural management practice. This great initiative obtained support from the top Chinese leadership. The first "No. 1 Document" about rural economic policy issued by the CPC in January 1982 made a summary of the fast-growing rural reform, and explicitly announced that the various forms of household responsibility system "were all production responsibility systems of socialist collective economy, and reflected the strong desire of hundreds of millions of farmers to develop socialist agriculture based on the reality of the Chinese countryside." It also declared that "it will be long-term policy for the collective economy to implement a production responsibility system." The "No. 1 Document" in 1983 further made it clear that the household responsibility system "is a great innovation of Chinese farmers under the CPC leadership, and a new development of the Marxist theory of agricultural cooperation in the practice of China." The approval and promise of the top CPC leadership stabilized farmers' institutional expectations and further expanded the household responsibility system. This system was practiced in 98 % rural collectives in China in late 1983.

The household responsibility system has overcome disadvantages of the highly centralized management in collective production, such as the widespread phenomenon of "free riding." As a result, rural households have really become independent operation entities and claimers of part of residuals, which provides institutional stimulus for farmers and reduces supervision costs. To strengthen the stimulus for farmers to continuously invest in land, the land contract term was constantly extended during the household responsibility practice. The term was at first a period of 1–3 years, which was extended to 15 years in 1984. In 1993, it was decided that the first round of land contracts shall be prolonged for another 30 years after the contract expired. Thereafter, legal means were sought to protect rural households' rights in land contract and use in order to establish stable land contract relations. In particular, the release and enforcement of the Rural Contract Law in 2003 "entitles Chinese farmers with the long-term and guaranteed rights to use their contracted land," which marks that the rural land contract system in China has genuinely embarked on a road of rule of law. This continuity and stability in policy has increased the political credibility of reform.

The rural management system reform, with the adoption of the household responsibility system as the main content, has remarkably liberated rural productivity, released a large amount of surplus labor, and led to the surge of township enterprises, which became a one-time mainstay supporting the rapid economic growth of China. Statistics show that during the short period of 1979–1984, all the major agricultural products in China achieved large increases in output. For example, the output of grains increased by 33.6 %, with an annual rise of 4.95 %; the output of cottons increased by 188.8 %, with an annual rise of 19.33 %; the output of oil plants increased by 128.2 %, with an annual rise of 14.75 %; and the output of meat increased by 79.9 %, with an annual rise of 10.28 %. Such notable output increases were closely related to the practice of the household responsibility system. Empirical research has shown that almost half of the output growth rate of 42.2 % in China's planting sector during 1978–1984 was attributable to reform-caused productivity change, which, in turn, almost totally resulted from the implementation of the household responsibility system.[1]

### 2.1.2 *The Rapid Growth and Timely Transformation of Township Enterprises*

Starting from the 1980s, surpluses arising from the rural household responsibility system and rural product price adjustments and the labor released by increased rural productivity provided important capital and labor resources for township enterprises. At the same time, the relaxation of control of the traditional planned allocation system rendered more opportunities for township enterprises outside this system to obtain major raw materials and access markets. Township enterprises developed rapidly in this context. During 1981–1991, township enterprises increased by 26.6 %, 11.2 % and 29.6 % in terms of number, employee and total output value respectively. The annual growth rate for the total output value was three times that of state-owned enterprises (SOEs) in the same period. In 1993, the output of township enterprises accounted for 38.1 % of the total industrial output. Township enterprises thus became an important driving force for China's high-speed economic growth from the 1980s to the early 1990s, and for some time a main channel for the transfer of surplus rural labor. Therefore, it is argued by some researchers that the emergence of township enterprises is one of the greatest achievements of China's reform.[2]

Because of the unique historical background, China's township enterprises, especially those with a collective ownership (represented by enterprises in South Jiangsu), have from the outset kept a close dependency relations with the community (township) government. In particular, during the establishment of township

[1] For empirical studies, see McMillan et al. (1989), Fan Shenggen (1991), Lin (1992), Wen (1993), Huang and Rozelle (1996).

[2] Sun (1997).

enterprises, the community government was responsible for the initial investment of factors such as capital, land and labor, and appointed "able persons" to head the enterprises. This management pattern of cooperation between community governments and local enterprises is labeled by some scholars as "local state corporatism." [3] China's township enterprises are also regarded by some as a "hybrid organizational form": being both local administrative organizations and market organizations simultaneously. This ownership is also viewed as an intermediate form between state socialism and market economy, as well as a result of weak market structure and incomplete transition to the market economy.[4] These enterprises are also sometime referred to as "vaguely defined cooperatives" or "community organizations."[5] Historically, such a unique ownership structure was indeed more efficient than that of traditional SOEs. It is estimated that during 1980–1992, the annual TFP growth rate of the state-owned industry was 2.5 %, compared to 7.15 % of the collective industry (including township enterprises).[6] The high efficiency of collectively-owned township enterprises has attracted great interests from scholars both in and beyond China. Various theoretical frameworks, including the incomplete contract theory, mechanism design theory, and principal-agent theory, are used to examine these enterprises from different perspectives, especially the aspects compatible with the transitional economy.[7]

In an incomplete market, this "obscure ownership" of township enterprises was useful or can be viewed as a rational choice to cope with the special institutional environment during the transitional period. Nevertheless, with the advancement of marketization, township enterprises have gradually lost the advantage of obscure ownership and troubled by its increasingly obvious disadvantages. The most salient problems included ambiguous definition of the boundary of rights and risk-taking, and insufficient stimulus and supervision. In the meantime, the closedness of township enterprises which tended to allocate resources within communities also impeded the trans-regional flow of factors and the formation of a unified market. Against this background, township enterprises have started the wide-range "second institutional innovation" since the mid-to-late 1990s focusing on the clarification of ownership. According to statistics of the Ministry of Agriculture of China, 95 % of the 1.68 million township enterprises had carried out various forms of ownership reform by 2006, with 200,000 turning to joint stock or stock cooperative enterprises, and 1.39 million to private enterprises. This marks the completion of the transition of the special organizational form of township enterprises, and reflects in a vivid way the progressiveness of China's reform.

[3] Oi (1992).

[4] Nee (1992)

[5] Weitzman and Xu (1994).

[6] Jefferson et al. (1995)).

[7] See Naughton (1994), Chang and Wang (1994), Walder (1995), Li Daokui (1995), Tian (1995), Che and Qian (1998).

### 2.1.3 Respect for Farmers' Reform Initiative

During the past 30 years of rural reform, the basic point of departure has been respecting the will, protecting the interests and mobilizing the initiative of farmers. Paying respect for the will of the people, a guideline emphasized by the Decision on Some Issues about Facilitating Agricultural Development approved in the Third Plenary Session of the 11th CPC Central Committee, has always played a crucial role throughout the whole process of rural reform. These principles, i.e., putting people first and assigning priority to farmers' choices during the making of rural policies, and evaluating these choices in accordance with whether they can improve productivity, comprehensive national power and people's livelihood, have given full play to the creativity of farmers. From the outset of the rural reform, Chinese top leadership has established the basic principles of economically guaranteeing the material interests and politically respecting the democratic rights of farmers. Therefore, some most basic and significant issues, such as those about business entity, the direction of reform, and institutional construction, have been gradually clarified, with farmers' innovation coming first, followed by the summarization, normalization and promotion by the leadership. This is also true for the three important achievements of most remarkable significance in institutional innovation during the rural reform, namely the two-layered management system based on family contract operation and the combination of centralization and decentralization, the rise of township enterprises, and the construction of rural grassroots democratic system. They first emerged out of the experiments of farmers, and were summarized and normalized by the Chinese leadership, and then finally generalized to become theories, policies and institutions. It shows that farmers are not only the subject of agriculture and other rural economic activities, but also the subject of rural reform. Allowing farmers to break away from ideological and institutional fetters and try institutional innovation, it is fair to say, is one of the basic experiences for the rural reform to go smoothly.[8]

In short, the years from 1979 to 1983 were a period of great changes. In this period, the agricultural management pattern was transformed from unanimous collective management to two-layered management combining both centralization and decentralization, with household management becoming an important level of agricultural production. The rural reform greatly advanced rural productivity and served as a role model for the reform of the whole economic system. Marked by the Decision of the CPC Central Committee on the Economic System Reform released in October 1984, the major battle field was turned from the rural to urban areas.

[8]About the summarization of this experience, please see Chen (1999).

## 2.2 Enterprise Reform and Development of Non-public Economy

The marginal evolution of China's reform is, in a sense, strongly manifested in the development of market entities. It was easier to develop new economic sectors than to directly reform the old system. And the system of non-state-owned economy, which matched better with the market economy, differed greatly with that of state-owned economy. As a result, China did not start with making major changes to the existing state-owned economy in the early years of the reform. Instead, it chose to facilitate the rapid growth of non-state-owned economy. Through competition and demonstration effects, creating favorable conditions, and allowing the opening and transfer of ownership, China facilitated the reform of state-owned economy. This progressive advancement has gradually changed SOEs under the planned economy into micro-level business entities meeting the demand of socialist market economy.

### *2.2.1 The Development of Non-public Economy*

In the early years of China's reform and opening up, some self-employed people and private entrepreneurs began to break through the fetters of the planned economy to seek the space for survival and development. They were innovative, adventurous, hard- working and willing to make reformations, and hence became the forerunner of China's reform. Having gradually recognized the potential of reform in individual and private economy, the Chinese leadership begun to progressively ease the previously suppressive policy towards individual and private economy, and accepted and legitimized their existence and development. As the reform deepened, they continuously provided favorable conditions to encourage the development of individual and private economy and made consistent efforts to help them equally engage in market competition.

China's policy towards non-public economy has undergone four stages of evolution since the reform was launched in 1978.

Stage I: 1978–1984, allowing the existence and development of individual economy. It was stipulated in the Constitution of the People's Republic of China approved in 1982 that "The individual economy of urban and rural working people, operated within the limits prescribed by law, is a complement to the socialist public economy. The state protects the lawful rights and interests of the individual economy. The state guides, helps and supervises the individual economy by exercising administrative control." Individual economy was hence legitimatized.

#### 2.2.1.1 Feature

The Emergence of Individual Economy

At the beginning of the reform, China was under immense pressures because a large number of *zhiqing* (educated youth) returned to the city and the urban unemployed accumulated to seven to eight millions. In February 1979, the State Administration for Industry and Commerce convened a conference of heads of local administrations, the first of its kind after the end of the "Cultural Revolution," in which it was proposed to recover and develop individual economy. It made a report to the CPC Central Committee and the State Council, suggesting that "considering market demands of a region, local authorities shall approve, on the precondition that permission of related administrations in charge is obtained, idle labor with formal *hukou* to engage in self- employed work such as repair, service and handiwork; but employment of workers shall be forbidden." In March of this year, this report was approved by the CPC Central Committee and the State Council and dispatched to all regions in China. This is the first report about individual economy approved by the CPC Central Committee and the State Council. Despite various limitations, in particular the prohibition of employment of workers, this report gave public permission to the development of individual economy. It was exactly by the end of this year that the self-employed increased to 310,000, more than twice the number in 1978. In August 1980, the CPC Central Committee held a nationwide labor employment conference, putting forward that "with the overall planning and guidance of the state, a policy shall be implemented which allows employment recommended by the labor department, employment through voluntary organization, and self-employment." Self-employment means work in individual economy. As a result, individual economy in both urban and rural China grew rapidly. At the end of 1980, people engaged in individual economy totaled 806,000, more than doubled compared with the last year. The Sixth Plenary Session of the 11th CPC Central Committee adopted in June 1981 the Resolutions on Some Historical Issues of the Party since the Founding of the People's Republic of China, stating that "state-run economy and collective economy are the basic economic forms of China; individual economy of laborers within a certain range is a necessary complement to the public economy." This is by far the earliest publicly published CPC central document that can be found using the expression of "necessary complement." In October 1981, released was the document Some Decisions of the CPC Central Committee and the State Council on Creating More Opportunities, Reinvigorating Economy and Solving Urban Employment Problems. With the aim of developing productivity, this document endeavored to eradicate the residual influence of the "leftism" in economic systems and legitimize individual economy. It announced that "self-employed laborers are socialist laborers in China. Their work is as necessary to the construction of socialism and glorious as that of employees in state-run and collective enterprises. They should be treated equally with the latter in social and political status." By the end of 1981, urban individual economy in China had covered 1.83 million households and 2.27 self- employed people, more than twice the number of 1980.

Stage II: 1984–1992, allowing the existence and development of private economy. It was proclaimed in the 13th CPC National Congress in 1987 that "It is determined by the reality of productivity at the primary stage of socialism to develop economy of various ownerships with public ownership as the main body, and even allow the existence and growth of private economy. Only this way can we promote the increase of productivity." And "The development of other economic components other than ownership by the whole people is not too much, but too inadequate. We shall continue to encourage the development of urban-rural cooperative economy, individual economy and private economy." Thereupon the 1988 Amendments to the Constitution prescribed that "The state permits the private economy to exist and develop within the limits prescribed by law. The private economy is a complement to the socialist public economy. The state protects the lawful rights and interests of the private economy, and exercises guidance, supervision and control over it." The legitimacy of the existence and development of private economy was thus clearly affirmed.[9]

Stage III: 1992–2002, gradually endowing non-public economy the equal status to participate in the market competition, and clarifying the important status and role of the various forms of non-public economy in the socialist market economy. The 14th CPC National Congress in 1992 again confirmed the necessity of establishing an ownership structure composed of multiple economic sectors. The Decision on Some Issues of Establishing Socialist Market Economic System, which was adopted in the Third Plenary Session of the 14th CPC Central Committee in 1993, made it clear that "the state creates conditions for all kinds of ownerships to equally engage in market competition, and treat all types of enterprises equally." In 1997, the 15th CPC National Congress summarized the experience in the ownership reform over the past two decades, and pointed out that "it is a basic economic system of China at the primary stage of socialism to take the public ownership as the main body and allow the co-development of economic sectors of diverse ownerships"; and that "Non- public economy is an important component of the socialist market economy. We shall continue to encourage and exercise guidance over non-public sectors of economy such as individual economy and private economy in order for them to develop healthily." This is fundamentally different with the traditional socialist theoretical explanations which excluded non-public economy from the socialist economic system. It changed the traditional thought that only public ownership was socialist, integrated multiple ownerships into socialism, and brought non-public economy from outside to inside the socialist economic system. The status of non-public economy as a complement was raised to be an important component of and playing an important role in the national economy. This marks a great breakthrough to the traditional socialist conception of ownership. In the 1999 Amendments to the Constitution, it was prescribed that "At the primary stage of socialism, the state adheres to the basic economic system with public ownership as the main body and economic sectors of diverse ownerships developing together." It also stipulated that

[9] From the second half of 1988 onwards, the development of private economy which had been legitimized was halted for some time because of changes in the situation.

"non-public economic sectors such as individual economy and private economy, operated within the limits prescribed by the law, are an important component of the socialist market economy"; and that "the state protects the lawful rights and interests of individual economy and private economy." This signals a change in the status of non-public economy: from being exclude from to being included in the socialist economic system.

Stage IV: 2002-present, further improving the policy environment for non-public economy. The 2004 Amendments to the Constitution, as the fundamental law of the country, strengthened the "encouragement" and "support" to non-public economy. Some Opinions on Encouraging, Supporting and Guiding the Development of Individual, Private and Other Non-public Sectors of Economy, the first governmental document released in 2005, indicated a change in the policy towards non-public economy, that is, from separate supportive policies to a systemic framework of supportive policies. In particular, with the aim of creating an institutional environment for fair competition, this document made explicit stipulations about the access of non-public economy into some important fields including monopolized industries. In 2007, the 17th CPC National Congress proposed to provide equal protection to real rights in order to give rise to a new pattern of equal competition and mutual advancement between economic sectors of diverse ownerships. The "equal" legal protection and "equal" economic competition became major pillars for promoting the development of non-public economy, further helping to realize equal opportunities in market access and financing of non-public economy. On this basis, Some Opinions on Encouraging and Guiding the Healthy Development of Private Investment was released in 2010, further expanding the scope and range for private investment, and making it clear to create a market environment for the fair competition and equal access of non-public economy.

It should be noted that during the transitional period, the market mechanism is still in a process of development, the investment environment remains unstable, and both the market and policy risks exist. To stabilize investment expectations and provide genuine incentives for investors, the Chinese leadership has to solve the problem of limited commitment, and use legal means to guarantee the credibility of their commitment. This requires that the leadership respect and implement contracts, restrain their future actions within the legal framework, avoid opportunist hold-up and transgression of investors' interests, and try to keep favorable records of political integrity. In particular, the leadership must first assure investors that individual property rights will be legally acknowledged and protected. The Chinese leadership has noticed this and consistently improved laws and regulations about the protection of individual property rights. The Amendments to the Constitution adopted in 2004 made it clear that "the legally obtained private property of the citizens shall not be violated." The Property Law promulgated in 2007 further made specific stipulations, laying a solid legal foundation for the protection of investors' property rights. This positively strengthens the investment incentive during the transitional period, and helps mobilize and attract social investment. It is fair to say that the vigorous growth of China's non- public economy during the transitional period is partly attributable to the relatively credible policy environment for investment.

This development strategy of first seeking breakthroughs outside the state-owned economy has greatly promoted the development of non-state-owned economy, which has become a dynamic part of the micro economic basis in China. According to circulars of the State Administration for Industry and Commerce about China's market entities, by the end of 2014, there had been 15.4637 million private enterprises with the registered capital of 59.21 trillion yuan and 49.8406 million individual businesses with the capital of 2.93 trillion yuan in China. Non-state-owned economy, mainly non- public economy, has occupied an increasing proportion in China's national economy. Currently, non-public economy has contributed nearly half of China's annual industrial added value, 3/4 or even more of annual newly added urban employment opportunities, about 3/4 of annual total foreign trade value, about 2/3 of annual total urban fixed-asset investment, and more than half of China's tax revenues. Non-public economy thus has become an important pillar of China's national economy.

The dramatic rise of non-state-owned economy has provided stimulus to the reform of state-owned economy in the following two ways. On the one hand, the development of non-state-owned economy has exerted external pressure on the reform of state-owned economy. Actually, non-SOEs serve as a standard and comparison for supervising and evaluating SOEs. Because of their market-dominated operations, these enterprises are generally more efficient than SOEs, which has brought strong competition pressures and facilitated the reform of the latter. A few significant reform measures in the management mechanism of SOEs, such as replacement of profit delivery by taxes, the implementation of the contracted managerial responsibility system, and the introduction of modern enterprise system, were to some extent responses to the competition pressures of non-SOEs.[10] It is argued by some research that the intensified competition between enterprises, especially between non-SOEs and SOEs, has provided positive stimulus to the increase of productivity of SOEs.[11]

On the other hand, the development of non-state-owned economy has created favorable conditions for the reform of state-owned economy. The booming of non-SOEs has accelerated China's rapid economic growth and provided more financial contributions, thereby relieving SOEs of financial pressures. And the rapid expansion of non-SOEs has created a large number of employment opportunities, hence helpful for the transfer of surplus employees in SOEs. These have effectively alleviated interest conflicts during the reform of SOEs. Meanwhile, the flexible and effective operation mechanisms of non-SOEs have "demonstration effects" on SOEs, and are easy to be introduced into the transformation of state-owned economy. This has in a sense reduced the operation cost during SOEs' transition to the market-oriented economic system.

Thanks to such stimuli, the reform of China's SOEs and economy has been deepening. As a result, a mixed ownership structure allowing the co-development of economic sectors of diverse ownerships has come into shape. If this mixed structure,

[10] See Jefferson and Rawski (1995).

[11] Li (1997).

more reflected at the macro societal level, is a structure with parallel development of different "sections," then it can be said that in recent years China has begun to seek a "gel-like" structure at the micro "cell" level. In another word, the closed ownership structure of the state-owned economy is broken, and China's domestic capital and foreign capital are allowed to participate in the reorganization and asset replacement of SOEs to the extent that state-owned capital and various non-state-owned capital are mixed and integrated. As a result, mixed-ownership economy with joint stock system as its main form has developed gradually. This marks not only that the mixed-ownership economy has been expanded and deepened, but that the public ownership and especially the state ownership has finally found effectives forms and approaches of integrating with the market economy.

### *2.2.2 SOE Reform*

SOE reform lies in the center of the reform of China's economic system. Different from the spontaneous reform of the rural micro management system, the reform of SOE management system has been driven by the government. This process has undergone three stages.

Stage I: 1978–1984, decentralization of power and transfer of profits. The Sichuan Province began in 1978 (it is 1979 for China as a whole) the pilot work of giving more power (mainly financial power) to SOEs. The contract-centered industrial economic responsibility system was then launched successively in 1981. Beginning in 1983, SOEs embarked on the first stage of reform for replacing profit delivery by tax collection, and in the next year started the next stage. This reform measure preliminarily broke the system under which everything was determined by planning, endowed SOEs with some decision-making power in production, and in a sense introduced material incentives.

**Feature 1** Sichuan's Stirring Pilot Program of Expanding Enterprises' Autonomy

In October 1978, Sichuan chose six local representative state-owned industrial enterprises, that is, Chongqing Iron & Steel Company, Chengdu Seamless Steel Tube Plant, Ningjiang Machine Tool Plant, Sichuan Chemical Plant, Xindu County Nitrogenous Fertilizer Plant, and Nanchong Silk Mill, to initiate the pilot work of "expanding enterprises' autonomy." The reform was mainly about checking and approving the profit target of each enterprise, setting the goal of yearly production and income increase, and allowing, after the goal was realized, the withdrawing of a small amount of profit as enterprise funds and the delivery of some few bonuses to employees at the end of the year. These rights, though insignificant, exerted unexpected effects on the outperformance in completing the fourth quarter's plan and showed great potential. Sichuan's pilot work marked the beginning of the reform of SOEs and even that of Chin's urban economic system.

On January 31, 1979, the Sichuan Provincial Party Committee issued the Opinions on the Pilot Work of Expanding Local Industrial Enterprises' Power to

Expedite Production and Construction. It increased the pilot industrial enterprises from 6 to 100, and extended this program to 40 state-owned commercial enterprises. Sichuan's pilot program included the following major measures. As regards planning, apart from state plans, enterprises were allowed to make their own supplementary plans based on market demands and revised the specifications in state plans which failed to meet the market demands. As regards material management, except for a small number of products related to national economy and people's livelihood, products in short supply and dangerous products such as explosive that shall still be purchased and allocated collectively by the state, most means of production could enter the market; enterprises could sign supply contracts directly with other enterprises without the involvement of material management departments, or satisfied their demands through market purchases, and they were permitted to sell part of their products by themselves. As regards the profit distribution between state and enterprises, on the precondition that national interests were guaranteed, enterprises could share some profits with the state based on their performance, and used these profits to develop the potential, make innovations and reformations, improve collective welfare and provide bonuses. And as regards personnel management, enterprises were granted the power to choose middle- level cadres, recruit workers based on their merits, and fire employees.

Immediately following Sichuan, Yunnan, Beijing and some other places began the pilot work of increasing autonomy among SOEs. At the end of 1979, the pilot enterprises rose to 4,200. The number grew to 6,000 in the next year, accounting for about 16 % of the on-budget industrial enterprises, 60 % of the output value, and 70 % of the profits. On September 2, 1980, the State Council approved the Report about the Pilot Work of Expanding Enterprises' Autonomy and Suggestions for the Future submitted by the State Economic Commission. It required that starting from 1981, the measures of expanding enterprises' autonomy should be adopted in all the state-owned industrial enterprises, and granted enterprises more decision- making power in the management of personnel, finance, materials, production, supply and sales.

Stage II: 1984–1992, the separation of ownership and management. Decisions on the Reform of Economic System issued by the Third Plenary Session of the 12th CPC Central Committee in 1984 put forward explicitly the theory of "appropriate separation of ownership and management." In the following 3 years, multiple modes of reform centered on this separation came out, new management mechanisms began to appear such as the rental system, contract system, and asset management responsibility system, and the pilot program of joint-stock system reform of SOEs was launched. In the meantime, enterprise alignment and merger was successively implemented, and enterprise bankruptcy emerged. These consequently gave rise to a small upsurge in SOE reform.[12] The separation of ownership and management,

[12] In the following period from the second half of 1988 to the end of 1991, as the situation changed, the SOE reform processed slowly except for continuing the contract management responsibility system. However, two important documents were released in this period, namely the Law on Industrial Enterprises of Ownership by the Whole People, which clarified the legal status of

which mainly involves the adoption of the contract system, further increased enterprises' management autonomy and established more direct incentive mechanism.

Stage III: 1992-present, the transition from "policy adjustment" to "institutional innovation." Both the reform of decentralizing power and transferring profits to enterprises at the first stage and the reform of separating management from ownership at the second stage were no more than improvement within the traditional system instead of fundamental change of the basis SOE system. These measures touched only upon the surface of the system, and failed to establish effective incentive and restraint mechanism, thereby resulting in serious problems of short-termism and insider control of enterprises. As a result, the SOE performance kept deteriorating. In the early 1990s, 1/3 of the SOEs had deficits, 1/3 had false profits, and only another 1/3 really made profits. Trapped in such a predicament, the SOE reform was in urgent need to find a new way out.

In 1993, the Decision on Some Issues of Establishing Socialist Market Economic System adopted in the Third Plenary Session of the 14th CPC Central Committee decided that the goal of SOE reform was to establish the modern enterprise system with "clearly established ownership, well defined power and responsibility, separation of enterprises from administration, and scientific management" in order for enterprises to genuinely become legal entities and competition subjects following market rules. It thus clarified a new approach based on the reform of property right system and innovation of enterprise institutions. As a result, the pilot program of establishing the modern enterprise system was launched in 1994. Priority was assigned to the corporate system and joint-stock system reform of enterprises, and the improvement of the corporate governance structure, such as improving corporate property system, defining investment subjects for state-owned assets, reorganizing enterprises into corporations, and establishing scientific and normative corporate internal governance structures. In 1995 the Fifth Plenary Session of the 14th CPC Central Committee further put forward that "with the view of invigorating the whole state-owned economy, we shall readjust its layout and structure, focus on the restructuring of large enterprises and relax control over small ones, and implement strategic SOE reorganization." Therefore, when the modern enterprise system was introduced into SOEs, the reform at the level of state- owned economy was also started with the focus on the strategic restructuring of the state-owned economy. In 2003, the Decision on Some Issues of Improving Socialist Market Economic System approved by the Third Plenary Session of the 16th CPC Central Committee proposed to establish modern property right system with "clear- cut ownership, well-defined power and responsibility, and strict protection and smooth transfer of the rights." In accordance with this design, the modern corporate property right system was established in SOEs; moreover, the mixed-ownership economy based on the modern property right system was also developed. The modern property right system was also adopted at the state level to reform the state-owned asset management system.

---

enterprises as commodity producers and transactors; and the Regulations on Transforming the Management Mechanism of Industrial Enterprises of Ownership by the Whole People, which facilitated the change in enterprise management mechanism.

In short, the approach of SOE reform since 1992 is to gradually abandon the traditional pattern relying on policy adjustment and interest redistribution, and instead seek breakthroughs at the profound institutional level for the sake of establishing socialist market economy.

After the reform at the above three stages, it can be preliminarily estimated that until now, the SOE ownership reform has involved about 85–90 % small- sized enterprises, 50–60 % medium-sized enterprises, and some large enterprises. In accordance with the statistics of the State-owned Assets Supervision and Administration Commission of the State Council, currently mixed-ownership enterprises established by central enterprises and their subsidiaries through introducing non-public capital account for 52 % of the total enterprises. At the end of 2012, there were 378 listed companies held by central enterprises and their subsidies, among which the non-state-owned shares accounted for 53 % of the total; 681 listed companies were held by local SOEs, among which non-state-owned shares exceeded 60 % of the total.

## 2.3 Dual-Track Pricing and the Price Reform

With the deepening of the reform at the micro-subject level, such as introducing the rural household-responsibility system and decentralizing power and delivering profits to enterprises, interest conflicts emerged and the conflict of different pricing systems was increasingly prominent. In the face of the seriously distorted price system, how to get price right became a problem that urgently needed to be solved in the economic system reform.

### *2.3.1 Dual-Track Pricing*

At the beginning of the price reform, there were two alternatives: one-step relaxation of control; or the active but prudent step-by-step approach. The former was not adopted in China's price reform, which instead chose the way of "combining relaxation of control with readjustment, readjustment coming first, and gradual relaxation of control." It underwent a transformation from "dual track" to "unitary track." Put differently, for some time coexisted within-the-plan price and out-of-the -plan price; then the two tracks combined and a unitary market price was applied. This was out of the following considerations: (1) The price reform needed to be in step with market maturity and should not run too much ahead of it. (2) It needed to take into account the characteristics of different industries and products and chose different reform strategies. (3) It needed to consider whether the governmental finance could deal well with the various price relations, whether the government was well equipped to keep the reform under control, and whether enterprises and residents were well prepared to face the reform.

The dual-track pricing including both state- and market-controlled prices was for a period prominently and typically reflected in industrial means of production. For industrial consumer goods, the dual-track pricing was not that prevalent or important, because the control over prices of small commodities was gradually lifted at the early stage of the reform. The buying and selling prices of most agricultural products began to get out of the state control in the mid-1980s; the dual-track pricing was long applied only to a few agricultural products, especially grains,[13] which was not of any typical significance. Nevertheless, from 1984 onwards, the dual-track pricing for industrial means of production was rapidly and extensively spread and became a successful example of the progressive market-oriented price reform in China.[14] At that time, within-the-plan price and out-of-the-plan price were simultaneously applied to the same city and the same kind of industrial means of production. The price of means of production within the plan was set by the state; for those overproduced or allowed to be sold by enterprises in accordance with the state-set proportions, the price was subject to market adjustment. Its purpose was, apart from reducing price distortion and providing necessary incentives and price signals, to keep some government control over the price level so as to guarantee economic stability. With the expansion of out-of-the- plan production and non-SOEs, the coverage of state-controlled price was constantly narrowed and market-controlled price was increasingly adopted. The two tracks of pricing were basically unified into one in the early 1990s.

This dual-track pricing played a role in demolishing the state-fixed prices. The subsequent practice shows that after this pricing system was implemented, the price gap between the two tracks was gradually widened, and the coverage of market control increased; with the deepening of the market economy, the two tracks were progressively combined into one and finally transformed to the market-controlled price mechanism. The dual-track pricing for means of production has been highly regarded by overseas scholars. Wlodzimierz Brus, a Polish economist, argued in the Bashan Cruise Conference[15] in 1985 that this pricing system was a useful invention

[13] The dual-track pricing for grains started in 1979 when the policy of "decreasing purchase and increasing prices" was implemented. By 1982, the grains purchased by the state through negotiation and those sold directly by farmers to non-farmers had accounted for 24.2 % of the total volume of purchase. The remaining part was state purchase by or beyond the plan, indicating that the dual-track pricing for grains came into shape. This pricing system in the strict sense was started in 1985, when the unified state purchase at fixed prices was abolished, and purchase by contract was implemented. For beyond-contract grains, the price was negotiated between farmers and grain management departments. Consequently, the dual-track pricing system was established including both contracted price and negotiated price. The grain market was not completely opened to market control until 2004.

[14] Of course, this dual-track pricing resulted to some extent in market disorder and the prevalence of rent seeking. Some empirical studies show that if the price gap were not that sharp, the dual-track pricing could have been more effective.

[15] On September 2–7, 1985, the "International Conference on Macro Economic Management" co-organized by the Chinese Academy of Social Sciences, China Society of Economic Reform, and World Bank was held on the "Bashan" Cruise from Chongqing to Wuhan. This conference was thereby referred to as "Bashan Cruise Conference".

of China; it served as a bridge through which China could transit smoothly from one price system to the other. Joseph Stiglitz, a US economist, wrote in the late 1990s that during the transition from a seriously distorted price system to one that could precisely reflect the scarcity of economic resources, China adopted a genius solution, i.e., the dual-track pricing, which provided suitable encouragement to the out-of-the-plan sections.[16]

**Feature 2** Mogan Mountain Conference: Price Reform Debates

Around 1984, Chinese economists had very intensive discussions on the price reform approaches. In particular, the "dual-track transition" of the reform, namely the dual-track pricing or dual-track approach, became a heatedly discussed topic among young economists in the Mogan Mountain Conference held in September 1984.

This conference advocated, one the one hand, to reform the price system for industrial products with the focus on raising the prices of mining industrial products; and on the other hand, to readjust consumer prices and public service charge by focusing on problems of price inversion and oversubsidy for agricultural products. However, about how to reform industrial product prices, there were at first two different suggestions: one is "combining readjustment with relaxation of control, but relying mainly on readjustment"; the other is "combining readjustment with relaxation of control, with relaxation of control coming before readjustment." Therefore the so-called School of Readjustment and School of Relaxation came into being.

Tian Yuan et al. from the Price Research Center of the State Council suggested that huge readjustments must be made to the seriously distorted price system, and they also conducted a large number of calculations and comparison of different plans. Zhou Xiaochuan, a PhD candidate in systems engineering at Tsinghua University, and Lou Jiwei and Li Jiange, graduate students at the Graduate School of the Chinese Academy of Social Sciences, proposed an approach of small but quick readjustments to constantly correct the price system, thereby both reducing the shock of reform and progressively approaching the market equilibrium price. In contrast, the School of Relaxation, represented by Zhang Weiying, a graduate student from the Northwest University, suggested lifting price control in one step or several steps in order to realize market-controlled pricing.

Fierce debates were conducted between the School of Readjustment and the School of Relaxation. The former questioned the latter based on the following reasons: when the planned economy dominated, it was unrealistic to lift the price control once for all, and the market development also took time. When the market was imperfect, the market equilibrium price was neither possible nor necessarily optimized. However, the latter disagreed with the former, arguing that the price problem was attributable to the current price system which cut off the relations between supply and demand and therefore distorted the price. Under such a price system, readjustment was not the fundamental solution. Before and after the Mogan

[16] Quoted from Zhang Zhuoyuan (1999).

Mountain Conference, both schools published actively to explain their views. Representative articles include "The Reform Direction of China's Price System and Its Related Models and Methods" by Lou Jiwei and Zhou Xiaochuan published in 1984 in the Economic Research Journal, the "The Goal Model of China's Price System Reform" by Guo Shuqing published in 1985 in the Journal of Graduate School of Chinese Academy of Social Sciences, and "On the Approach Centered on the 'Relaxation of Control' in China's Price Reform" by Zhang Weiying published in 1985 in the Review of Economic Research, to mention just a few.

When heated debates were underway between the two schools, there appeared a third approach. Some representatives, such as Hua Sheng, He Jiacheng, Zhang Shaojie, and Gao Liang from the Graduate School of the Chinese Academy of Social Sciences and Jiang Yue from the Department of Statistics of Renmin University of China analyzed and integrated the approaches of the two schools and put forward the approach of "combining readjustment and relaxation." They advocated that China should use the already existing dual-track pricing for means of production, and make the planned price and market price gradually close up. During this process, the planned part should be gradually decreased and the market part increased and eventually the two came into one. By the article "On the Price Reform with Chinese Characteristics" published in 1985 in the Economic Research Journal, Hua Sheng et al. again argued for the dual- track pricing approach.

### 2.3.2 *The Radical Price Reform*

To rationalize the price system and combine the two tracks of pricing in a short term, the CPC Politburo decided on the conference held on May 30–June 1, 1988 to "crash through barriers" in reforming the price and wage systems, and required the State Council to make specific plans. Subsequently, the Price Commission of the State Council presented an initial plan about the price and wage reform. It believed that price reform was inevitable, and suggested that the price relations shall be rationalized within about 5 years. It also proposed to raise and adjust wages and appropriately increase subsidies during the price reform in order not to lower the actual living standards of the majority of employees. After being discussed on the executive meeting of the State Council on August 5–9, this initial plan was submitted to the CPC politburo conference convened in Beidaihe on August 15–17, and this five-year plan was approved. The gazette of this conference was published in the *People's Daily* on August 19, laying out the basic content of the price reform plan. This aroused fear about price rise among the people, and finally led to massive panic buying and severe dissaving.[17] This agitation was deteriorated across China.

[17] Statistics show that in August 1988, the retail turnover of commodities in China increased year-on-year by 38.6 %. The year-on-year growth rates of the retail volume of major commodities are as follows: cotton cloth, 46.7 %; wool fabric, 53 %; silk fabric, 40 %; cotton wool shirts and trousers, 92 %; fleecy sweaters and trousers, 74 %; woolen yarn, 70 %; color televisions, 40 %; black-

On August 27, an emergency meeting was held by the CPC Central Committee, deciding to make adjustments and suspend the price reform plan. The State Council released a notice on August 30 that no more new price adjustment measures would be launched in the second half year, and the price reform in the next year would be conducted in small steps. This sudden halt actually put an end to this radical price reform.

This failure was largely attributable to the improper timing of reform. As regards the macro situation at that time, the price rose at an increasing monthly rate in 1988. In February it was 11.2 %, a double-digit rate. In the following 3 months, it was 11.6 %, 12.6 %, and 14.7 %, respectively. In particular, before the price and wage reform plans were approved on the CPC Politburo conference, individual reform measures had already been successively launched. For example, China lifted the control over the retail prices of four major kinds of subsidiary food, i.e., meat, common vegetables, eggs and white sugar in May to July; this then also applied to famous cigarettes and wines. This swarm of measures further quickened the rise of price. The price increase rate reached 16.5 % in June and rose to 19.3 % in July. Under such immense inflation pressures, the radical "one-step" price reform was launched, which quickly gave rise to people's inflation expectation and therefore made it more difficult for reform to be conducted.

In fact, economists had controversy over whether structural adjustments of price could be made under inflation. Some insisted that inflation would not pose any severe threat to Chinese economy at that time. In April 1988, it was argued that "if economic growth is the top priority for macro control, then some degree of inflation is not bad." "In the next three years, China's macro policy shall be changed from the demand-side policy targeted at stabilizing prices to supply-side policy aimed at economic growth and structural readjustment. Finance and banking should not shrink simultaneously, but should instead keep moderate expansion."[18] The *People's Daily* published on July 1 an article entitled "Risks Here, Success Ahead" advocating the relaxation of control over price.

However, most scholars believed that the price reform must be preconditioned on a tolerant environment, otherwise the risks would be too big and it might lead to the spiral increase of wage and price and even great social upheaval. For example, some argued that the inflation policy was neither conducive to sustainable and healthy economic growth nor helpful to the smooth advancement of economic reform, let alone "crashing through barriers" in the price reform.[19] Given the macro economic situation at that time, some economists proposed the plan of "remedy before reform" out of the following considerations: (1) The price rise first hitting agricultural products in the fourth quarter of 1987 was extending to other domains. (2) The

---

and-white televisions, 64 %; washing machines, 160 %; refrigerators, 100 %; electric fans, 68 %; recorders, 71 %; bicycles, 52 %; and sewing machines, 58 %. In the same month, urban and rural savings did not increase but reduced by 2.68 billion yuan. See Wu Li (2010) "Price reform and its failure". http://www.hprc.org.cn/, January 26, 2010

[18] See the *People's Daily* on pp. 4, April 8, 1988.

[19] See Xue Muqiao (1996), Liu Guoguang (1988).

bottleneck in transportation and the supply of means of production was getting worse. (3) Sporadic panic buying emerged and spread in China. (4) A negative increase in savings was found in April, indicating the inflation expectation was taking shape.[20] The research group in economics of the Chinese Academy of Social Sciences (CASS) also proposed to "seek improvement in stability." With regard to the suggestion that "both reform and development should be advanced speedily; moderate inflation can be used to support the super-high economic growth," the CASS scholars argued that 3 years (1988–1990) were needed first to improve the economic environment, which mainly involved inflation management, fiscal austerity and credit crunch, and the stabilization of economy. After the macro- economic proportion was again well coordinated, reform could be conducted in bigger steps.[21]

One prominent lesson from this radical price reform is that "stability is the basic precondition of reform." Put differently, reform needs stable political and social environments as well as a tolerant economic environment in order to ensure its success. Before major reform measures are launched, it is necessary to take into full account the possible impact on all fields, decide prudently on the timing, intensity and coordination of reform in order to make the reform affordable to the society. If the conditions are not ripe, reform should not start hastily but should wait until there is a ready environment and therefore a good timing. As commented by Deng Xiaoping in September 1988 about the problems of reform: "High speed is in itself a good thing. But if it is too high, it will bring trouble. Inflation was mainly caused by relaxed control; we did not have enough experience in this regard. Before the price reform, there was already the inflation problem, mainly because we did not address well the relations between aggregate supply and demand. Now we need to summarize our experiences and continue to go ahead, and control the increase in aggregate demand and the speed of development. We are bold enough, now we need stability. China is a big country with 1 billion population; we should ensure its stability. We make a step, and then summarize our experiences. If there are mistakes, we correct them, and should not let small mistakes develop into bigger ones. This is the principle that we follow."[22]

After the 30-plus years of reform, we can see clearly that this progressive strategy of "incremental reform" characterized by "different measures for different fields" and "sequential progress," while ensuring the existing interests pattern not to suffer from fundamental and drastic strikes, allows the market system to develop in a way of "marginal evolution" and finally "escape" from the planned economy. During this process, the power and advantages of the market gradually infiltrate into and diffuse within the traditional system through the "trickle-down effect" and "ink spreading effect," and finally provide ready conditions for the comprehensive transformation to the socialist market economy.

---

[20] Quoted from Wu Jinglian (2010b).

[21] See The Research Group of the Economic System Reform Outline of the Chinese Academy of Social Sciences (1991).

[22] See *A chronicle of Deng Xiaoping thought: 1988*. http://cpc.people.com.cn/GB/69112/69113/69683/4723408.html.

Of course, the progressive reform will inevitably prolong the confrontation between the old and new systems, and give rise to some new problems. For one thing, since reform is advanced step by step, this will leave enough time to the old system to fight against the new comer. During their confrontation, the old system (especially its most die-hard part) may contain or erode the new one and force the reform to stagnate and make it more difficult. For another thing, because of the cumulative measures of the marginal evolution, the coexistence and confrontation of the two systems will long last, therefore making interest arbitrage possible. Those vested interest groups benefiting from this arbitrage may stand by the vested interest groups of the traditional system and oppose the further deepening of the reform, which will also make it more difficult to reform. Therefore, during the advancement of reform as a whole, how to choose the right timing and crucial, prioritized fields and links to achieve "abrupt change" is a problem that has to be solved by the progressive strategy of reform.

At the very outset, when the Third Plenary Session of the 11th Central Committee of the CPC was sounding the clarion call for reform, the Chinese government did not have a clear blueprint as to which way to go. And the chief architect of reform Deng Xiaoping had not yet finished his "top-tier design." Like Wong Kar Wai's style of filmmaking, there was no written script for China to follow in its reform. Nonetheless, "crossing the river by feeling the stones" has yielded promising results to the Chinese people.

Looking back on the inauguration of reform, we find that China's reform took off precisely at a time between the end of Cultural Revolution and the eve of social and economic collapse, and at a time when the developed economies had just experienced a decade of stagflation before Ronald Reagan and Margaret Thatcher resorted to liberalization reforms as a rescue. Meanwhile, the wave of globalization was also beginning to gather momentum, which was about to sweep the world in the coming two decades. This time, finally, China got on the train of globalization and kept up with the wave of reforms. The reform initiated in the 1970s has since changed China in a dramatic and unprecedented way.

## References

Chang C, Wang Y (1994) The nature of the township-village enterprise. J Comp Econ 19:434–452

Che J, Qian Y (1998) Insecure property rights and government ownership of firms. Q J Econ 113(2):467–496

Chen X (1999) The economic system reform in rural China. In: Wang M (ed) The 20 years of economic transition in China. Foreign Language Press, Beijing

Fan S (1991) Effects of technological change and institutional reform on production growth in Chinese agriculture. Am J Agric Econ 73(2):265–275

Huang J, Rozelle S (1996) Technological change: the re-discovery of the engine of productivity growth in China's rural economy. J Dev Econ 49(2):337–369

Jefferson G, Rawski T (1995) How industrial reform worked in China: the role of innovation, competition, and property rights. In: Proceedings of the world bank annual conference on development economics 1994. World Bank, Washington, DC, pp 129–156

Jefferson G, Rawski T, Zheng Y (1995) The change trend of china's industrial productivity since 1978: estimates and reliability analysis. Econ Res J 12
Li W (1997) "The impact of economic reform on the performance of Chinese state enterprises". 1980–89. J Polit Econ 105(5):1080–1106
Li Daokui (1995) The theory of ambiguous property rights in a transitional economy. Econ Res J 4
Lin JY (1992) Rural reforms and agricultural growth in China. Am Econ Rev 82(1):34–51
Liu Guoguang (1988) Facing inflation issues. Economic Daily, 5 Apr 1988
McMillan J, Whalley J, Zhu L (1989) The impact of China's economic reforms on agricultural productivity growth. J Polit Econ 97(4):781–807
Naughton B (1994) Chinese institutional innovation and privatization from below. Am Econ Rev 84(2)
Nee V (1992) Organizational dynamics of market: hybrid forms, property rights, and mixed economy in China. Adm Sci Q 37(1)
Oi J (1992) Fiscal reform and the economic foundations of local state corporatism in China. World Polit 45(1)
Sun L (1997) Emergence of unorthodox ownership and governance structure in East Asia: an alternative transition path. Research for action, No 38. UNU/WIDER, Helsinki
The Research Group of the Economic System Reform Outline of the Chinese Academy of Social Sciences (1991) Two-way coordination, improvement in stability: medium-term economic system reform outline of China (1988–1995). In: Liu G et al (eds) Economic system reform and development in the 1980s China. Economy & Management Publishing House, Beijing
Tian G (1995) Ownership structure and reform in China's township enterprises. Econ Res J 3
Walder A (1995) Local governments as industrial firms: an organizational analysis of China's transitional economy. Am J Sociol 101(2):263–301
Weitzman M, Xu C (1994) Chinese township-village enterprises as vaguely defined cooperatives. J Comp Econ 18:121–145
Wen JG (1993) Total factor productivity change in China's farming sector: 1952–1989. Econ Dev Cult Chang 42(1):1–41
Wu Jinglian (2010b) A course in economic reform in contemporary China. Shanghai Far East Publishers, Shanghai
Wu Li (2010) Price reform "Breakthrough" and frustration. www.hprc.org.cn. Accessed 26 Jan 2010
Xue Muqiao (1996) Memoir of Xue Muqiao. Tianjin People's Publishing House, Tianjin
Zhang Xiaojing (1999) WTO and China's economy: an overview. Working paper No 99–005. Institute of National Economy, China Reform Foundation

# Chapter 3
# The Overall Advancement of Reform

In October, 1992, the reform target of establishing socialist market economy was made clear in the 14th National Congress of the Communist Party of China (CPC). With discussion and preparation for more than 1 year, the program of action on *Decision for Establishment of Socialist Market Economy* "50-Articles" was agreed in the Third Session of the 14th Central Committee of CPC in November 1993, deciding to change the reform strategy of "overall gradual advancement and periodical breakthrough", and setting forth the new policy of "the overall advancement and the key breakthrough". The Decision focus on supporting reform on such five key aspects as finance and tax system, banking system, foreign exchange management system, state-owned enterprise system and social security system, so as to form the framework for market economy system.

From the beginning of the market-oriented reform in the late 1970s to the overall reform advancement for establishing socialist market economy in the early 1990s, China made firmer and more powerful strides in its economic reform.

## 3.1 Planned Economy or Market Economy?

From the determination of reform policy in 1978 to the definition of reform target of establishing socialist market economy in the Report of the 14th National Congress of the CPC in 1992, China had faced with the choice of "planned economy or market economy", theoretically and practically.

During 1979–1981, encouraged by ideological line of emancipating the mind and seeking truth from the facts, the circle of economic theory became active in thinking and conducted discussion on relation between planned economy and market economy. When summarizing past experience and lessons, many economists criticized the left- wing views of attempting to perish the monetary relationship, and proposed to give more play to the role of law of value in economic life. For instance, Sun Yefang advanced again "law of value is the first of all laws"; Xue Muqiao



X. Zhang, X. Chang, *The Logic of Economic Reform in China*, China Insights,
DOI 10.1007/978-3-662-47404-4_3

proposed to learn to use the law of value and market regulation.[1] In April 1979, initiated jointly by Institute of Economics Chinese Academy of Social Sciences, Institute of Economics State Development Planning Commission and Jiangsu Institute of Philosophy and Social Sciences, the 2nd National Seminar on Economic Theories, the famous "Seminar on Role of Law of Value in Socialist Economy" was held in Wuxi, Jiangsu. The participants reached a consensus on such aspects as socialist economy is commodity economy, means of production are also commodities, law of value still plays a role in socialist economy, and competition is the inherent mechanism of socialist economy, affirmed the position of commodities, value and law of value as well as competition mechanism in socialist economy, and made a point of combing planned regulation with market regulation.[2] Whereafter, the theoretical circle further affirmed the position of market regulation in socialist economy, defining market regulation as an economic adjustment means, which has no positive connection with capitalism and can be used to serve socialist economy.

The reform principle of "ensuring the leading role of the planned economy supplemented by market regulation" was officially put forward in the Report of the 12th National Congress in 1982. It decided to reform the traditional centralized planned economy system and allowed part of products not to be planned for production and circulation, but to be regulated by market, which broke through the traditional understanding that had deemed planned economy and market economy as incompatible like water and fire and the absolute monopoly status of planned economy. However, the wording of "ensuring the leading role of the planned economy supplemented by market regulation" actually still took planned economy as the essential characteristic of socialist economy, emphasizing the role of plan means and regarding the market mechanism as a "supplement".

In the process of exploring the theory of socialist market economy, it was the theoretical development on compatibility between market regulation and planning system in 1984 that had the break-through significance. *Decision of the CPC Central Committee on Reform of Economic System* as a programmatic document was agreed in the Third Plenary Session of the 12th CPC Central Committee, confirming China's socialist economy is the "planned commodity economy" based on public ownership, emphasizing that full development of commodity economy is an impassable stage in socialist development and the prerequisite for China's economic modernization; emphasizing on proceeding in accordance with economic law, especially law of value and taking full advantage of market mechanism to develop socialist economy. The theory of planned commodity economy broke through the traditional view of taking planned economy and commodity economy as opposite to each other, which indicated the duly establishment of law of value, as one of the major laws for market economy, in the economic life. It was a major breakthrough in the theory of socialist economy as well as a major theoretical breakthrough in the exploration for the reform target of economic system. Deng Xiaoping set a high

[1] See Zhang Zhuoyuan (1999).

[2] See Editorial Office of Economic Research (1979).

value on the *Decision of the CPC Central Committee on Reform of Economic System*, pointing out: this decision is the political economics that integrating the basic principle of Marxism with the social practice in China.[3]

With the theory of "planned commodity economy" proposed, the theoretical circle started the exploration on the issue of corresponding economic mechanism. In 1987, the 13th National Congress of the CPC emphasized the inherent unity of planning and market forces in the socialist planned commodity economy and further proposed the new economic mechanism of "state regulates market and market guides enterprises"[4] in the socialist planned commodity economy, which further improved the status of market mechanism in China's economic life.

Later, the theoretical circle had a warm discussion on which was the basic mechanism: planning or market. More and more theoretical workers no longer merely regarded market mechanism as a kind of auxiliary means but the inherent operation mechanism of socialist economy. They held that socialist economy cannot do without the function of market and law of value, and market functioned in the whole society, rather than existed merely as the supplement to plan mechanism.

In his statement made in "Southern tour" in 1992, Deng Xiaoping further elaborated his view on planned economy and market economy: "The proportion of planning to market forces is not the essential difference between socialism and capitalism. A planned economy is not equivalent to socialism, because there is planning under capitalism too; a market economy is not capitalism, because there are markets under socialism too. Planning and market forces are both means of controlling economic activity".[5] It profoundly answered the question constraining people's thought for a long time, and eventually resolved such fundamental problem as market economy is not necessarily the exclusive nature of capitalism, which enabled the argument on planning and market forces over the years to get rid of ideological restraint and cleared away the theoretical barriers for the 14th National Congress of the CPC to establish the target of socialist market economic system.

## 3.2 Organic Combination of Socialism and Market Economy

The essence and core of socialist market economic system is: to make market forces play a decisive role in the allocation of resources under the socialist macro- control and cause the economic activities to follow requirements of law of value and adapt to the changes in supply-demand relations; to allocate resources to the segments with better benefits, and put pressure and power on enterprise to select the superior and eliminate the inferior, through the functions of price leverage and competition

[3]Yang Junchang (2004, p. 1006).

[4]This wording was initially presented by GuiShiyong, Wang Jiye and Li Chengrui at "National Conference on Macro Economic Management" held by the State Development Planning Commission in October 1986.

[5]Deng Xiaoping (1993, p. 373).

mechanism; to timely balance production and demand by taking advantage of sensitive response of market to different economic signals.

Socialist market economic system is the organic combination and compatibility of basic system of socialism and market economy. It reflects the system features of socialism as well as general characteristics of modern market economy. The system features are mainly reflected in: (1) with regard to structure of ownership, public ownership is the mainstay and economic entities of diverse ownership develop together; (2) with regard to distribution system, distribution according to work is dominant and a variety of modes of distribution coexist; co-existence of multiple distribution modes with distribution on the basis of labor as the main part; with regard to principle of distribution, encouraging some people to get rich first by working honestly and running business lawfully to rationally widen differences in personal income to promote efficiency, and to prevent great disparity of income, and eventually achieving the goal of common prosperity. As the general characteristics of modern market economy, it is mainly reflected in: (1) in view of the resource allocation mode, market is taken as the decisive means; (2) in view of the economic mechanism, stress is placed on giving play to the role of price, supply and demand, and competition; (3) from the micro level, enterprise is the independent market entity and the legal entity; (4) from the macro level, the government is required to make necessary regulation over economic activities with economic and legal means. The institutional characteristics of socialism and the general characteristics of market economy can be integrated to give full play to the superiority of socialist system and the promoting effect of market economy to development of productivity.

The target of establishing socialist market economic system is mainly based on such three basic aspects in which the modern market economy is superior to the traditional planned economic system.

1. Market economy has the powerful incentive function. The motive of seeking advantages and avoiding disadvantages is the original power to promote economic operation. The traditional planned economy assumed "the whole society is a big factory", which could hardly produce an incentive function, because it denied completely the material interest of individuals and excluded the basic regulating effect of market mechanism in economic operation, as a consequence, enterprises could engage passively in production and operation according to country's instructions. However, in market economy, the pursuit of market entities to material interests and the effect of price mechanism and competition mechanism are integrated to produce a great incentive effect. Under such incentive effect, the energy of the whole society will be adequately excited.
2. Market economy has the function for efficient transmission of information. Information is one of the necessary conditions for economic activity and the transferability and shareability are its marked features. In planned economy, information is vertically transmitted according to instruction of the planning organ, by which many segments are included to bring slow information feedback, high cost and serious information distortion. In market economy, information is horizontally transmitted among different economic entities to bring extremely

wide channels and relatively short distances for transmission of information. Additionally, in market economy, price is the "barometer" for market activities. Enterprises can make decisions by mastering necessary information, so demand for information is far less huge and complex as in planned economy. Therefore, in market economy, information can be transmitted in a quick and immediate manner, so as to reduce costs and distortion degree.

3. Market economy has the function of promoting the flow of production factors. In planned economy, with stagnation, production factors cannot flow freely according to the actual economic needs. Under such rigid structure, the factors in need of complementation cannot complement freely and factors in need of interchanging cannot interchange freely, which result in a significant gap between the total of nominal production factors and that of playing an actual role. However, in market economy, being promoted by profit motive of market entities and driven by competitive pressures, production factors flow continuously among enterprises, sectors and regions. In this case, the gap of social demand will be filled and idle resources will be fully used, so as to constantly optimize resources allocation and use at peak efficiency.

## 3.3 The Overall Advancement of Reform

With the target model of socialist market economic system established, the decisive effect of market was affirmed in resources allocation under macro-control by government and the effect of market mechanism was further amplified. On this basis, the market-oriented reform was advanced in microeconomic base, market system, government management, income distribution system and social security system, to name a few. Based on the earlier ownership structure reform, state-owned enterprise reform, rural reform and price reform, the contents of reform were further extended and widened. The harmony and systematic arrangement among the reforms in different fields were highlighted.

### *3.3.1 From Development of Commodity Market to Development of Factor Market*

#### 3.3.1.1 Market-Oriented Reform of Capital Factor

Firstly, development of capital market: since the issuance of treasury securities was restored in 1981 and the treasury securities held by residents were allowed for circulation in 1988, China's capital market has developed from the market merely for issuing the government bonds to the national capital market system with stocks and bonds as the main part, with co-existence of multiple securities forms and with coordination of centralized trading and over-the-counter distributed trading.

As SME Board was established in 2004, GEM Board established in 2009, and National Equities Exchange and Quotation ("New Three Board"), a national over-the-counter market, and regional equity markets (known as "4th Board") in 2013, a multi-level capital market system had already begun to take shape. Taking stock market as an example, since Shanghai Stock Exchange (SSE) and Shenzhen Stock Exchange (SZSE) were established in 1990 and 1991, the scale of stock market has continuously expanded. The number of domestic listed companies (Stock-A and B) increased from 53 in 1992 to 2,613 at the end of November, 2014 and market capitalization also increased from RMB 108.4 billion to RMB 37.3 trillion. Especially, since May 2005, the listed companies started non-tradable share reform. At the end of 2007, 1,298 listed companies of SSE and SZSE had completed or had been under the reform, sharing 98 % of the listed companies which should be reformed. Consequently, the stock market entered a brand- new stage of development.

Secondly, marketization of interest rate: since the middle 1990s, China has steadily advanced the process of market-oriented reform for capital price-interest rate- formation mechanism with the concept of marketizing money market rate and bond market rate at first and then gradually advancing the marketization of deposit and loan rates. Currently, money market rate (bank call loan, discount and transfer discount and so on), bond market rate (national debt, financial bond and enterprise bond and so on) and foreign-currency market rate have been basically marketization. Based on relaxing the float range for loan rate twice successively in the middle of 2012, the lower limit of 0.7 times of loan rate was cancelled in July 2013 for financial institutions except for commercial individual housing loan; with the control over the loan rate being comprehensively released, the space has been further expanded for the financial institutions to set price independently. The deposit rate is subject to the upper-limit control, but is also partially open in such alternative modes as trust wealth management, agreement deposit and treasury deposit tender. In the middle of 2012, the deposit rate was allowed to float upwards by 1.1 times of the base rate, which is a breakthrough trial in reforming the upper-limit administration of deposit rate. In November 2014, the upper limit for the floating range of deposit rate for financial institutions was adjusted from 1.1 times to 1.2 times of the base rate.

Thirdly, marketization of exchange rate: in early 1981, the double-track price system was introduced into the field of exchange rate, for co-existence of double exchange rates: trading internal settlement price and official market quotation, with the hope to correct partially the level of exchange rate that had been over-valued for long, by adopting the internal settlement price. Since 1985, with the foreign exchange retention ratio being increased and the foreign exchange swap center being established locally, a situation was formed for the co-existence of the official exchange rate and the foreign exchange swap market rate. The double-track price system for exchange rate was implemented to allow the market exchange rate (swap exchange rate) to float with supply and demand in the foreign exchange market. On this basis, to guide the official exchange rate through swap exchange rate to increase the influence of market forces on Renminbi exchange rate. At the end of 1993, 80 % of the foreign exchange was allocated by the foreign exchange swap center. Since

January 1, 1994, the foreign exchange control system has seen significant changes: cancelling the foreign exchange retention and turning over; implementing the banking exchange settlement and sale system; establishing the national unified inter-bank foreign exchange market, actualizing the integration of the official exchange rate and foreign exchange swap market exchange rate; implementing the unitary and managed floating exchange rate system based on the market supply and demand. Thus, the leading role of market in allocation of foreign exchange resources has been primarily established.

#### 3.3.1.2 Market-Oriented Reform of Labor Factor

Since the reform and opening up, with the adjustment of ownership structure and the rapid development of non-public sectors of the economy, the reform of enterprise employment system and gradual decrease of barriers for mobility and employment of agricultural surplus labors, China's labor market has developed rapidly. Especially, the situation of isolating completely urban and rural populations and prohibiting migration and mobility under the traditional planned economic system has been thoroughly broken; the policy environment gradually tended to be relaxed for non- local employment and non-house registration migration of agricultural surplus labors. Since 1990s, the number of peasants going out for employment has increased rapidly by millions annually and going out for employment has been the main channel for transfer of agricultural surplus labors (in the per capita net income of rural residents, the proportion of wage income increased from 20.2 % in 1990 to 43.5 % in 2013, with a rise of 23.3 % points). It is estimated that peasant workers have by now shared more than one third of the total industrial workers. At present, there are still such problems as barrier of household registration system and especially welfare difference by identity in household register, but it cannot be denied that the integration of urban- rural labor market has been continuously deepened.

During this process, marketization of labor price strengthened continuously. From the very beginning of the reform, the situation started to be broken for the unified allocation of labor resource and the range was gradually expanded for market allocation of labor resource. On the one hand, for non-state-owned economy and especially non- public ownership economy growing outside the traditional system, labor resource has been allocated through market from the very beginning and the labor price (wage) has been also determined according to supply and demand in labor market as the important reference for the wage level of the state-owned sector. On the other hand, from 1980 when the pilot work conducted for labor contract system to 1986 when the *Provisional Regulations for State-owned Enterprise Implementing Labor Contract System* was published, the labor contract system had been adopted for additional employments in state-owned economy, forming the double-track system for allocation of labor resources. Since 1995, with *Labor Law* and the supporting regulations published, the labor contract system for all employees was implemented in state-owned economy, thus basically actualizing the integration of allocation modes of labor resource, and both sides of supply and demand making independent choices based on the labor contract; the wages of contract employees were no longer under the instructive control of government, but were determined independently by the enterprises and laborers under the wages guidance policy of government.

#### 3.3.1.3 Market-Oriented Reform of Land Factor

Firstly, the commodity attribute of land resources was restored and the system of compensated use of land was implemented. The *Land Administration Law* published in 1986 specified the mode of land use in two forms: administrative allocation and compensated transfer. Secondly, the open trading system of land use right was gradually introduced and the market-oriented formation mechanism was established for the land price. In 1987, the invitation to bid and auction system was introduced for the right to use state-owned land for the first time. The *Interim Regulations of Assignment and Transfer of the Right to the Use of the State-owned Land in the Urban Areas* issued in 1990 stipulated that the right to the use of land can be assigned and transferred by means of reaching an agreement, bid invitation and auction. From the mid and late 1990s, the advancement was accelerated for the market-oriented allocation of land factor and the range was gradually expanded for the market-based land price. In 1999, bid invitation, auction and listing system for state-owned land was established in Guangdong, Zhejiang and Jiangsu. In 2002, the *Regulation on* Assigning *the Right to the Use of the State-owned Land by Bid Invitation, Auction and Listing* was implemented. Issued in 2004, *Notice for Further Undertaking the Enforcement and Supervision over* Assigning *the Right to the Use of Operating Land by Bid Invitation, Auction and Listing* specified "all lands for operation shall be assigned by bid invitation, auction and listing" and bid invitation, auction and listing system for state- owned operating land nationwide. In 2006, land for industrial purpose was covered by bid invitation, auction and listing system for the first time. It should be said that the price reform of land resources has been continuously deepened from priceless to price and from non-market oriented pricing of assigning by allocation and agreement to market-oriented pricing by public bidding and auction. In total assigned land area, the proportion of land area assigned by bid invitation, auction and listing increased continuously. In 2013, the land area assigned by bid invitation, auction and listing shared 92.3 % of the total state-owned land area for construction. Additionally, in the rural areas, the circulation of right to the use of land started in late 1990s. In practice, peasants created many modes for circulation such as subcontracting, transferring, leasing (including back-leasing and reverse contracting), exchanging and pooling of land. Furthermore, circulation market for the right to the use of land in the rural areas was also under exploration and establishment, and the mode of "three rights separation" (ownership, contracting right and operating right) of contracted land was gradually formed. According to the data of Ministry of Agriculture, by the end of June 2014, 38 billion mu of the circulation area of household-contracted cultivated land, sharing 28.8 % of the total area of household-contracted cultivated land.

## 3.3.2 *From Micro Reform to Macro Reform*

With micro reform making progress, constraints at macro level became prominent, which mainly reflected in: distortion of macro signals, failure of micro entities with marketization improved to respond rationally, thus the acceleration of macro reform was put on the agenda. Hence, the reform mainly focused on correcting the distortion of macro signals so that the macro policy environment cohered with the mechanism for the market to allocate resources and the reform of micro operation system. At the macro level, another keynote of reform is to reform the macroeconomic management system of the government. One of the important progresses is, with a large number of explorations made in establishing and perfecting the macro-control system, since the target was established for the socialist market economic system, direct administration has changed to indirect administration as the main measure and the macro-control system has been basically established with the economic leverage as the main administrative means.

### 3.3.2.1 Reform of the Finance and Tax System

Over the last three decades, China has undertaken the reform of finance and tax system mainly in the financial distribution relationship between the central and local government, the tax system and the budget system. The reform of financial relationship between governments is the core area. Around this reform, three stages have been basically experienced:

At the third stage, starting from early 1980s, the financial contract system was implemented for "serving meals to different diners from different pots" between the central and local governments by decentralizing power and transferring profits from the central government to the local governments. i.e. the scopes of budget revenue and expenditure of the central and local governments are determined respectively in advance, including the contracting base for the local budget revenue and expenditure. According to the base, local governments implement the revenue and expenditure contract and keep the balance within the determined scope. The reform of financial decentralization aroused the local enthusiasm of organizing financial revenues and increasing sources of financial revenues (developing economy), but also caused "two proportions" to drop: the proportion of national financial revenues in Gross Domestic Product (GDP) and the proportion of central financial revenues in the national financial revenues, thus weakening the fiscal function of the state due to lack of necessary financial capacity and especially weakening the capacity of the central government to regulate and control the national economic development, forming the feudal economy.

At the second stage, according to the reform target of establishing the socialist market economic system, a major breakthrough was achieved in the reform in 1994: the reform of tax-sharing system was implemented between the central and local finance. In other words, the scope of expenditures was determined for finance at different levels according to powers of office for the central and local government; in line with the principle of combing the power of office and financial power, the central tax, local tax and tax shared by central and local governments were divided according to the tax types, and two sets of institutions for tax collection and management were established: central and local; with the local revenue in 1993 as the base, the amount was verified for return of tax revenues to the local governments, which would increase annually. Meanwhile, the relatively official central-to-local transfer payment system was established. The reform of financial system in 1994 took an important step in building frame for finance and tax system according to the target requirement of socialist market economic system, thus strengthening the overall financial capacity of governments, especially the central financial capacity. However, some problems were also exposed, especially in: firstly, as for the local governments, the financial power tended to be transferred upward, while the power of office downward, and the financial power and power of office were not symmetric for the central and local governments; secondly, the function of public services within the scope of power of office for governments at all levels was weakened and the supply of basic public services was inadequate; thirdly, the rules were not clear for the transfer payment of the central finance and the policy making was highly subjective.

At the third stage, starting from the late 1990s, exploration was made for the reform of public financial system with the target of actualizing the equality of basic public services. On this reform, the expenditure proportion was gradually increased for compulsory education, public health and basic medical, basic social security and other basic public services. Additionally, the process has been accelerated for the public finance to cover rural areas: e.g., rural compulsory education is brought into the scope of public financial security and the scope of social security is also further extended to the country from cities and towns. Since the division standard of the power of office for governments at all levels is further specified to meeting the public needs, the reform oriented for public finance can also be considered as the further deepening of the reform of tax-sharing system.

In addition to the foregoing reform of financial system, (1) in terms of reform of tax system, in 1994, with the fair tax burden and simplification of tax system as the core, the turnover tax system was established with value-added tax (VAT) as the main part and consumption tax and business tax as the supplement; in recent years, studies have also been conducted for further reform of tax system, including the reform of changing VAT from production to consumption and scope expansion of VAT, reform of unifying the corporate income tax for domestic and foreign-capital enterprises, perfecting resource tax and reforming tax and surtax for petroleum products, and carrying out experiment for property tax. (2) In terms of reform of budget system, reforms were implemented for departmental budget, central payment system of national treasury, government procurement system and double-line management system for revenue and expenditure; additionally, attempts were made to establish double-entry budget system composed of governmental public budget, governmental fund budget, state-owned capital operating budget and social security budget.

#### 3.3.2.2 Reform of Financial System

The reform of financial system involved the financial organization system, financial market system, and governmental financial macro-control system (actually, the reform concerning the governmental functions also includes the reform of financial supervision system and of state-owned financial asset management system). As for reform of financial macro-control system, upon establishing the target of socialist market economic system, it was carried out mainly at three levels as per concept of establishing and perfecting the indirect financial regulation and control.

In terms of regulation and control subject, the position and duties were first defined for the People's Bank of China as the central bank to implement financial macro- control; afterward, in order to enhance authority of the central bank, the management system of the People's Bank of China was reformed in 1998, by changing the setup from provincial branches to regional branches; additionally, in order to enable the central bank to focus on the implementation of monetary policies as well as to enhance the independence of the People's Bank of China, the regulatory function of securities, insurance and banking were disengaged from the functions of the People's Bank of China, respectively in 1992, 1998, and 2003. Thus, the separation was actualized for monetary policy and financial regulation, especially the regulatory function of banking.

In terms of regulation and control objects, policy finance and commercial finance were separated, by organizing the policy banks, changing the previous special banks into state-owned commercial banks and developing gradually joint-stock and regional commercial banks and different non-banking financial institutions. In recent years, the reform has been further deepened for the exclusively state-owned commercial banks, with the four major state-own commercial banks: ICBC, ABC, BOC and CCB all completing the reform for joint-stock system; meanwhile, the reform was advanced for policy banks, with State Development Bank being the first commercial bank transformed from a policy bank. In addition, innovation was further advanced for financial organizations, by developing new rural financial institutions and small-credit companies, as well as such new financial organization form and financial service mode as Internet finance is also continuously developed.

In terms of regulation mode, it was managed by applying the deposit rate, central bank re-lending interest rate, open market service and other monetary instruments instead of by mainly relying on the management of credit scale; for the purpose of perfecting the market-oriented financial regulation and control mode, in 1998, the limit control was cancelled for the loan scale of state-owned commercial banks and the statutory deposit reserve accounts and provisions accounts of financial institutions at the central bank were generally merged into the reserve deposit account; in order to enrich the money policy instruments, the central bank bills were issued to hedge the base money release resulting from the growth of foreign exchange reserve, and form the operating frame for open market services with the Chinese characteristics; the central bank also created the oriented regulation and control monetary policy instruments, including the two short-term interest rate regulatory instruments for the open market introduced in early 2013: Short-term Liquidity Operations

(SLO) and Standing Lending Facility (SLF), as the necessary supplement for the regular operation of the open market, and such regulation and control instrument exploring for guiding the mid-term interest rate as Pledged Supplementary Lending (PSL) in the mid-2014.

By the foregoing reforms, the frame has been basically formed for the financial regulation and control system that meets requirements of the socialist market economic system.

### 3.3.3 *Laying More Stress on Fairness from Focusing on Efficiency*

The relation between fairness and efficiency is the key issue for research on economic theories as well as the focus in practice of reform. Since the reform and opening up, China has continuously deepened the theoretical understanding to relation between fairness and efficiency and also continuously adjusted principle of dealing with the relation between them along with development of the practice.

At the first stage, it focused on overcoming disadvantages of equalitarianism and persisting in "give priority to efficiency with due consideration to fairness".

China's traditional system deviated on fairness and efficiency, by excessively stressing on fairness, but ignoring efficiency; furthermore, the understanding of fairness is also on the narrow side, excessively emphasizing the equalitarianism in income distribution. According to the estimates of World Bank, in 1980, 0.16,[6] the Gini coefficient of urban residents in China, indicated a high quality of income distribution. Since such income distribution system substantially blurred out the difference among individuals and caused inequity between contribution and remuneration of different production factors (mainly referred to labor factors), it is unfair either. In turn, such unfairness caused, to a certain extent, the economy to lack of necessary vigor and power and low efficiency.

In view of such disadvantage of equalitarianism under traditional system which seriously affected the efficiency, China started theoretical self-examination on relation between fairness and efficiency. The *Decision on the Reform of Economic System* adopted at the Third Plenary Session of 12th National Congress of the CPC analyzed scientifically the theoretical misunderstanding of equalitarianism and simultaneous prosperity for long and the inherent logic of "rich first" and "rich together" and proposed that "socialism shall ensure to promote gradually the level of material and cultural life for the social members and achieve the goal of common prosperity. However, common prosperity is not equal to complete equity and doesn't mean all social members being rich at the same speed at the same time. If common prosperity were understood as complete equity and simultaneous prosperity, it would not only be impossible, but also would definitely result in common poverty.

[6] Cited from Zhang Zhuoyuan (1999).

Only by allowing and encouraging some regions, some enterprises and some people to be rich first by working hard will it be possible to encourage most of people to get rich."

Being promoted by the foregoing ideological emancipation, efforts were made to overcome disadvantages of equalitarianism and "big rice bowl" system which reflected in dealing with relation between fairness and efficiency i.e. give priority to promoting efficiency and efforts made by factor suppliers, especially laborers and strive to actualize the allocation of production factors (At the beginning of the reform, the labor factor was the focus; with the reform and opening up going further and the economic structure, especially ownership structure changing, materialized capital and technology, management and other factors that represent the human capital were also included gradually.) in line with their contributions in creating wealth so as to adequately stimulate their enthusiasm and creativity and promote the increase of social wealth to actualize the fairness at a higher level. The 13th National Congress proposed, for the first time, to "reflect the social fairness on the premises of promoting efficiency". The *Decision for Establishment of Socialist Market Economic System* adopted at the Third Plenary Session of the 14th National Congress of the CPC further put forward explicitly the principle of "give priority to efficiency with due consideration to fairness", which was re-affirmed at the 15th National Congress of the CPC.

The implementation of the principle of "give priority to efficiency with due consideration to fairness" has, to a great extent, broken the set pattern of "equalitarianism", strongly stimulated the social vigor and promoted the rapid development of social productivity. During the rapid accumulation of social wealth, individuals also enjoyed the rapid growth of absolute income and remarkable improvement of individual welfare.

At the second stage, in view of the realistic contradiction of increasingly expanded income gap, "laying more stress on social fairness" was emphasized.

Since the earlier reform laid stress mainly on improving efficiency and increasing economy and relatively ignored fairness, especially the fairness of social wealth distribution, which directly leaded to expansion of income gap. Besides the expansion of urban-rural income gap and unbalanced development in regions, the income gap between different industries, different ownerships and different social groups was also relatively prominent. It should be said the expansion of income gap includes rational and inevitable factors, and there are irrational factors and even unfair factors. The unfair problems especially existed in opportunities (or starting point) and rules (or procedures) for distribution. Such unfairness was mainly reflected in irregular income due to the institutional and legal flaws and policy faults, such as the illegal income obtained by capitalization of power and unreasonable income obtained by monopoly. If such unfairness goes further without control, it will not only easily create social contradictions, but also will strangle the economic incentives for social development, thus resulting in low efficiency.

Under the background of worsening income distribution and increasing poor-rich gap, the appeal of the whole society for fairness became increasingly strong. In view of this, when expounding the relation between fairness and efficiency, the 16th

National Congress of the CPC no longer insisted on the principle of "give priority to efficiency with due consideration to fairness", but started to emphasize on "stressing on efficiency for initial distribution and on fairness for re-distribution", with the aim to resolve the unfair problems in the process of re-distribution. According to the requirement for building a socialist and harmonious society, the Fourth Plenary Session of the 16th National Congress of the CPC emphasized to "lay stress on social fairness". The Fifth Plenary Session of the 16th National Congress of the CPC further proposed "based on the economic development, to lay more stress on social fairness so that all the people will benefit from achievements of the reform and opening up and the construction of socialist modernization". The 17th National Congress of the CPC specified "the relation between efficiency and fairness shall be properly dealt for both initial distribution and re-distribution and more stress shall be laid on fairness for redistribution". The keynote changes emphasized in these wordings represent the further deepened understanding of fairness and efficiency.

On laying more stress on social fairness, efforts were made to advance the reform of income distribution system and social security system.

In terms of income distribution system, the basic direction for reform is to change from equalitarianism and "big rice bowl" system to the integration of distribution as per work and distribution as per production factors, with the distribution as per labor as the main and with the co-existence of multiple distribution modes; consideration is given to both efficiency and fairness, protecting the lawful income, banning the unlawful income, regulating the high income and assuring the basic life of low-income people. Upon reforming for more than three decades, the traditional equalitarianism distribution system is already broken basically, the distribution system with distribution as per labor as the main part and co-existence of multiple distribution modes is primarily established, capital, land (right to use) and other traditional production factors are gradually brought into the category of income distribution, and technology, management and other modern production factors also start to be transformed into share capital, in the mode of "human capital", for participation in distribution. Hence, the composition of income sources for residents and especially urban residents is also observed with changes accordingly: wage income from working is still the main source of income for urban residents, but its proportion declines to some extent; the proportion of such non-wage income as operating income and property income increases to some extent. Additionally, since consideration is given to both efficiency and fairness, a great change is observed in the distribution pattern of national income among sectors of residents, enterprises and governments. In view of the macro distribution pattern for national income in 2012 as supported with the available data, income of residents shares about 62 %, income of enterprises shares about 18.5 %, and income of governments shares about 19.5 %. It indicates that residents already become the important main body of savings, some of the enterprises in proper performance are also capable to self-development and governments also accumulate continuously the fiscal capacity for income regulation. Such changes are in compliance with the requirement for changing from planned economy to socialist market economic system.

In terms of social security system, the basic direction of reform is to establish the multi-level social security system covering social insurance, public relief, social welfare, special care and placement and social mutual aid, personal savings accumulation assurance. As from the mid-1990s, as per requirement of providing the market economy with "shock absorber" and "safety net", the reform of social security system was further advanced with endowment insurance, medical insurance, unemployment insurance and minimum subsistence as the keynote. Especially, in recent years, certain progress has been made in implementing the new rural cooperative medical system, urban resident basic medical insurance system, rural minimum living security system and establishing the national unified endowment insurance system for urban-rural residents (by combining the new rural social endowment insurance system and social endowment insurance system of urban resident). In terms of endowment insurance, as by the end of 2013, nationwide, the participants in basic endowment insurance for urban staff and workers numbered to 322.12 million and the participants in the basic endowment insurance of urban-rural residents numbered to 497.50 million. In terms of medical insurance, as by the end of 2013, the participants in basic medical insurance numbered to 573.22 million, including 274.16 million for the basic medical insurance of staff and workers; the participants in the resident basic medical insurance numbered to 299.06 million. As by the end of 2013, 2,489 counties (cities and districts) implemented the new rural cooperative medical system, with a participating rate of 99.0 %. As by the end of 2013, the participants in the unemployment insurance numbered to 164.17 million, the participants in the industrial injury insurance numbered to 198.97 million and the participants in the maternity insurance numbered to 163.97 million. Additionally, in terms of minimum living security, as by the end of 2013, the urban household enjoying the minimum living guarantee nationwide numbered to 10.972 million and 20.642 million persons; the rural household enjoying the minimum living guarantee numbered to 29.311 million and 53.88 million persons. As a whole, the frame of new social security system has been basically formed and the coverage of social security is expanding continuously.

## References

Deng Xiaoping (1993) Selected works of Deng Xiaoping, vol 3. China People's Publishing House, Beijing

Editorial Office of Economic Research (1979) A special collection of discussions on law of value in socialist economy. Editorial Office of Economic Research, Beijing

Yang Shengqun (2004) Chronicle of Deng Xiaoping. Central Party Literature Press

Zhang Zhuoyuan (1999) Price reform in China. In: Wang Mengkui (ed) The 20 years of economic transition in China. Foreign Language Press, Beijing

# Chapter 4
# Development of Open Economy

At the beginning of reform and opening up, Deng Xiaoping pointed out: the present world is open. One important reason for China's backwardness after the industrial revolution in western countries was its closed-door policy. After the founding of the People's Republic, we were blockaded by others, and the country remained virtually closed, which created difficulties for us. The experience of the past 30 or so years has demonstrated that a closed-door policy would hinder construction and inhibit development. There could be two kinds of exclusion: one would be directed against other countries; the other would be directed against China itself, with one region or department closing its doors to the others. Both kinds of exclusion would be harmful. We are suggesting that we should develop rapidly, but not too rapidly because that would be unrealistic. To do this, we have to invigorate the domestic economy and open (Deng Xiaoping 1993).

Often used as a single word in China, "reform and opening up" actually contains two meanings: one is "reform" and the other is "opening up". However, opening up is the essential of reform. There are two major driving forces of China's reform: one is the internal driving force of China, the top-down reform led by the government and the other is the external driving force (or pressure) after China integrating into globalized economic system, the influence of globalization on China's reform from bottom to top and from the outside to the inside. On one hand, globalization has accelerated economic development in China, without which it would not be possible for China to move on the road to modernization in 30 years, which has taken other countries 200 years. On the other hand, globalization has forced and deepened China's reform.

## 4.1 Background and Trend of Economic Globalization

The term "economic globalization" carries rich meanings. On the macro level, economic globalization is a process for governments, enterprises, residents and other economic entities of all countries to break through the national boundaries, on the

 
X. Zhang, X. Chang, *The Logic of Economic Reform in China*, China Insights,
DOI 10.1007/978-3-662-47404-4_4

basis of generally accepted economic principles, to carry out the economic activities in an equal and mutually beneficial manner. On the micro level, it is the tendency of economic interdependence among countries and regions continuously deepening, with product, service, capital, technology, information, population and other elements flowing on a global scale, the barrier being lowered and the scale being enlarged. All such cross-border economic phenomena as international trade, international direct investment, transnational production and financial market integration are all in the category of economic globalization.

Economic globalization is not newly emerged in recent decades. Based on research, as early as 200 B.C., the ancient Greek philosopher Polybius once talked about the concept of globalization: "in the past, what happened in the world have nothing to do with each other. Since then, they depend on each other". From this maxim, we can deduce that the economic globalization has a long history. As to the history of the real world, in the book "Reorient", Franck pointed out: from 1400 to 1800, the globalization based on division of labor in agriculture was dominated by China and India, before the western world emerged, forming a basic pattern of "exchange of needed goods". Since the nineteenth century, the transatlantic and intercontinental trade and financial network with West Europe, especially UK as the center has been formed, and the trade between core industrial countries and marginal agricultural countries for industrial products, agricultural products and raw materials has been formed. As Maddison (2003) pointed out, the annual average growth of global export was 3.4 % from 1870 to 1913. It should be particularly noted that the trade growth of almost all countries was faster than their income growth, which was the most important feature of globalization deepening, and of countries getting closer. However, many scholars believe such globalization limited to developed countries and was not a global sense.

Since the 1970s, represented by modern transport, communication and information technology, the technological progress has significantly overcome transaction costs caused by geographical distance and greatly expanded the radius of market transactions and the breadth of globalization. As a consequence, the "Global" feature of various economic activities has been increasingly strong; resource allocation has been conducted on a global scale; international division of labor has broken through the national boundaries and into all production processes of products. Accordingly, the nationality and regionality of economic activities tends to be weakened. At the moment, the new round of economic globalization has really aroused extensive concern in the international community.

As per further analysis, the current economic globalization over the last three decades or so has the following prominent features:

Firstly, the current globalization is mainly driven by transnational corporations. These transnational corporations are the real "international citizens". The revolutionary significance of their prosperity for the development of globalization lies in that, by breaking through the boundaries of countries and nations, the division of work is no longer confined to manufactured products but different production processes of products. Hence, more and more transnational corporations has been actively looking for the most suitable production bases around the world for all production stages of their products by slicing the value chain, so as to expand and accelerate international industrial transfer. With the production system of intra-product specialization promoted by transnational corporations, different economies are divided into different production stages and cooperate and share interests under the framework of global production chain and value chain. The international division of work based on intra- product specialization has been the most obvious in the East Asia region since 1980s. Roughly, the production network in East Asia is as follows: core components are produced mainly in Japan, general components are produced in South Korea and ASEAN-5 and products are assembled in China.

Secondly, the current globalization is accompanied with dramatic changes in the system structure. Since the 1980s, the ideological trends of marketization, liberalization and integration have spread all over the world. Especially with the former Soviet Union and the Eastern Europe disintegrating, many economies in the world have undergoing great changes in the system transformation towards the market economy: the enclosed planning system has been gradually substituted by open market system; barriers of international trade have been continuously cut down; the international rules for economic globalization have increasingly tended to maintain the fair competition; all the countries have also changed their restriction to encouragement for foreign direct investment. All changes have promoted the deepening of international division of work, enhanced the dependence of countries on foreign trade and accelerated the international capital flow, thus advancing the economic globalization to a new stage.

Thirdly, the current globalization is the globalization of labor. Since the 1980s, the trend of developing economies and transforming economies participating in international economic division system dominated by developed countries has triggered the new globalization of labor to increase the supply of labor. As the American economist Freeman once estimated, if China, India and the former Soviet Union Group were still outside the global economic system, the number of labors in the world would be about 1.46 billion by 2000. With joining the world economic system, the number of the labors would be doubled by 2000, from 1.46 billion to 2.92 billion.

## 4.2 Unveiling the Curtain for Opening Up

In synchronization with the current-round globalization, over the last three decades since 1978, China has advanced the sustainable and rapid development of economy by implementing the strategy of opening up, making use of two types of resources and two markets, improving efficiency of factors allocation and driving the reform process through opening up.

Before the reform and opening up, China implemented the centralized planned economic system, with all trading activities under control of the central government with the precise quantitative standard. State Planning Commission (SPC) was responsible to formulate the plan for import and export and some state-owned foreign trade companies under Ministry of Foreign Trade and Economic Cooperation were responsible to implement such plan. In terms of foreign trade, it was run by the state- owned foreign trade companies and the power to engage in import and export trade was granted only to the special foreign trade corporations and their branches, while no other institutions had the right to engage in import and export trade. According to statistics, as by the end of 1978, there were about 130 special foreign trade companies nationwide, including provincial and municipal foreign trade branches and sub-branches, and their business activities were subject to the monopoly and interference of the administrative authorities, without separating the government and enterprises. In terms of domestic trade, the export procurement system and import appropriation system were implemented. Foreign trade companies bought out the exported commodities from the suppliers or producers, while the producers were not responsible for the marketability, prices and profit and loss of the commodities. The commodities imported by foreign trade companies were allocated and transferred, as planned, to the users that would not undertake any responsibility for import quality and benefits. The state implemented the strict directive plan for foreign-trade purchase, allocation and transfer, export, import, foreign exchange receipt and expenditure and all the business activities; in terms of financial management, the national finance generally took on the profit and loss and the working capital of foreign trade companies was also generally verified and appropriated by Ministry of Finance. In terms of foreign-trade pricing system, domestic operation was subject to the planned price and foreign operation was subject to the international market price, cutting off the contact between domestic and overseas market price. Under such a system, since the quantity of import and export was not so much related to the foreign exchange rate and relative prices of commodities, so the foreign-trade structure was not so much associated with the comparative advantages of China. As a prominent case in point, it was until the early 1980s the capital-intensive and resource- intensive products had always played an important role in the export of China with relatively abundant labor resources. In addition to distortion of trade structure, the relative scale of foreign trade was also shrinking. According to the estimation of Lardy (1994), the share of China's trade volume in the world trade decreased from 1.5 % in 1953 to 0.6 % in 1977.

The distortion of foreign trade system and shrinkage of the total volume was an epitome of the rigid economic system and poor performance of overall economic development in China in those days. After the great calamity of the Cultural Revolution, it was an urgent need for the whole nation to accelerate the economic development and reform the traditional planned economic system. At that time, it was found that when China was observed with economic and political turbulence one after another, the science and technology developed rapidly all over the world and some of the developing countries, especially the neighboring Asian newly industrializing countries and regions made outstanding achievements in development, with the living standard of their people obviously improved, showing a sharp contrast with the situation in China: economic development was stagnated and improvement of people's living standard was slow. One important experience of these countries and regions in accelerating the development was to open up, undertake the transfer of international industry, absorb foreign capital, introduce foreign technologies, develop foreign trade, promote financial opening and enhance competitiveness in international competition. Based on the foregoing international experience, it was necessary to actively develop the equal and mutual-benefit economic cooperation with all the countries in the world on the basis of depending on China's own efforts and strive to use the advanced technologies and equipments in the world. Hence, China unveiled the curtain for open economic development.

Opening up was a new thing in the economic construction of New China, without any ready-made experience to follow, and therefore there were many economic risks and uncertainty and many doubts and worries about political ideology. Under such conditions, it was neither feasible nor possible to open up comprehensively as one package, and to explore for a moderate and creative strategy of opening up was the only way to go. In 1979, with the favorable conditions that the southeast coast is near to Hong Kong, Macao and Taiwan, the central government decided to demarcate part of the areas in Shenzhen, Zhuhai, Shantou and Xiamen to establish special economic zones for pilot opening up and accumulating partial experiences to exploring feasible approaches. Within a few years after establishment, the special zones were observed with great changes and especially Shenzhen developed from one small frontier town to a modern metropolis and being an example for development by opening up.

With success in the experiment of establishing special zones, the open area entitled to the preferential policy expanded gradually, from the coastal regions, regions along rivers and borders and inland provincial capital cities and then to the central-west regions, gradually forming the opening pattern regionally.

Meanwhile, the reform of foreign trade system was also advanced gradually. Similar to the other reforms in economical field, the reform of foreign trade system in the early 1980s was also mainly featured for decentralization of power and transfer of profits. According to such concept of reform, the state successively approved the departments under the central government and provinces and municipalities to found foreign trade companies and expand rapidly trade channels. After 1987, it became the key field for development of open economy to cultivate foreign trade enterprises as the real market entities. As from 1988, the contract responsibility system for foreign trade was implemented mainly in provinces, municipalities and autonomous regions nationwide. The orientation of the reform was: establish the foreign trade system with responsibility for their own profits and losses, open operation, integration of industry and foreign trade and the promotion of agent system. The reform focused on promoting the foreign trade enterprises to be responsible for their own profits and losses by establishing and perfecting the economic regulation system with exchange rate and tax as the main lever.

In addition to the foreign trade management system, China was also observed with great changes in absorbing foreign businessmen for direct investment. Since the reform and opening up, China has encouraged foreign investment in a wider scope and more forms, by introducing policies for encouraging the compatriots from Hong Kong, Macao and Taiwan to invest in Mainland China and the taxation law for foreign-invested enterprises. During 16 years from 1979 to 1994, China formulated and promulgated more than 500 regulations for foreign economy, including more than 70 regulations and rules for utilization of foreign capital, and concluded the investment protection agreements with 65 countries in the world (Pei Changhong 2009).

## 4.3 The Key Step for Opening Up: Accession to WTO

2001 was an important time point of China for opening up. In the year, China officially accessed to the World Trade Organization (WTO). The integration of 1.3 billion people into the world economy brings about not only the huge demographic dividend, but also the flourishing consumer market. To some extent, China's accession to WTO has fundamentally changed the development process of China's economy and become an important watershed for the stage of China's opening up and economic reform.

China was originally the contracting party of GATT (General Agreement on Tariff and Trade), the predecessor of WTO. On March 6, 1950, Taiwan authority declared to withdraw from GATT. Upon restoring the legitimate seat in UN in 1971, China was once invited to return to GATT, but in the circumstance that the reform and opening up was not yet launched at that time, the decision makers considered GATT as a club of the rich, which was not much necessary for China to participate in.

With the policy of reform and opening up established in the early 1980s, China's foreign trade developed rapidly and the comparative advantage of China's economy in textile and other labor-intensive industries was also manifested through international trade with the textile export once sharing 30 % of the total export volume. However, without the textile agreement of GATT (i.e., the Multi-fiber Agreement), the necessary quota could not be lawfully obtained from the textile business for the Chinese government. With consideration to export expansion and economic development, the Chinese government signed the Multi-fiber Agreement and then decided to apply for rejoining GATT.

In July 1986, the Chinese government further demonstrated China's determination and confidence for opening up and integrating actively with globalization, by applying for restoring the position as the contracting party of GATT. However, while becoming gradually a big country of export, China has been deemed by many countries as the competitor, the anti-dumping action against China increased continuously, and foreign- invested enterprises also encountered many problems on operating environment when entering into Chinese market. Under such environment, the obstruction for China to rejoin GATT was also getting larger. Especially, due to WTO Uruguay Round negotiations, when accessing to WTO, the developing countries had to promise to advance the wider and more adequate opening up and improve continuously the operating environment for foreign-invested enterprises.

In the 1980s, the query about China's economic system also became a barrier for accession to WTO. According to the recall of Mr. Long Yongtu, a country for joining GATT was required to submit a copy of explanation for the economic and trade system before being reviewed. Generally, such review would take a period of 1 ~ 2 months, but it took 6 years for China. The key reason lied in that many countries did not recognize China as a market economic entity and China's "commodity economic system integrated with planned regulation and market regulation" could not be understood by western countries. It was until 1992 when the 14th National Congress of the CPC determined the reform target for the socialist market economic system that the review over China's economic system was over.

In order to integrate with the rules of WTO and win trust from the negotiation partners, China accelerated the process of trade liberalization. China fundamentally resolved the problem of compatibility with the multilateral trade system of WTO by perfecting the system frame of open economy from 1994 to 2001, selecting the unilateral trade liberalization strategy, and lowering sharply the tariff level. The reform of China at this stage mainly included: (1) cancelling the foreign exchange turning over and quota control system for foreign trade enterprises; cancelling foreign exchange retention for export, and implementing the unified bank exchange settlement and sale system; (2) implementing, as from July 1, 1994, the *Foreign Trade Law of the People's Republic of China*; bringing the foreign trade management to the legal track; granting the power to engage in foreign trade to qualified state-owned production enterprises, research institutions and commercial goods enterprises, and opening the operation of import and export commodities to a maximum extent; annulling the directive plan for foreign trade enterprises; (3) according to modern enterprise system, re-organizing the state-owned foreign trade enterprises, actively implementing the pilot work for joint- stock system and allowing the qualified foreign trade enterprises to change gradually to limited liability companies or joint-stock limited companies.

The reason for the Chinese government to do so was to promote the reform by opening up. During his visit in USA in April, 1999, Premier Zhu Rongji once expressed: more adequate competition was the most important source of pressure that can force Chinese state-owned enterprises and banks to implement the structural reform, and the competition resulting from the identity being a WTO member would promote the fast and healthy development of Chinese economy.

During the process for China's accession to WTO, the completion of negotiation with USA in November 1999 was another critically important milestone. On November 13 and 15, 1999, Zhu Rongji, acting then as the premier of the State Council, met twice with the US government delegation led by Charlene Barshefsky, United States Trade Representative, and Gene Sperling, Chairman of the United States National Economic Council, which came over for the bilateral negotiation on China's accession to WTO, and negotiated with them in person. Eventually, by seizing the historical opportunity, the two sides reached a consensus on a series of issues such as trade in goods, trade in service, finance, telecommunication, audio and video products, bancassurance and distribution and came to an agreement on China's accession to WTO between China and America.

The afterward period of 1999–2001 was the final stage for China's accession to WTO, during which the multilateral documents were drafted and approved for

China's accession to WTO. On November 10, 2001, China's accession to WTO was examined and voted at the WTO's Fourth Ministerial Conference held in Doha.

After 2001, with keeping promise for accession to WTO, the Chinese government continued to comprehensively adjust foreign trade system and foreign trade policy: (1) checking up and amending a number of laws and regulations concerning foreign trade and keeping foreign trade policies transparent: as by the end of 2002, nearly 30 departments under the State Council checked up and amended the laws and regulations in connection with foreign economic contact, by checking up 1,400 regulations, of which 559 were abolished and 197 were amended; (2) changing the administrative functions of the government and further rationalizing the foreign trade management system: classifying uniformly the qualification for import and export into foreign trade circulation and self-run import and export, of which the former was subject to the verification and approval of Ministry of Foreign Trade and Economic Cooperation and the latter was decentralized to the provincial administration of foreign trade and economic cooperation for implementation of the registration system; (3) intensifying the trade liberalization and perfecting the management measures for import and export: according to the commitment for accession to WTO, China took action to lower substantially the tariff in a relative wide range and reduced and regulated the non-tariff measures; from January 1, 2002, the import tariff was lowered for more than 5,300 commodities, with the arithmetic average tariff rate lowered to 12 %, including the average tariff rate of industrial products from 14.17 % down to 11.16 %; for agricultural products from 18.19 % down to 15.16 %, with the weighted average tariff rate lowered from the prevailing 99.15–51.56 %, at a decrease rate of 41.15 %, and the tariff items involve sharing 73 % of the total tariff items; in terms of non-tariff barriers, restriction on import quantity was cancelled for part of commodities; (4) strengthening the construction of rule of law: on April 6, 2004, according to China's commitment for accession to WTO and the rules of WTO, the eighth meeting of the Standing Committee of the 10th National People's Congress amended the *Foreign Trade Law* with respect to any content incompliant with the commitment for China's accession to WTO and the rules of WTO and stipulated new provisions for the implementation mechanism and procedure for China to enjoy the rights as a WTO member.

With the regulations on foreign trade being perfected, the tariff being lowered sharply, trade in service being opened gradually and great progress being made in utilization of foreign investment, protection of intellectual property and enhancement of transparency, China already completed the integration with WTO system and basically actualized the requirement for trade liberalization under the rules of WTO. Being driven by the system reform and trade liberalization force initiated by accession to WTO, China's foreign trade, FDI and foreign trade dependence grew rapidly after 2002; open and competitive external environment also caused China to effectively make use of its own factor endowment, give play to its own comparative advantages and second-mover advantages and gain huge globalization dividend.

## 4.4 China's Experience in Opening Up: Gradual and Orderly Opening Up

As part of the whole gradual reform, the orderly opening up was the successful experience of China for actively responding to the trend of globalization, fully participating in global competition and benefiting from globalization. In summary, the orderly opening up includes: protected trade opening and gradual and orderly financial opening. In the final analysis, the orderly opening up helped to actualize the opening up in compliance with the economic development level of China, benefiting from participation in globalization and avoiding the possible sharp impact and even crisis resulting from globalization.

### *4.4.1 Protected Trade Opening Up*

Opening up may not naturally bring about economic growth. Only by paying attention to protection, opening up gradually and persisting in reform can benefits be earned from opening up. Overall liberalization and opening up would only result in conflicts and crises, without any supporting reform and consideration to the realistic conditions but by believing everything books or foreign experts said. As early as in his theory of immature industry, Friedrich List underlined the protection in opening up. Historically, all the countries successful in opening up had been aware of it. For instance, Amsden (1989) and Wade (1990) pointed out: the economic policies taken in the 1960s by South Korea and Taiwan well-known for implementing the successful export-oriented strategy were far beyond the range for market and comparative advantage to freely play a role. In their opinion, South Korea and Taiwan defined the priority for development of industry and took, without the least hesitation, the intervening measures (including subsidy, trade restriction, administrative guidance, state-owned enterprises, credit distribution and other policies) to re-invent the comparative advantage according to the intended target of government. Intervention is a part of the transition stage rather than to support the declining enterprises. The target is to establish powerful and prosperous enterprises that can compete with equal conditions in the global market, without being protected further.

Developing countries successful in economy would be often ready to take measures to protect their industries and give every industry or trade time for diversified development in new fields. Emphasis on protection in opening up actually means that trade opening up shall match the level of economic development.

China's opening up is the protected opening up. If the reduction of tariff rate is used to measure the degree of opening up for trade, it may be observed that China's trade has been opened up gradually. According to the relevant analysis, with previous reductions of tariff, the degree of China's trade protection decreased gradually.[1]

[1] Jin Xiangrong and Lin Chengliang (1999).

Figure 4.1 also shows China's overall tariff level dropped from 42.1 % in 1992 to less than 10 % in 2007. All these indicate there is protection in opening up, but the degree declines gradually.

China's trade protection should be noted in two aspects: firstly, the trade protection is structural, i.e., the tariff rate is much different for different industries. For instance, in 1994, the tariff was 0 for Color TV and 120 % for motorbikes (excluding the non- tariff trade restriction) (see Table 4.1). Secondly, in addition to tariff, trade protection also included non-tariff trade restriction.

Foreign exchange control and exchange rate subsidy used to be the main means for trade protection. For instance, in 1994, the central government imported such products as wheat, fertilizer, edible oil and sugar at the exchange rate of RMB 5.8/US$, while the single exchange rate was RMB 8.6/US$ in average at that time, which is a typical exchange rate subsidy. Furthermore, before the integration of exchange rates in 1994, domestic enterprises were allowed to retain a certain proportion of foreign exchange earning in their retention quota account. Such system was cancelled in January 1994. However, the retention quota of foreign exchange previously held by the enterprises could be still used to import products as per official exchange rate of RMB 5.8/US$ before integration.

If consideration is given to the non-tariff restriction measure resulting from the foreign exchange control and exchange rate subsidy, China's actual tariff level would be nearly doubled in 1994. As Table 4.1 shows, in 1994, the tariff rate was 21.74 %, and the non-tariff rate converted from measures would be up to 21.55 %.

Trade protection is mainly for import, but "protection" can also be actually reflected in export. For instance, the export rebate implemented by China as from 1985 is a kind of taxation policy for encouraging export, to enhance the competitiveness of export enterprises.[2] Export rebate was mainly meant for the segment of

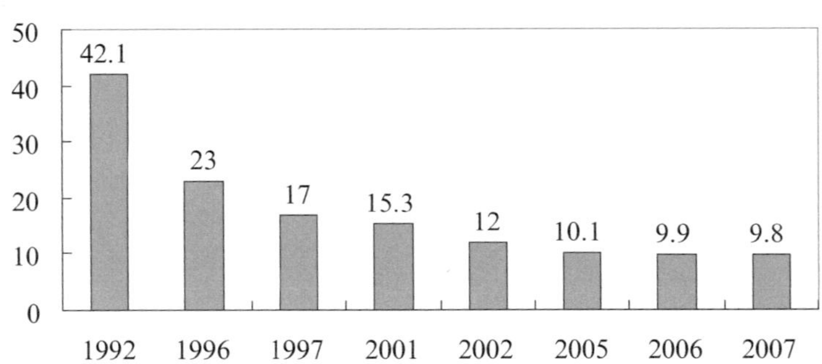


**Fig. 4.1** Actual tariff reduction by China (%) (Data source: data before 2001 are sourced from Zhang Xiaojing (1999); data after 2001 are sourced from the website of Ministry of Commerce)

[2] It is also viewed that in principle, rebate is not a policy for encouraging export, but help export enterprises to be entitled to the benefits general enterprises should be entitled to. Cancellation of rebate for exported commodities will constitute prejudice to export enterprises, thus causing the market distortion. However, it cannot be denied that the export rebate policy is currently implemented, with a relatively high rate of export rebate, just to encourage export.

**Table 4.1** China's trade protection (tariff and non-tariff restriction measures) %

| | Total trade protection (t+n) | Tariff rate (t) | Non-tariff restriction (n) |
|---|---|---|---|
| Rapeseed oil | 113.6 | 25 | 88.6 |
| Sugar | 141.4 | 30 | 111.4 |
| Non-alcohol drinks | 105.56 | 65 | 40.56 |
| Plywood | 46.1 | 20 | 26.1 |
| Wool and wool tops | 19.2 | 15 | 4.2 |
| Color TV | 18.59 | 0 | 18.59 |
| Tape recorder | 54.27 | 8 | 46.27 |
| Motorcycle | 131.2 | 120 | 11.2 |
| Air conditioner | 104.73 | 90 | 14.73 |
| Steel products | 38.76 | 15 | 23.76 |
| Copper and copper products | 17.15 | 10 | 7.15 |
| Alumina and alumina products | 27.49 | 18 | 9.49 |
| Gasoline | 35.24 | 9 | 26.24 |
| Diesel | 24.7 | 6 | 18.7 |
| DAP | 72.4 | 0 | 72.4 |
| Synthetic fibre | 22.01 | 15 | 7.01 |
| Natural rubber | 42.9 | 30 | 12.9 |
| Synthetic rubber | 42.9 | 30 | 12.9 |
| Plastics | 36.59 | 25 | 11.59 |
| Car | 134.2 | 110 | 24.2 |
| Crude oil | 18.19 | 1.5 | 16.69 |
| Microcomputer | 13.02 | 7 | 6.02 |
| Chromatron | 33.59 | 15 | 18.59 |
| Wheat | 72.4 | 0 | 72.4 |
| SPC exchange | 20.98 | 12 | 8.98 |
| **Total** | **43.29** | **21.74** | **21.55** |

Data source: Zhang Shuguang et al. (1997)

production and processing at home, with the rebate applicable to the general export trade, but only to the domestic raw materials used for processing imported materials in improvement trade. With the export rebate increasing obviously, the competitiveness of China for general export trade and export of domestic products was greatly enhanced.[3]

Restriction for market access is another evidence for protection in opening up. Such sequence as from trade opening up to financial opening up has represented the concept of protection. As for the development stages of one nation, manufacturing generally comes before service industry. The industrial gradient transfer in developed countries also basically follows such law. Thus, at the early stage, by their

[3] However, with the huge trade surplus aggregating and the crude mode of trade growth becoming prominent, the Chinese government adjusted some policies of encouraging export, including gradual reduction and cancellation of export rebate.

comparative advantage in labor force, the developing countries can compete with the developed countries in manufacturing, especially labor-intensive manufacturing industry and there will not be any major problem for opening up in these fields firstly. Thus, China opened up trade first. However, since service industry, especially financial service is one of the industries with the weakest competitiveness in China, so it has been gradually opened up according to the commitment in the relevant agreement after China's accession to WTO.

In view of the course of China's opening up, obvious achievements have been made by certain protection, especially fitting the level of opening up with the development level. With export increasing, some industries have also developed and the overall industrial competitiveness has been enhanced. In general, such protected opening up has been successful. Yet, it should be also understood that protection will naturally lead to economic distortion. How to minimize such distortion and improve efficiency is also a question one nation has to consider prudently when determining the level of trade protection.

### *4.4.2 Orderly Dual Financial Opening Up*

The sequence of opening up from trade opening up to financial opening up synchronizes with the sequence of that in industry. After the 1990s, the share of China's total import and export in GDP rose up rapidly, thus gradually forming the export-oriented economy. Meanwhile, China has been relatively prudent in financial opening up. In 1996, China implemented the current convertibility, but has not yet by now a clear timetable for capital convertibility. Figure 4.2 shows that after the Asian Financial Crisis, China has gradually relaxed the capital control. However, compared with other Asian countries, the intensity of capital control is still high in China (Fig. 4.1).

Still, China's gradual relaxation for capital flow channel has been obvious to all.

In 2001, China relaxed the restriction for the native enterprises and residents to buy foreign exchange, allowing them to buy foreign exchange for early repayment of local and foreign-currency loans or repayment of loans converted from foreign debts and foreign debts. Additionally, the government also allowed the native enterprises to buy foreign exchange for strategic investment overseas. Students for overseas studies at their own cost (college undergraduates or above) were allowed to buy, in lump sum, the foreign exchange equal to US$20,000 (the buying limit before was US$2,000) for paying the tuition fees and school sundry fees (as from January 2005, the limit for other school sundry fees than tuition fees increased to US$20,000) (Fig. 4.3).

In 2002, China started to introduce the system of Qualified Foreign Institutional Investors (QFII) into the capital market, allowing non-native residents for investment in China's stock market (Stock-A) on the premises of observing the certain restrictive provisions.

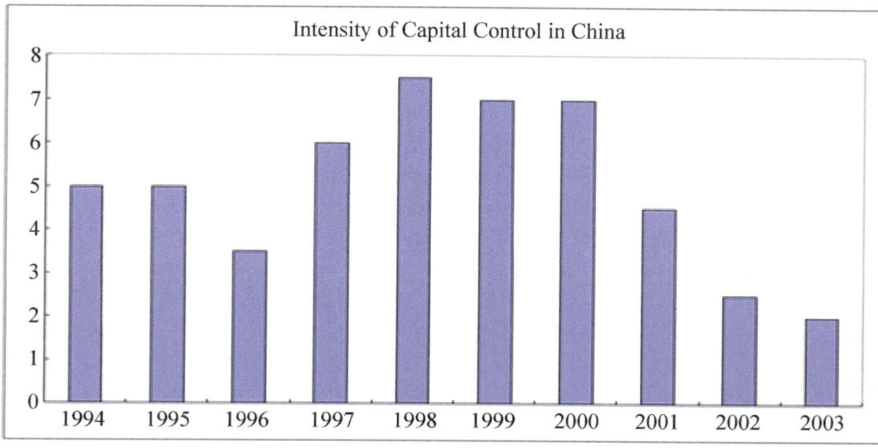


**Fig. 4.2** Gradually weakening intensity of capital control in China (Data source: Jin Luo (2004))

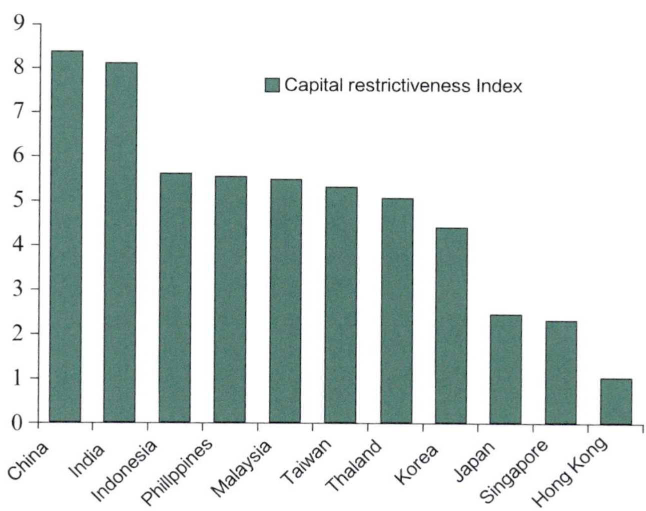


**Fig. 4.3** Capital restrictiveness index (Data source: CEIC, IMF, UBS estimation)

In 2003, the Chinese government permitted that when repaying the principal, the residents that obtained foreign exchange loans from the Chinese financial institution may not necessarily register with and obtain the approval from the government; the domestic enterprises were allowed to retain, in the foreign exchange account, the foreign-currency income from the overseas contract projects, overseas freight transport and commission and international bidding projects. In some provinces and regions, the limit for overseas investment (US$ equivalents) increased from US$1 million to US$3 million. Without LCFCA, residents could leave the country carrying foreign exchange; the maximum amount (US$ equivalents) of foreign exchange for individuals for leaving the country increased from US$2,000 to US$5,000; the limited amount (US$ equivalents) requiring for approval from State Administration of Foreign Exchange (SAFE) also increased from US$4,000 to US$10,000. The maximum amount (US$ equivalents) of foreign currency residents could carry in without declaration increased from US$2,000 to US$5,000.

In 2004, China approved, in principle, the National Social Security Fund (managing the capital of about US$17 billion) and domestic insurance companies to invest a limited part of portfolio overseas. The Chinese government permitted international financial institutions to raise Renminbi capital in China for overseas uses. China permitted the institutions of transnational companies to collect the foreign exchange capital for re-allocation in China in the form of trust loans, or lending to the overseas affiliated institutions. At present, the Chinese citizens migrating overseas and non- residents granted with legacy are also allowed to transfer the personal assets.

In 2005, to practically meet the demand of enterprises for exchanges and reduce their exchange settlement and sale cost, SAFE decided to adjust the administrative measures for the limit of current foreign exchange account: (1) the period for out-of- limit exchange settlement was extended form 10 working days to 90 days; (2) the scope of enterprises was expanded for the limit of current foreign exchange accounts verified as per 100 % of actual foreign exchange income.

On June 20, 2007, China Securities Regulatory Commission (CSRC) promulgated the *Trial Measures for the Administration of Securities Investment outside the Territory of China by Qualified Domestic Institutional Investors*. Consequently, the gate was fully open finally for Qualified Domestic Institutional Investors (QDII) of securities dealers and funds. China's QDII service developed steadily and gradually, with the total quota of QDII up to US$42.17 billion as by the end of September 2007.

In addition, to fulfill the commitment for accession to WTO, the Chinese government opened up the domestic finance gradually as from 2001. By the end of 2006, finance was comprehensively opened up. After 2006, China would cancel all the restrictions on foreign-capital banks in terms of establishment form of ownership and operating right, including ownership system, allowing foreign-capital banks to provide Chinese customers with services for Renminbi business and granting foreign-capital banks with national treatment. During the transition period of WTO, since the opening up of banking and insurance as well as securities were advanced gradually, no major impact was caused to the domestic finance thereof.

Due to the orderly and gradual financial opening up, China had, to a great extent, avoided the impact resulting from Asian Financial Crisis. However, as the "go global" strategy was implemented and the capital out-flow encouraged under the background Renminbi revaluation and excessive liquidity would cause a relatively big impact on the domestic economic and financial stability, it is extremely necessary to lay stress on orderly and gradual opening up of capital accounts.

## 4.5 The New Trend of the Development of Open Economy

### *4.5.1 New Challenges for Open Economy*

Generally speaking, over the last three decades or so, China has formed multi-level pattern of open economic development by opening up in the sequence of the special economic zones, coastal regions, areas along rivers and borders and inner land. In the systematic environment for integration with the rules of WTO and other international organizations, China has already involved deeply in economic globalization, benefiting much and making great achievement. In view of the scale of open economy, China's international trade grew sharply. China not only ranks the first by export in the world, but also being the second biggest country of import in the world. The overseas direct investment has also developed rapidly in recent years. In 2014, with the actual overseas investment exceeding the scale of utilizing foreign capital, China became the country of net capital output (according to the information disclosed by Ministry of Commerce, if the third-place financing for re-investment is added, the scale of China's overseas investment was about 140 billion in 2014, up by about US$20 billion than China's utilization of foreign capital).

Although great achievements have been made, China's open economic development will still face severe challenges in the future.

In view of international industrial division, according to the studies of Gill et al. (2007) and World Bank (2010), the medium-income countries at the intermediate level of international industrial division may be squeezed between the low-income countries with the lower-cost advantage and the high-income countries at the innovative frontier, thus being observed with "vacancy of comparative advantage" and facing the danger of being marginalized and consequently thrown out the international division system. However, it is only the primary meaning of the "middle-income trap" concept. In recent years, as China has been ranked as the middle-income country by GDP per capita, China's comparative advantage in labor-intensive industries is being gradually lost, but has not yet obtained the comparative advantage in technologies and capital intensive industries. It is imminent to resolve the problem of "middle-income trap". Facing such challenge, it will be an inevitable choice for China to build up the new advantage in international industrial division and stride over the "middle-income trap" by further expanding opening up, forcing the market-oriented reform, devoting to enhance the market vigor by establishing the mechanism of "creative destruction" and selecting efficient enterprises with market of liberal competition as the mechanism.

Meanwhile, in the post-crisis era, in order to maintain the favorable potential in the pattern of international competition, the developed economies are actively advancing the transform of economic development mode and global governance system and painstakingly excluding China from the scope of makers of new rules. For instance, "Trans-Pacific Partnership (TPP)", "Transatlantic Trade and Investment Partnership (TTIP)" and "Trade in Service Agreement (TiSA)" led by the developed economies have clearly shown that as a collective, the developed economies are not satisfied with present mode of globalization and its operating rules. They are forming the new "Holy Alliance" and striving to establish new rules. Such "new rules" have all excluded China, as shall be a new challenge for China in opening up in the new period.

### 4.5.2 Shanghai Free Trade Zone and Its Expansion

With the foregoing background, China has put forward the concept of constructing Shanghai Free Trade Zone. It clearly indicates the active attitude of the Chinese government to the foregoing new situations and new changes at home and abroad and shows the positive strategy of the Chinese government for the new pattern of international economy: on the one hand, China will positively request for participation in negotiation for all the new rules in formation; on the other hand, China selects one most important region on its territory for testing the reasonable rules in TPP and other new rules, "actualizing the promotion of development, reform and innovation by opening up, forming the reproducible and promotable experience for serving the development nationwide", and seeking the new competitive advantage for China in the international industrial division system. On September 27, 2013, the State Council officially published the overall program for China (Shanghai) Pilot Free Trade Zone, which indicates that China is in a brand-new period for opening up.

Historically, for opening up, China has basically experienced the following progressive stages: (1) by starting to, in 1980, establish Shenzhen and three other major special economic zones, followed by establishment of the coastal belts for opening up and then developing and opening Pudong, China firmly made a move for opening up. From then to China's formal accession to WTO was the period for China's "policy opening up". Its basic characteristic is that China positively selected a number of fields, regions and industries for introducing selectively foreign capital, technology, management and market mainly by taking the special preferential policies, so as to establish gradually the export-oriented economic system. (2) Upon making unremitting efforts for 13 years, China accessed to WTO officially in late 2001 and started the era of "systematic opening up". The basic characteristic of this period is that China comprehensively accepted a set of rules, systems, measures and "best practice" preset by the developed economies, for total integration into the world economic system of globalization; additionally, based on the "brining in" strategy implemented for years, Chinese enterprises started to go global. (3) The start-off for the construction of Shanghai Free Trade Zone should be deemed as a new stage for China to open up. At a level of implementing the systematic opening up in the last decade, China set up a more grand target of "constructing comprehensively the open economy" in order to ensure China grows steadily to playing an important role in the international community and to make contributions in enhancing the welfare of the whole mankind. (4) The experience of Shanghai Free Trade Zone is spreading in a larger range. In view of the system and mechanism innovation of Shanghai Free Trade Zone in negative list management of foreign investment, trade facilitation, opening up of financial service, and improvement of the governmental supervision system, and the reproducible and promotable experience and methods gathered thereof, the Chinese government decided, on December 12, 2014, to promote the experience of Shanghai Free Trade Zone in a larger range to advance the implementation of a new round opening up at a higher level. Firstly, deepen the reform and opening up of Shanghai Pilot Free Trade Zone, compress further the negative list, take a number of measures for further opening up in such industries as service and advanced manufacturing, and extend part of the opening up measures to Pudong New District. Secondly, except for the matters involving the amendment of laws, nationwide, promote the experience of 28 pilot reforms in opening up and mid and post-event supervision of investment, trade, finance and service; promote six innovative measures for custom supervision and inspection and quarantine system in other customs special supervision areas. Thirdly, based on the existing new zones and parks, set up three other free trade parks in the specific areas of Guangdong, Tianjin and Fujian and substantiate new pilot contents with the pilot contents of Shanghai Pilot Free Trade Zone as the main part and with reference to the local features. The new free trade zones will attach more importance to the local development and their tasks: e.g., Shenzhen Qianhai Free Trade Zone of Guangdong lays stress not only on finance, but also on modern logistics, information service and technological and cultural innovation. Since Tianjin Free Trade Zone mainly actuates more trade facilitation, its breakthrough direction may focus on trade in service and financial opening up.

With China in a critical period for industrial transformation and promotion, free trade zones such powerful engines will, to a great extent, innovate in the form of open economic development, win dividend from the new round globalization and accordingly advance the domestic reform and promote China's economic growth in the future.

### *4.5.3 "One Belt, One Road" Strategy*

If the construction and expansion of Shanghai Free Trade Zone is the domestic arrangement for China to cope with the new pattern of international economy in the post-crisis era, "One Belt, One Road" strategy can be considered as the global arrangement for opening up in an all-round way.

The so-called "One Belt, One Road" means the silk-road economic belt and the twenty-first century maritime silk-road. This strategy has been proposed to conform to new requirements of the new economic development stage[4] for regional

[4] That is the new normal of economy mentioned hereinafter.

development and opening up. On the one hand, after the current-round crisis, the external demand reduces obviously and China's export-focused foreign economic development is constrained. On the other hand, with China's economy developing rapidly, the structural contradiction and new-round excess capacity has already generated huge pressure and risk. Furthermore, such developed economies as USA, Europe and Japan seeks to establish the new rules for international trade and economic cooperation and rebuild the new order of international economy, which restrains the development of China. In order to positively adapt to and lead the domestic new normal and the new pattern of international economy, the central authorities proposed the strategic concept of "One Belt, One Road", which not only defines the new approach for regional development and opening up, but also will become a new growth point for economic development under the new normal.

"One Belt, One Road" strategy (i.e., the silk-road economic belt) is implemented to, on the one hand, strengthen the trade and economic cooperation of China, especially the western region with Central Asia, West Asia and East Europe by expanding the opening up westward and, on the other hand (i.e., the maritime silk-road), consolidate and develop the relation between China and Southeast Asia in trade and economic cooperation and gradually extend to such regions as South Asia and Africa. "One Belt, One Road" is a critical move for China to form the pattern for opening up in an all- round way. Through the connectivity of infrastructures in the countries along the line, it will optimize the allocation of trade and production factors promote the integration of regional economy and provide a wider market space for the development, transform and transfer of the domestic industries. In order to resolve the capital bottleneck for connectivity of infrastructures, the financing mechanism should be innovated. As the favorable supplement to World Bank, Asian Development Bank and other existing financial institutions, China has founded, jointly with the relevant countries, Asian Infrastructure Development Bank (AIIB) and the open silk-road fund. It will be helpful for Chinese capital to go global, effective use of excessively high foreign exchange reserve (nearly 4 trillion US dollars) and advancement of Renminbi internationalization. By the initial large-scale infrastructure construction followed by development and utilization of resources and energies and then all-round trade and economic cooperation, "One Belt, One Road" strategy will become a new growth point for China's economic development under the new normal. Meanwhile, considering the new order of international economy (represented by TPP, TTIP and TiSA) to be formed by such developed economies as Europe, USA and Japan, "One Belt, One Road" strategy will be also beneficial for breaking through the "encirclement" established by the developed economies and seeking the cooperation for resources and market in a larger range. "One Belt, One Road" construction can form a situation of "tripartite confrontation" with EU and North American Free Trade Zone and accelerate the new pattern of international economy, thus making a profound influence on economic globalization (Li Yang and Zhang Xiaojing 2015).

### 4.5.4 Emphasis of Open Economic Development

In view of the future, the keynote fields of China's open economic development cover mainly four aspects:

(1) Catch up with the technological revolution of the world and respond to the challenge from the international division. It means to respond to the huge challenge resulting from the re-building of international division system caused by the strength accumulation of the developed countries for prior dominance and the catch-up and competition of emerging economies, by grasping the opportunities brought by the third industrial revolution, to make full use of and cultivate advantages of China in a number of R&D fields for new technologies, to positively promote the industrial level of entities, especially improve the technical level and independent innovation capacity of manufacturing, to make efforts to extend to the two ends of the international industrial value chain with higher added value, and to actualize the change from "Made in China" to "Created in China".

(2) Actively participate in preparation and revision of the international rules and more frequently reflect intention of China in future global governance. It means to, in the process of forming new rules for the international economy, find the accurate starting point, make efforts to promote the participation in and the right of speech for the international affairs, and create an excellent and safe external environment for the sustainable and healthy development of domestic economy in advancing the establishment of more impartial new order of international economy, currency and politics.

(3) Expand the opening up of services and improve the productive efficiency of services. It means to improve the opening up level of finance and other modern services, promote the internationalization of Renminbi, and force the enhancement of labor productivity of services in China, especially promote the control relaxation and rapid development of productive services and further enhance their role in supporting the real industries, with the external competition as the power.

(4) Promote Shanghai Free Trade Zone (and its expansion) and "One Belt, One Road" strategy and break through the "encirclement" of the developed economies. The domestic arrangement of Shanghai Free Trade Zone (and its expansion) as well as the global arrangement of "One Belt, One Road", advancement of constructing Asian Infrastructure Investment Bank (AIIB), SCO Bank, BRICS Bank and Silk-road Fund and creation of regional collective financial security network all aim to positively conform to and lead the new normal of the pattern for opening up, break through the "encirclement" of the developed economies led by USA, and explore a new road for China's foreign trade, overseas investment, industrial transform and promotion and future development space in the new era.

## References

Amsden AH (1989) Asia's next giant: South Korea and late industrialization. Oxford University Press, New York

Deng Xiaoping (1993) Selected works of Deng Xiaoping, vol 3. China People's Publishing House, Beijing

Gill I, Kharas H et al (2007) An East Asian renaissance: ideas for economic growth. The International Bank for Reconstruction and Development/World Bank, Washington, DC

Jin Luo (2004) Studies on strength of China's capital control. J Financ Res 12

Jin Xiangrong, Lin Chengliang (1999) An empirical analysis on China's previous tariff adjustments and effective protection structure. J World Econ 8

Lardy N (1994) China in the world economy. Institute for International Economics, Washington, DC

Maddison A (2003) The world economy: a millennial perspective. Peking University Press

Pei Changhong (2009) An empirical analysis on China's establishment of an open economy. Res Financ Econ Issues 2

Wade R (1990) Governing the market: economic theory and role of government in East Asian industrialization. Princeton University Press, Princeton

World Bank (2010) Robust recovery, rising risks, East Asia & Pacific update. World Bank, Washington, DC

Zhang Xiaojing (1999) WTO and China's economy: an overview. Working paper No 99–005. Institute of National Economy, China Reform Foundation

Zhang Shuguang, Zhang Yansheng, Wan Zhongxin (1997) An empirical analysis on cost for China's trade protection. Econ Res J 2

# Chapter 5
# Reform of Macro Management System

The evolution of China's macro management system is observed with a process of mutual influence and mutual learning with the west. At the beginning of the reform, macro-control was introduced from the west, when China was still "a primary school pupil" with the main task to learn. Within a relatively long period of time, the Chinese government was worried for failing to master the macro-control policy. Actually, the fundamental reason rested in different "soil" of China and the west. However, since the international financial crisis in 2008, this situation has changed. The west started to consider learning macro-control from China. It is associated with the impact of the crisis on the western mainstream economics and macro policy idea as well as surely with the characteristics and strong points of China's macro-control.

China's macro management system is still in the continuous evolution. China cannot be self-satisfied or stop advancing forward when others come over to learn. Actually, some characteristics of China's macro-control are often the products at the specific development stage and under the institutional system. Such specialty should be distinguished from the general macro management experience of China which is really worth of reference for the international community. Especially, it is necessary to define which will be eliminated and required for improvement along with institutional changes, such as the decisive role of market in allocation of resources, and which fit with the institutional changes and thus following up with the step of the times. It also constitutes the basic logic for the future reform of China's macro management system.

## 5.1 "Learning from China on Macro-control"

After the modern economics were again introduced into Mainland China, since the reform and opening up, the economic circles of China have always been considered as the listener, follower and imitator of the western mainstream macro-economic



X. Zhang, X. Chang, *The Logic of Economic Reform in China*, China Insights,
DOI 10.1007/978-3-662-47404-4_5

theories and policies. Some people believe the really important issue is how to transform China's economy into such "standard" market economy as prescribed in the mainstream economic textbooks, so as to create conditions for implementation of the mainstream macroeconomic policy. Therefore, if the enlightenment and referential significance of China's experience in macro-control for the world were discussed 10 years ago, it would be much likely to sound ridiculous. However, the global financial crisis bursting out in 2008 changed such situation to a great extent.

Like the Great Depression in 1929, the crisis was not only a crisis of the world economy, but also a crisis of the macroeconomic ideology and economic policy. Theoretically, different trends of macro economy are now in a fierce and confused debate: on the one hand, the neoclassical macroeconomics that used to hold the mainstream position suffers from denounce to the fullest extent, with such Keynesians as Krugman and Stiglitz claiming theory for "back to Keynes" and Soros organizing "Institute for New Economic Thinking" and gathering numerous non-mainstream scholars to criticize and introspect the Neoclassical Economics. On the other hand, facing the criticism one after another, Lucas, Taylor, Maskin, Mishkin and other leaders of the mainstream economics took a clear-cut stand in refuting the viewpoint of "the out-burst of financial crisis represents the failure of economic theory" and stated the lesson resulting from the financial crisis has not, from any angle, eroded or overturned the basic principle of the macroeconomic developed before the crisis, but in turn proved the correctness of "EMH (Efficient Markets Hypothesis)".

Like the melee at the theoretical level, at the policy level, the economists and policy makers have also intruded into the "Brave New World", facing far more problems than effective solutions, while the outline is not yet clear for the new macroeconomic policy frame. The former chairman of the Federal Reserve, Bernanke once pointed out that the roots of the current crisis may not necessary rest in the system of mainstream economic theory, but the big problem observed at the level of making and implementing the economic policy (Bernanke 2010). Therefore, it can be considered that the impact of crisis has really set forth new requirements for studies on macroeconomic policy, although it is hard for the theoretical argument to come out with a result for the time being, i.e., rebuilding the management frame of macro economy, by studying the science of economic policy, and gradually making up the gap between economic theory and policy practice so as to enhance the effectiveness of macro policy.

In the process of establishing the system for the science of economic policy and rebuilding the frame of macroeconomic policy, many mainstream economists observed that the traditional macro policy that paid close attention to the price stability and other aggregate indicators could hardly ensure the actualization of macro stability, so attention should be also paid to the output composition, asset price change, leverage level, external unbalance and other structural indicators. It was the ignorance of structural problems by the developed economies in their macro policies that led to the out-burst of the crisis.

The performance of China's macro economy over the last 10 years has formed a situation of echoing with such trend of theoretical introspection. When the major developed economies fell into depression successively, China's macro-control practice has just showed an excellent performance, without copying the frame of the western macroeconomic policy and with the structural regulation and control as its characteristics: as Fig. 5.1 shows, since the mid-1990s, by measuring with GDP growth rate and inflation rate, China's macroeconomic fluctuation has gone smooth and steady, with the economic growth rate fluctuating smoothly at an appropriately high level with a growth rate always above 7 %; the relatively high inflation rate of more than 10 % repeatedly observed during the mid-1990s no longer appears. The overall operating pattern of macro economy can be summarized as "high growth, low inflation and steady fluctuation". According to the studies of some Chinese scholars, China's steady macro economy is associated with the optimization of China's economic structure and deepened system reform, and benefits from the well development and perfection of China's macro-control system (Dong Yun 2011; Fuqian et al. 2012; Lin Jianhao et al. 2013; Jianfeng 2010). This stage is rather consistent with the period of the global "great moderation", indicating the "good luck" of the global economy also as a prooting factor to ensure steady operation of macro economy in China.

Due to the huge contrast of macro economy performance in China and the West, the concept, category, principle and system of the western macroeconomics that used to be considered as the golden laws and precious rules suffered from being questioned to the fullest extent, and the rules, guidance and systems of all the mainstream macroeconomic policies respected as the criterion are also cast into the shade. Meanwhile, the economist of Harvard University, Frankel proposed to save the mainstream macro-economic theory by summarizing the experience of the emerging markets (Frankel 2010); the former chairman (Asia) of Morgan Stanley, Roach wrote an article directly with the title of "Learn Macro-control from China", stating China "gives the world a lesson in terms of macro strategy, which should listen to by other regions in the world." These views indicate that China's successful

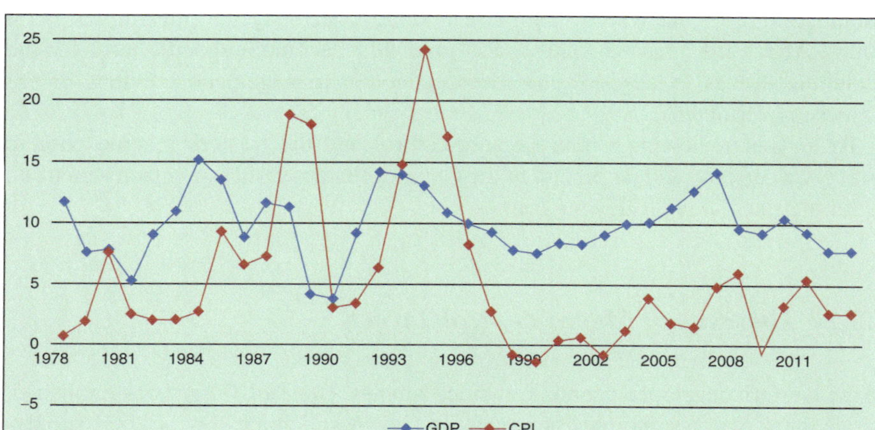


**Fig. 5.1** Changidency of China's GDP growth rate and CPI (1978 ~ 2013)

experience in macro-control has come into the vision of the western mainstream economists and China's experience and ideology of macro management is of great referential significance for restructuring the frame of mainstream macro policy and rebuilding the mainstream macroeconomics (Zhang Xiaojing and Dong Yun 2013).

## 5.2 "Macro-control" with Chinese Characteristics

Actually, China's macro-control system is similar, in some aspects, to the macroeconomic policy of the western developed economies, but also shows distinct characteristics of the transforming economies and developing economies. As for the former aspect, according to the description of Wu Jinglian (2014), since the 1980s, the design and construction of China's macro management system has been profoundly influenced and impacted by the western economic theories, and the proposals made by many western scholars for China's macro policy framework design have also been adequately discussed and adopted by the decision makers, as will be involved hereinafter. In this section, we will emphatically analyze the latter issue, i.e., the Chinese characteristics implied in macro-control.

Literally, the uniqueness of China's macroeconomic management system can be visited. "Macro-control" itself is a term of economic policy full of Chinese characteristics, as has not been found in the western countries. With respect to the source, it was the concept initially presented by such economists as Edwin R. Lim and Wu Jinglian at Bashan Cruise in 1985, with the original intention to combine the two words "regulate" and "control" for describing the Chinese meaning of "macro-management". The wording of "macro-control" was eventually selected because the "regulate" idea conformed to the idea of modern macro management, emphasizing on the economic management by indirect means; "control" idea highlighted the Chinese characteristic and transitional character, emphasizing on the effective administration of the whole national economic system by the government (Lim 2008). Afterward, "macro-control" has gradually become a specific term for the economic circles to describe the macroeconomic management activities of the Chinese government.

By further reviewing China's macro-control and the western macroeconomic policy, we can have a clear picture of the Chinese characteristics of "macro-control", as summarized in the following four aspects:

### *5.2.1 Diversity of Macro-control Target*

In the western developed economies, since Keynes' *General Theory* was published, mainstream macroeconomics have mainly shown solicitude for the total supply-demand relation and economic fluctuation, in other words, the changes in such aggregate indicators as economic growth rate, inflation rate and employment rate resulting from the changing relation between total demand and total potential supply. Correspondingly, the macroeconomic policies of the developed economies were also dedicated to resolve the problem of economic fluctuation, to keep the total demand and total potential supply consistent by means of "make good omissions and deficiencies" and "refund surplus" and make up shorthandled and resolved by other economic policies: e.g., taking anti- monopoly policy to resolve the structural problem of industrial organization; resolving the incentive problem of entrepreneurs by strengthening property definition and protection. In this sense, the western macroeconomic policy is a very "narrow" concept, which cannot cover all the problems, but can only resolve the short-term fluctuation of economic aggregate.

On the other hand, China's macro-control target is diversified. *Decision of the CPC Central Committee on Some Major Issues Concerning Comprehensively Deepening the Reform* approved at the Third Plenary Session of the 18th National Congress of the CPC pointed out: "the main task of macro-control is to keep the economic aggregate in balance, promote the coordination of the major economic structure and the optimization of productivity arrangement, reduce the impact of economic periodical fluctuation, keep watch for regional and systematic risks, stabilize market expectation and realize the sustainable and healthy development of economy." As mentioned above, China's macro-control tasks include: smoothing aggregate fluctuation, promoting the upgrading of structure, actualizing short-term macro stability, and advancing long-term sustainable and healthy development. Furthermore, in such transitional economy as China from the planned economy to the market economy, it is a material issue for the successful reform to keep the macro stability. However, to realize the macro stability, it is necessary to find the systematic cause for economic fluctuation and reform accordingly, and depends on the decision makers continuously reforming the existing macroeconomic management system, thus forming the scientific and efficient macro- control decision system and idea. Therefore, systematic study for system reform should be included when discussing macro-control in China. In a word, the most important task of China's macro-control is to deal well with relation among reform, development and the stability, with reform as the means, development as the purpose and stability as the premises.[1] The discipline fields involved in such tasks already beyond the category of macroeconomic theory in the sense of the western economics, covering the microeconomics, industrial economics, growth economics and transitional economics. All the economic issues involving universality, vitality, integrity, overall importance and strategy are in the scope of macroeconomic regulation and control. Obviously, China's macro-control has shaken off the yoke of the western theoretical doctrine, with changing such characteristics of the western macroeconomic theories and policies of stressing on short term but ignoring long term, on aggregate but structure, on fluctuation but development, on situation but base, and on

[1] In 1995, the Fifth Plenary Session of the 14th National Congress of the CPC expounded systematically the relation between reform, development and stability for the first time, which was considered as the first relation should be properly dealt with among "relations to be correctly dealt with in the construction of socialist modernization".

countermeasures but mechanism, to stressing on coordination, in the process of actualizing reform, development and stability, as between short term and long term, aggregate and structure, fluctuation and development, countermeasures and mechanism, economy and society, and man and nature.

### 5.2.2 Structural Macro-control

Since the developed countries are observed with the relatively perfect market system, relatively high homogenization and are on the path of relatively balance growth, they mainly focus on aggregate regulation and control and rarely apply the structural policies. Furthermore, according to the western mainstream economics, the structural policy would often lead to market distortion, such as industrial policy. While developing countries are much different. Underdeveloped market, structure changing sharply, high heterogeneity and unbalanced growth urges the developing countries to adopt the structural regulation and control policy.

All in all, China's structural problems are in two aspects. One is the institutional structure, covering the relation between the state-owned and non-state owned, between institutional transform and double-track transition, central and local governments. and government and market, the other one is the economic structure in a broad sense, including: (1) age structure of population (aging problem); (2) urban-rural structure; (3) industrial structure (unbalanced development of tertiary industry); (4) regional structure (unbalanced regional development); (5) distribution structure (distribution pattern of national income and gap between the rich and the poor); (6) growth impetus (unbalanced internal and external demands and irrational structure of factor input), etc. It is because of the existence of a series of structural problems and the changing structures that the structural regulation and control becomes extremely necessary: firstly, the sharp structural change means the change of macro-control base and policy conduction mechanism, as may result in the failure of aggregate regulation and control; secondly, the rapid structural change causes the change of factor return and the flow of factors, as may easily result in structural unbalance in the circumstance of inaccurate and imperfect price signal, which makes the structural regulation and control indispensable; thirdly, due to the sharp structural change and structural unbalance, many problems are not merely a problem of short-term macro stability, but the harmony between the short-term macro-control and the mid and long-term development, so the structural adjustment becomes extremely critical for the mid and long-term sustainable development.

Different structural problems will lead to different concepts of structural regulation and control.

With respect to the institutional structure, since the economic transform is not yet completed and the double-track transition is observed, so the idea of double- track regulation and control is formed accordingly, i.e. combination of administrative regulation and control and market-oriented regulation and control. On the one hand, with the market-oriented reform being advanced step by step, the establishment and development of macro-control system has always persisted in market orientation, emphasizing on the indirect regulation and control by economic and legal means. On the other hand, although the traditional planning administrative means continue to be withdrawn, it not be completely abandoned, and eventually integrated into the macro-control in a certain form, finally forming the integrated macro-control system with planning control, fiscal control and financial control. The role of state-owned enterprises, local governments and National Development and Reform Commission (NDRC) in macro-control and the combination of market-oriented regulation and control and the administrative regulation and control have just characterized the macro control of China.

Due to the existing problem of economic structure in a broad sense, the structural regulation and control and aggregate regulation and control are in parallel: industrial policy, trade policy, exchange rate policy, regulatory policy (such as energy saving and emission reduction), capital control, strict financial supervision and balanced finance and other policies obviously with the characteristics of administrative intervention and the features of structural regulation and control have all played an important role in promoting the economic growth and macro stability (Zhang Xiaojing et al. 2010).

### *5.2.3 Unification of Reform, Development and Stability*

Essentially, the course of China's economic transformation and development is the process for unification of reform, development and stability, while the macro-control is the handle for dealing correctly with the relations among reform, development and stability. The method for consideration of the three may give up growth rate appreciably and pay some short-term cost, but have finally actualized the long-term sustainable growth of China for more than three decades. Comparing with the Shock Therapy that laterally stressed on rapid privatization and rigid fiscal disciplines, it may be observed that China can make the situation of long-term stable growth just in close association with the macro-control policy implementing and the approach of gradual reform by insisting on the unification of reform, development and stability and acting according to circumstance. Such three-dimension unification is also much different from the one- dimension vision of the western mainstream economics stressing on efficiency. In the coming period, China will continue to insist on the unification. At the symposium of economic experts on July 8, 2014, General Secretary Xi Jinping pointed out to "accurately hold the balance point of reform, development and stability, accurately hold the balance point of short-term target and long-term development, accurately hold the stressing point of reform and development and accurately hold the bonding point for the economic and social development and the improvement of people's life". Because of this, it is extremely critical for accurately holding the cause, characteristics, limitation and future improvement direction of China's macro-control system to interpret the reform course of China's macroeconomic management system from the vision of unifying reform, development and stability.

### 5.2.4 *Strategic Planning in Parallel with Fiscal and Monetary Policies*

In view of the macroeconomic management system, upon development and evolution for more than three decades, the framework for China's macroeconomic management system has been basically established. In view of the decision making and implementing mechanism, in China's macro-control system, the top decision-maker is the Central Leading Group on Financial and Economic Affairs and the State Council, and the main executors are "three carriages": National Development and Reform Commission (NDRC), Ministry of Finance and the People's Bank of China. Of the "three carriages" for China's macro-control, NDRC is the leader and dominator, with the functions covering most of the macro and micro fields in the operation of national economy; Ministry of Finance and the People's Bank of China are subject to the guidance and constraint of NDRC in terms of formulating as well as implementing policies; economic policies shall be subordinate to the national strategic planning. Without the approval from NDRC, the money from Ministry of Finance and bank loans cannot be investment.

Such three-in-one regulation and control mode is of strong Chinese characteristics, laying stress on "national development strategy and planning as the orientation, fiscal policy and monetary policy as the main means, and intensifying the coordination and collaboration of the fiscal policy and monetary policy with industrial, price and other policy means". It is much more abundant than the fiscal policies and monetary policies in the western mainstream macroeconomics. It should be noted that nowadays, even some of the developed economies have also started to lay stress on strategic planning and industrial policy and no longer regard such practices of the government as a kind of distortion for market like the western mainstream economics, as obviously happens to coincide with the practices in China.

## 5.3 Reform of Macro Management System and Evolution of the Macro-control Philosophy

The change of macro-control system and the evolution of macro-control ideology influence and promote each other. The interaction of them constitutes the basic power for China's macro management evolution. The course of China's macro stabilization over the last three decades or so can be basically divided into three stages: the first stage is from the late 1970s to the early 1990s, during which the macro-control started to be introduced and primarily applied; the second stage is from the early 1900s to the beginning of the new century, during which the macro-control system was primarily shaped; the third stage is from the early twenty-first century to the 18th National Congress of the CPC, during which the macro-control ideology is relatively stable. At present, China is at the stage of new normal for macro-control after the 18th National Congress of the CPC.

### 5.3.1 Introduction of "Macro-control" and Its Impact with the Ideology of Planned Economy (1978–1992)

In China, macro-control emerged as the governmental function along with the transition process of economic system.

In the discussions of Marxist classic writers, elimination of capitalist economic period and economic crisis is the necessary core of the communist society, which will be realized by planned production as per proportion. Therefore, plan and proportion became the golden laws and precious rules of the planned economy. During the period from 1950s to 1970s, all the economic activities in China were subject to the micro intervention and control of the central planning, while the central government played a decisive role in allocation of economic and financial resources. Hence, all economic problems became "macroeconomic" problems and micro policy and macro policy were not essentially distinguished. It was of neither space nor necessity for the aggregate regulation and control and market-oriented regulation policy in the sense of modern macroeconomics to operate. With the economic management institution as an example, SPC played a decisive role of the agent for the central government in allocation of resources, Ministry of Finance was merely a "cashier" in collaboration with SPC in allocation of resources, and the central bank was merely the "waitress" of Ministry of Finance. Before 1978, China had only one bank as the People's Bank of China, which used to be temporarily merged into Ministry of Finance, as its subordinate department which is in charge of monetary affairs during the period of the Cultural Revolution. Under such institution, fiscal policy and monetary policy were out of the question. Starting to sprout from this historical point, China's macro-control management system would, without doubt, carry the transitional character of the transition economy. It was also the most important institutional background for the target of China macro-control policy to be far beyond the category of ironing economic aggregate fluctuation and for the means of structural regulation and control to appear frequently.

With the low-efficiency flaw of planned economy being gradually shown in allocation of resources, it became an important issue for the attention of China's top decision makers to correctly understand and deal with the relation between planned economy and market regulation. In the late 1970s, China started the transition process from the planned economic system to the market economic system. The spirit of entrepreneurs was gradually inspired accordingly; enterprises started to be able to make microeconomic decisions independently to some extent; the difference between macro economy and micro economy also started to appear; the macroeconomic management system being continuously developed and perfected in the institutional transition process also became the necessary core of economic reform. In 1978, the People's Bank of China was dependent from Ministry of Finance, indicating the beginning of China's modern monetary and financial system construction.

In the early period of reform and opening up, the planned economy and state-owned sector held an absolutely ruling position in the national economy and "planned and proportional" was still the leading ideology for the government to administrate economy. Facing the situation of overheated economy with CPI rising by 7.5 % in 1980, the central government practiced the macro-control by administrative order: compress the scale of capital construction, reduce the fiscal expenditures, intensify the bank credit management, and freeze the deposits of enterprises. In view of the macroeconomic management institution, it was until 1984 that the People's Bank of China still integrated the functions as the central bank, commercial bank and administrative organ of the government. Based on such institution, discussion on the formulation and implementation of monetary policy was still like climbing trees to catch fish.

At the level of economic management idea, from 1982 to 1985, the function of market was officially approved to some extent. In 1982, the *Report of the 12th National Congress* officially proposed to "carry out the principle of ensuring the leading role of the planned economy supplemented by market regulation". Accordingly, "planned" in the ideology of "planned and proportional and comprehensive balancing" was gradually weakened and actually became "proportional and comprehensive balancing". For instance, in 1985, the *Proposal of the CPC Central Committee for Formulating the 7th Five-year Plan for National Economic and Social Development* set forth "persist in the basic balance of total social demand and supply, keep the accumulation and consumption at an appropriate proportion. … Ensure their respective balance and mutual comprehensive balance of national finance, credit, materials and foreign exchange." In the fields which the market gradually interposed in and the plan gradually faded out, the role definition of the government became a critical issue. Then, due to the profound experience of the malpractice with the direct administration under the planning system, the decision makers assumed to carry out the indirect regulation and control by applying the economic leverage for macro-control. It was during this period that the idea of market-oriented indirect regulation and control sprouted. For instance, the *Decision of the CPC Central Committee on the Reform of Economic System* (1984) pointed out, "the more the economy is invigorated, the more attention shall be given to macro regulation … we were used to promoting the economic operation by administrative means, but ignored, for long, the application of economic leverage for regulation."

Under the guidance of the market-oriented macro-control ideology, the People's Bank of China exercised, from January 1, 1984 the function as the central bank of the state, while its general industrial and commercial credit services were separated and transferred to newly established Industrial and Commercial Bank of China. After that, the deposit reserve system was also established in 1985. Such reform of the macroeconomic management institution was launched to indicate the original form of monetary policy in China. At that time, however, since the People's Bank of China operated only savings, credit and cash issuance, such term as "currency" was not yet observed in the terminology of Chinese economic theories and policies and thus, it was hard to say China had already had the monetary policy in the real sense.

In terms of learning the macroeconomic management experience from the western developed economies and defining the orientation for the major policies of China' macro-control, Chinese Academy of Social Sciences (CASS), State Commission for Restructuring Economy and the World Bank jointly held the "International Seminar on Macro-economic Management and Reform" (historically known as "*Bashan Cruise*" Meeting) in September 1985. The meeting was of the milestone significance and attended by a number of world-class economists and some of the Chinese economic officials and economists. The meeting formed a common view in the following aspects:

1. After the micro economy is relaxed, for the macroeconomic management, the government shall change the previous direct management and planned management to the indirect management only, i.e., mainly managing by economic and legal means supported with administrative means. It is also the major part of the reform of the macroeconomic management institution.
2. The economic means for macroeconomic management is mainly to implement the appropriate fiscal policy and monetary policy. Generally, when the macro economy is overheated, i.e., total demand is more than total supply, it is better to implement the tight macroeconomic policy for tightening the public finance and credit; when the macro economy is supercooling, i.e., total supply is more than total demand, it is better to implement the expansive macroeconomic policy, for financial deficit and credit expansion. Its fundamental significance is to implement, according to the changes of macroeconomic situation, different fiscal policies and monetary policies and realize the proper matching of them. In 1985, facing the danger of severe inflation, China shall govern with tight policies for public finance, money and revenue.
3. Market coordination mechanism under macro control is beneficial for the optimal allocation of resources and the system with highest efficiency, as the important reference for China to select the mid and long-term reform target. Since it is consistent with the market-oriented reform after 1979, it is necessary to reform fundamentally the planned economic system with the directive plan as the main indication.
4. To ensure the effective indirect management of macro-economy by the government, it is necessary to deepen the reform of state-owned enterprises and develop the non-public ownership economy so that every enterprise becomes an independent market entity, which is able to respond sensitively to the market signals, especially such signals as interest rate, exchange rate and price and adjust the interest subject of the behavior accordingly. For this purpose, state-owned enterprises shall change the status of soft budget constraints, without gazing at the market with one eye and at the government with the other.

5. Establish an effective macroeconomic management system as well as establish and perfect the market system, especially the financial market and labor market, actively reform the pricing mechanism and price system, establish and perfect the economic information and economic supervision system; perfect the revenue distribution policy and prevent excessive expansion of consumer demand.

The foregoing common views had an importance influence on China's macro-control policy and some of the core viewpoints were adopted by the decision makers of China. In 1985, the *Proposal of the CPC Central Committee for Formulating the 7th Five-year Plan for National Economic and Social Development* set forth the guiding principle for the "primary stage" of economic reform to take the steady macroeconomic policy, so as to create conditions for the successful advancement of reform. It also explicitly presented "the state's administration of enterprises will gradually turn from direct control to indirect control as the core, and the economic operation shall be controlled and regulated mainly by economic means and legal means and taking necessary administrative means."

In consistence with the foregoing macro-control ideology, in responding to the situation of overheated economy with CPI rising by 9.3 % in 1985, the government cut down the investment scale and controlled the consumption funds as well as adjusted upward the interest rate twice consecutively, adopted the tight monetary policy and introduced the economy measures in governance. However, such macro-control measures were not properly implemented, leaving a problem for the next overheated economy.

While the last tight macro-control measures could not be properly implemented, in the mid-1987, the "decentralization" reform for the state-owned enterprises developed to the stage of total "contracting system", thus showing a sign of overheated economy in 1987. The "price breakthrough" in 1988 made the circumstances even worse, with a tide of running on banks and rushing to purchase. In the year, CPI rose by 18.8 %, resulting in the third inflation after the reform and opening up. From the third quarter of 1988, the government started to sharply cut down the investment scale of fixed assets and stop approval for any non-planned construction project; clear and rectify companies, especially trust and investment companies; control the purchasing power of public organizations; intensify the administration of prices and implement the maximum price for the important means of production. The central bank also took the tight monetary and credit policies, including the rigid control and inspection over loans, stopping once the lending to township enterprises; increasing the deposit reserve rate; raising the interest rate twice; implementing the premium saving. Due to the rigid measures, the regulation and control became promptly effective. The money supply growth obviously slowed down, CPI dropped rapidly and the economic growth rate also declined to about 4 %. As another consequence, the regulation and control led to the second peak of unemployment since the reform and opening up. In one word, the result of the regulation and control was the "hard landing" of national economy.

This period was also a period for the fierce impact between the ideology of planned economy and the ideology of market economy in the field of macro-control.

With the co-existence of the proportional and comprehensive balancing ideology of planned economy and the market-oriented indirect regulation and control, it was obviously a stage of ideological mixtures. Especially, under the impact of economic fierce fluctuation and political disturbance, the ideology of administrative regulation and control rose to some extent, while the market regulation was merely an auxiliary mean for the governmental macro-control. In 1987, the *Report of the 13th National Congress* proposed the mechanism of 'the state regulates the market and the market guides the enterprises', with the government still as the final controller of resource allocation and macroeconomic operation and the market and enterprises as the players on the economic stage only. This feature can be reflected by the discussion in the *Proposals of the CPC Central Committee for Formulating the Ten-year Planning and "8th Five- year Plan" for the National Economic and Social Development* adopted at the Seventh Plenary Session of the 13th National Congress in 1990: "the main task of the national economic management is to make rationally the planning and macro-control target of national economic development, formulate the correct industrial policy, regional policy and other economic policies, make comprehensive balance, coordinate the major proportional relation, and guide and regulate and control the economic operation by economic, legal and administrative means comprehensively and auxiliary."

### 5.3.2 Primary Formation and "Soft Landing" of Macro-control System (1993–2002)

Upon governance and rectification for 3 years and after the afterward "Speech of South Cruises" and the 14th National Congress of the CPC, China's economy took off rapidly again from 1993 to 1994 and soon moved in a new round of overheat. This overheat was summarized as "4-F, 4-H, 4-T and 1-C".[2] The domestic economic theoretical circles started a fierce debate on the overheated economy. In June 1993, "International Seminar on China's Macroeconomic Management" was held in Dalian, which was another milestone international seminar after the *Bashan Cruise*, having the important influence on the orientation of macro-control at that time. The "Dalian Meeting" was prepared for more than 6 months and invited Modigliani, Winner of Nobel Prize for Economics, Prof. Stern of LSE, Prof. Lau Juen Yee of Stanford University and Kwoh-Ting Li known as "Important Pusher of Taiwan's Economic Miracles" for presence. "Dalian Meeting" proposed a package of reform measures such as increasing the deposit and loan interest rate to the level of positive interest rate, implementing the credit line restriction and carrying out price reform.

[2] "4-F": real estate fever, development zone fever, capital raising fever and stock fever; "4-H": high investment inflation, high industrial growth, high currency issue and credit availability, and high inflation of prices; "4-T": tight communications and transport, tight energy, tight important raw materials and tight capital; "1-C": chaotic economic order, especially chaotic financial order (Liu Guoguang and Liu Shucheng 1997).

After the meeting, Zhu Rongji held a special meeting with Kwoh-Ting Li. Kwoh-Ting Li presented such proposals as defining the rational proportional relation between the central and local taxation, rectifying the central bank, integrating the exchange rates and joining IMF. At the critical time for advancing the comprehensive economic reform, the leading views discussed and generated at Dalian Meeting became the importance reference for formulating policies. Soon after the meeting, upon consultation and discussion repeatedly, the State Council finally formed the *Opinions Concerning the Current Economic Situation and Strengthening of Macro-control* (16-Articles) for distributed on June 24. Upon implementation of the "16-Articles" for half a year, the effect was primarily observed. The number of new projects started to decrease, growth of money supply dropped obviously and the gap for chaotic lending and chaotic capital- raising was basically blocked. It should be noted that of the "16-Articles", 13 articles are economic means, emphasizing on intensifying the indirect regulation and control, taking more economic measures, economic policy and economic legislation as the practice of reforming the macro-control mode under the conditions of market economy. With the target defined for the socialist market economic system, the indirect regulation and control mainly by economic means can be called as the "first test". It was a good start as well as created conditions for issuing the series of macro reform policies. The Third Plenary Session of the 14th National Congress of the CPC held in November 1993 adopted the *Decision of the CPC Central Committee on Some Issues Concerning the Establishment of a Socialist Market Economic Structure.* The *Decision* presented the measures for reforming state-owned enterprises, public finance and taxation, financial and investment institutions, with the attempt to eliminating the systematic roots of overheat by deepening the reform. The effect of the "16-Articles" and the *Decision* was gradually shown: by 1996, the trend of CPI became stable, the economic growth rate remained high and "soft landing" was actualized for economy. Liu Guoguang and Liu Shucheng (1997) pointed out: since the second half of 1993, the macro-control of the government with inflation governance as the prime task succeeded and "soft landing" was actualized for the national economic operation. "Soft landing" was actualized under the correct guiding principle of the government for despiking timely, tightening appropriately, applying micro regulation at the right time and grasping the main line.

In addition to the changes at the level of macro policy orientation and operating means, this period was of the landmark significance for the reform of macroeconomic management institution. The major reforming events from 1994 to 1998 expedited China's modern macroeconomic policy system. These events include: reform of tax- sharing system for the fiscal system, reform of financial system for defining the position and tasks of the central bank, monetary supply indicator system defined and announced for the first time, separation of policy banks and commercial bank, floating exchange rate system for foreign exchange management and cancellation of restriction on loan limit. With this series of reforming actions taken, it was possible to implement the fiscal policy and monetary policy in the sense of macroeconomics and thus form primary macro-control system of Chinese characteristics with SPC, department of finance and Central Bank in mutual collaboration and the macro-control capacity of the government intensified. Afterwards, China's macro-control policy was operated gradually to get rid of the shackles of the traditional planning system and turned to a new pattern mainly with indirect regulation and control.

In 1997, China's macroeconomic situation was observed with an important change: with the undersupply for a relatively long period changing to inadequate periodical effective demand as well as with the external impact of the Asian financial crisis, economic decline and currency inflation became a realistic threat, and it seemed to be far harder to start-off the economy than before. From 1998, the subject of the governmental macro-control changed to expansion of internal demand, the "active fiscal policy" and "steady monetary policy" was implemented and the total demand management became the main handle of macro-control. Due to such reasons as the non- performing asset ratio of state-owned commercial banks on high side and international financial turbulence resulting from the Asian financial crisis, the monetary policy was implemented with various constraints and thus the fiscal policy played a major role in the regulation and control. The decision-makers were aware of that, as long as the fiscal solvency is ensured, the implementation of proactive fiscal policy is the direct and effective means for expansion of internal demand.[3] The following wording shows explicitly the ideological logic of the decision makers: "we take measures of intensifying the infrastructure construction and expanding the fiscal investment ... highway, railway, environmental protection, urban construction and so on which are not duplicate construction. ..., since such construction has a long payback period, investment depends on the state only. ..., in this way, the surplus productivity can be utilized. Such concept was already generated last year.[4] Keynes was the inventor and Roosevelt was the initial executor of such theory for allowing the government to adopt the expansive fiscal policy and promoting the economic development by expanding the demand. It is an art to use properly the money of the government."[5]

As a whole, from 1993 when the soft landing started to 2003 when a new round of regulation and control was actuated, the 10 years were a period for the primary formation of China's macro-control institution under socialist market economic system. In view of the institutional reform, the problem of relation between planning and market was thoroughly resolved during this period. The basic position of market in allocation of resources was duly affirmed and planning withdrew again and again, with part of its functions gradually brought into the category and becoming one of the important means for macro-control. Finally, the three-in-one macro-control system was primarily formed, with the planning, financial and fiscal sectors assigned with specific jobs. The macro-control at this stage laid stress on mutual collaboration between the measures of reform and the measures of regulation and control measures, thus integrating properly reform, development and stability.

---

[3] *Report on the Work of the Government* (2000).

[4] It refers to the year of 1997, noted by the author.

[5] Cited from "Issues on Current Economic Situation", recorded in *Memoir of Zhu Rongji's Talk*, vol. 3, 20 Oct 1998.

### 5.3.3 Relatively Stable Macro-control Ideology (2003–2012)

The decision makers had always paid close attention to the fiscal risk. The *Report on the Work of the Government* (2003) pointed out: "It is the important principle for economic work to persist in keeping the fiscal balance and making both ends meet. The implementation of proactive fiscal policies for issuance long-term state bonds over the years are the special policies implemented under the specific circumstances. We always insist on current budget without deficit and constructive budget with deficit not beyond the scale defined at the beginning of the year." In terms of monetary and financial policies, the central government published a series of measures such as separate operation of financial institutions, classification of loans by five grades and clearance and rectification of non-banking financial institutions to actively prevent any financial risks. The decision makers understood that conditions can be created for giving play to the monetary policy in the future by diffusing the financial risk.[6]

While the total demand management was strengthened, the relation between state-owned enterprises and macro-control became the keynote in the reform of macroeconomic management institution. The *Decision of the CPC Central Committee on the Reform and Development of State-owned Enterprise*, adopted at the Fourth Plenary Session 15th National Congress of the CPC in 1999, provided an excellent explanation of the relation between reform of state-owned enterprises and macro- control. According to the *Decision*, firstly, the macro-control shall "maintain the economic aggregate basically in balance. Expand the internal demand, develop the urban-rural market, increase employment, promote the sustainable, rapid and healthy development of national economy, prevent the economic growth from fluctuating sharply, and create beneficial macroeconomic environment for the development of state-owned enterprises." Secondly, "state-owned economy hold a dominant position in the important industries and key fields in relation with the lifeline of the national economy, supporting, guiding and driving the development of the whole society and playing an important role in realizing the national macro-control target." In other words, on the one hand, macro-control shall create a stable macro environment for the reform and development of state-owned enterprises; on the other hand, state-owned enterprises shall play a role in realizing the target of the government for macro-control.

After 2003, at the level of basic policy frame, the macro-control ideology of the decision-makers became relatively stable, without any major changes; at the level of particular operation, the government attached more and more importance to macro-control and gained increasingly experience in operating and the connotation of macro- control seemed to be increasingly extensive. From 2003 to 2012, China's macro-control idea and mechanism is worth of attention in three keynotes:

---

[6] *The Report on the Work of the Government* (2000): "deepen the financial reform, rectify the financial order, intensify the financial supervision and rule of law, prevent and defuse the financial risk, strive to increase the operation benefits and create excellent conditions for giving further play to the role of monetary policy."

Firstly, special attention was given to the implementation of appropriately tight pre-adjustment in the flourishing period. For instance, the *Report on the Work of the Government* (2004) pointed out: "in regulation and control, make sure to carry out appropriate micro regulation and treat in a distinguished way. ... For proper macro-control, it is necessary to maintain the continuity and stability of macroeconomic policy as well as adjust the intensity and keynote of policy implementation appropriately at the right time. The right time means to control properly the time for publishing the regulation and control measures, recognize the whole through observation of the part and nip any hazard in the bud; appropriateness means to relax or tighten properly, without slamming the brake or making a clean cut." It indicates that differing from the developed economies that gave up the antiperiodic regulation principal and turned for laissez-faire policy, China's macro-control decision makers strived to build more thoroughly the world of Keynes: while developing the private economy, relaxing the prices and encouraging the competition at the micro stratum, firmly adopt the antiperiod policy for intervening and ironing the economic fluctuation at the macro stratum.

Secondly, the direct administrative means are still playing a great role and are indispensable in the current macro-control system. For instance, the *Report on the Work of the Government* (2005) pointed out: "strictly control such two gates as land approval and credit availability, control the investment demand inflation, and contain some of the industries from blind investment and duplicate construction at a low level." The *Report on the Work of the Government* (2007) pointed out: "intensify and improve the macro-control. The keynote is to control the fixed asset investment and credit scale and promote the balance of economic aggregate in optimizing the structure." The *Report of the 17th National Congress* (2007) explicitly proposed to "give play to the guiding role of the national planning, plan and industrial policies in macro-control." Obviously, China's decision makers had always persisted in the methods of laying equal stress on structural instrument and aggregate instrument and combining the administrative regulation control and the market-oriented regulation. It is because China is a developing country with heavy tasks for development and faces various problems for institutional reform. Therefore, it will be possible for resolving more problems to place more spare tools in the toolkit of regulation and control.

Thirdly, since the decision makers have a relatively broad understanding of the macro-control connotation, "macro-control" becomes a concept opposite to "market mechanism", meaning in general all the major decisions made by the government to make up the market failure, including macro stability policies as well as micro regulation policies. In another word, since the decision makers equate the government to macro and deem all the functions of the government for administrating the economic society as macro-control, macro-control thus becomes a synonym of governmental intervention. The *Report on the Work of the Government* (2011) pointed out "both perfect market mechanism and effective macro-control are indispensable important part of the socialist market economic system. It is necessary to the select the functions of market and government according to the circumstances. In responding to the impact of the international financial crisis, it is completely correct, as practice has proven, to strengthen and improve the macro-control, promptly correct the market distortion, make up the market failure and prevent the economy from any sharp rise and fall."

### 5.3.4 *Macro-control Under New Normal (2013–)*

Since 2013, under the co-effect of such major structural factors as increased factor cost, reduced post-developing advantage, decreased globalization dividend and transfer of leading industry from manufacturing to service, the potential growth rate of China's economy has been consecutively lowered and its macroeconomic operation has also turned from the stage of previous "structural speedup" to the new normal with "structural slow-down" as the main characteristic. In the new normal of economy, to continuously maintain the sustainable and healthy development of economy, in terms of macro- control, it is necessary to control properly the dropping range of potential economic growth rate, adjust the orientation of macro policies appropriately at the right time and prevent the economic growth from dropping sharply. Accordingly, the guiding principle of China for macroeconomic operation is changing from "stable and relatively fast" to "stable rate and synergy". The so-called "stable speed" means to stabilize the economic growth rate within a reasonable range (potential growth rate range), and adjust the target of growth rate according to its changing trends. The macroeconomic policy will never pursue sedulously to surpass the potential growth rate. In such relatively stable and ease macro environment, we are ready to promote the strategy of comprehensive and deep structural adjustment and practically carry out the scientific outlook on development. The so-called "synergy" means to place the quality improvement, cost reduction and labor productivity promotion to a more important position so as to improve the distribution pattern of national income and prevent financial risks. The key of stable rate and energy is to make up the gap of declining economic growth rate by enhancing the quality and benefit, so as to further intensify the aggregation of national wealth and promote the happiness and benefits of people. Correspondingly, the stressing point of China's macro-control policy is changing from depending much on total demand management previously to applying rationally the demand management, comprehensively strengthening the supply management, and strengthening the coordination and collaboration of fiscal policy and monetary policy with industrial, price and other policy means. When the economic operation is close to the upper or lower limits, the total demand management shall still play a basic role in ironing the fluctuation, while when the economic operation remains in a reasonable range, the supply management shall be the main handle of macro policy for improving quality and efficiency. Without doubt, supply management will not do without the adjustment of industrial policy, but its key significance rests in implementing the institutional reform for stimulating the vigor of enterprises and market, clarifying the relation between government and market, mostly encouraging entrepreneurs for structural adjustment by market mechanism, breaking through the old equilibrium and actualizing new equilibrium so as to create and obtain new reform dividends, practically improve the supply efficiency of China's economy and realize the real and solid economic growth. Such new changes will surely require for advancing and promoting the further reform of macro-control system.

With China's economy in new normal, the macro-control shows new features. In view of the decision-makers, the following points are emphasized: keep the power of mediation and advance steadily; ensure micro vitality, macro stability, and social backup; carry out interval regulation and control and oriented regulation and control; imply reform in regulation and control; plan, as a whole, the coordination mechanism construction with macro-control policy; advance the institutionalization of macro- control target and policy formulation. Obviously, all these are innovations of macro- control mode under new normal.

## 5.4 The Basic Logic of the Reform of Macro Management System

There are multiple forces that have promoted the reform of China's macro management system, including the change of decision makers' ideas, evolution of institutional structure, change of stages for economic development and impact of internal and external macroeconomic fluctuation. It is these factors that promote the reform of the macro-control system and its gradual maturity and perfection.

Firstly, the change of decision makers' idea is the direct factor promoting the institutional reform of macro-control.

From 1979 to 1997, the decision-makers' macro-control ideology was observed with a great change, from "planned and proportional and comprehensive balancing" to "state regulates market and market guides enterprises", and then to "ensure the market to play a basic role in allocation of resources under the macro-control of socialist country". Such changes directly affects the change of macro-control means at the systematic stratum: market-oriented regulation and control means change from not being accepted to holding the leading position; the planning means are continuously split up and cleared up, but part of them are retained, thus forming eventually the new macro-control system under the socialist market economic system. From 1998 to 2012, the basic frame of such system remained basically stable, with being developed and improved to some extent. The decision-makers had a clearer understanding of the effect of proactive fiscal policy, necessity of regulation and control in the flourishing period, applicability of administrative regulation and control and other issues, obtained increasingly mature skill for regulation and control and accumulated a lot of treasured experience. "Three-in-one" regulation and control mode was basically formed. In 2013, the decision-makers' macro-control idea was observed with a new change, manifesting the macro-control innovation after the economy entering into new normal, including: highlight quality improvement and efficiency and lay stress on supply management; keep the power of mediation and advance steadily; ensure micro vitality, macro stability, and social backup; carry out interval regulation and control and oriented regulation and control; imply reform in regulation and control; plan, as a whole, the coordination mechanism construction with macro-control policy; advance the institutionalization of macro-control target and policy formulation.

Secondly, the process of institutional transition becomes the fundament force affecting the institutional reform of macro-control.

In order to ensure the smooth and successful transition from the planed system to the market system, it is extremely necessary to provide a relatively stable macroeconomic environment, as the macro stability is the prerequisite for the completion of reform. As China's system transition was gradually advanced and the economic structure changed, with the co-existence of state-owned sector and non-state owned sector and planning and market, the double-track regulation and control was thus indispensable. On the one hand, with the market-oriented reform being gradually advanced, the market-oriented force became gradually strong, the decision-makers also took the market-oriented forces as the main tool for macro-control accordingly, and market orientation is insisted for the building and development of macro-control system, emphasizing indirect regulation and control by economic and legal means. On the other hand, since China's economic system was still in the process of transition, the traditional planning means continued to withdraw, but had never been completely abandoned by the decision makers and instead entering eventually into the macro- control in a certain form as one of the optional policy tools in the hand of the decision makers. Under the great flag of macro-control, planning and market were properly integrated to eventually form the macro-control system integrated with planning, fiscal and financial sectors. The role of state-owned enterprises, local governments and NDRC in macro-control and the integration of market-oriented regulation and control and administrative regulation and control represented therein had just formed the uniqueness of China's macro-control.

Thirdly, the change of economic structure caused by the change of development stages has important influence on China's macro-control. With different issues of economic structure, the government is required to resolve one by one with different policy instruments. Consequently, equal stress is laid on structural regulation and control and aggregate regulation and control: some typical structural regulation and control policies such as industrial policy, trade policy, exchange rate policy, capital control and even regulation policy are all included in the toolbox of the government for macro-control.

It should be pointed out that the current macro-control system was observed with such problems as inadequate indicators reflecting economic development quality and benefit, improvement of residents' living and ecological construction, casual overlapping of effective offsetting or negative effect between policies, hysteresis of formulation and regular of regulation and control policies and mechanism-oriented construction, unsmooth conduction mechanism of policies, and inadequate legal assurance and authentication and execution of macro-control policies. The existence of such issues affected the scientificity and efficiency of macro-control. Therefore, in the coming period, China shall, according to the requirement set forth at the Third Plenary Session of the 18th National Congress of the CPC, comprehensively deepen the reform, change the governmental functions, build the more efficient solid institution of macro-control system of Chinese characteristics, with indirect market-oriented means as the main tool, so that it can fit with the need for the general target for "market plays a decisive role in allocation of resources". Particularly, with respect to the reform of macroeconomic management institution, the following works shall be seriously advanced: (1) perfect the macro-control system with the national development strategy and planning as the guidance and the fiscal policy and monetary policy as the main means, and intensify the coordination and collaboration of fiscal policy, monetary policy with industrial, price and other policy means; (2) advance the institutionalization of macro-control target and policy formulation; (3) speed up to form the mechanism in coordination with the international macroeconomic policy; (4) deepen the reform of investment system and establish the position of enterprises as investment entities; (5) perfect the examination and evaluation system for development achievements.

China's macro-control system has the characteristics and advantages of its own and is also in relatively good performance of regulation and control, but since the process of institutional transition was not yet completed, the government had no choice but adopted various administrative means in regulation and control in the circumstances that the institutional reform was not yet properly completed and the conduction mechanism was not smooth for market-oriented regulation and control. These non- market oriented means could be used to mobilize resources rapidly and cope with the external impact within a short period, but in view of the long term and overall situation, excessive dependence on administrative means would easily cause a negative effect in various aspects, including hindering the basic role of market mechanism in allocation of resources, increasing fiscal risks, distorting economic structure, causing corruption and forming new sources for economic fluctuation. China's macro management system is still in the continuous reform. We cannot be satisfied or stop going forward because others want to come and learn. Actually, some characteristics of China's macro-control are the products at the special development stage and under the specific institutional structure. Such particularity should be distinguished the general experience of China's macro management really worth of reference for the international community. Especially, it necessary to define which will be eliminated as the system changes, e.g., the market plays a decisive role in allocation of resources, and which can keep abreast with the times because of fitting with the institutional changes. It also constitutes the basic logic for the reform of China's macro management system in the future.

## References

Bernanke B (2010) On the implications of the financial crisis for economics. Comp Stud 5

Dong Yun (2011) Institutional transition and changes in China's economic fluctuation forms. China Open J 2:101–104

Frankel J (2010) Monetary policy in emerging markets: a survey. NBER working paper, No 16125
Fuqian F et al (2012) State-owned economic reform and tranquilization of China's economic fluctuations. Manag World 3:11–22
Jianfeng Y (2010) Studies on tranquilized phenomenon of China's economic cycle in 21st century. Soc Sci China 4:56–73
Lim ER (2008) Mind opening up in China's reform and opening up process. Comp Stud 38
Lin Jianhao et al (2013) 'Great moderation' of China's macroeconomic fluctuations—time-point identification and cause analysis. Chin Econ Q 2:577–604
Liu Guoguang, Liu Shucheng (1997) Discussion of 'soft landing'. People's Daily, 7 Jan
Wu J (2014) China: government's role in the transition of economy. Hebei Acad J 4:39–46
Zhang Xiaojing, Dong Yun (2013) Reconstructing policy framework of macro- economy: exploration and controversy. Comp Stud 3:55–61
Zhang Xiaojing, Li Cheng, Chang Xin, Zhang Ping (2010) China's macro-control in post-crisis Era. Econ Res J 11:4–20

# Chapter 6
# System Transition and Development Transformation

For more than three decades in the past, China has always carried out the reform with the economic construction as the focus and closely in line with economic development, provided new incentives and behavioral constraints by adjusting the system, continuously liberated and developed productivity, and took the improvement of economic performance and public welfare as the standard for judging the success and failure of reform. While reforming in line with the economic development, China continuously developed and deepened the denotation and connotation of development, gradually formed the "four-in-one" modern development framework including economic development, social development, harmonious development of man and nature and human comprehensive development, and focused on the change of economic development mode and advanced the reform further vertically.

## 6.1 The Development Orientation of the Reform

Reform is carried out for the purpose of development. "Development" is primarily economic development, as the base for all developments. At the very beginning of reform and opening up, China already defined the economic construction as the focus and gave the first priority to economic development. It was set forth on the basis of summarizing the historical experience and lessons. Deng Xiaoping once pointed out: "the key for China to resolve all the problems is to rely on its own development"[1] and "Development is the absolute principle".[2] In line with economic development, China has correctly defined the road for development—the socialist road with Chinese characteristics, stage of development—primary stage of socialism, and the development strategy—"three-step" strategy.

[1] Deng Xiaoping (1993), p. 265.

[2] Deng Xiaoping (1993), p. 377.



X. Zhang, X. Chang, *The Logic of Economic Reform in China*, China Insights,
DOI 10.1007/978-3-662-47404-4_6

The "three-step" strategy itself is continuously developed. Deng Xiaoping initially proposed the "three-step" strategy as: the first step is from 1981 to 1990 for doubling GNP and resolving the problem of food and clothing for people; the second step is from 1991 to 2000 for doubling GNP again and enabling people to have a well-off life; the third step is to the mid-twenty-first century when GNP per capita reaches the level of medium developed countries, people have a relatively prosperous life and modernization is basically realized. The *Outline for the "9th Five-year" Planning of National Economic and Social Development and the Prospective Target for 2010* adopted at the Fourth Meeting of the 8th National People's Congress in 1996 presented the major target for 5 years and 15 years as: firstly, during the "9th Five-year" period, comprehensively complete the strategic arrangement for the second step of modernization, control the population within 1.3 billion and quadruple GNP per capita (as compared with 1980) by 2000; secondly, basically eliminate the phenomena of poverty, with the people's living up to the well-off level; thirdly, speed up the construction of modern enterprises, primarily establish the socialist market economic system, and lay a better material and technical base for the step-3 strategic arrangement to be implemented in the next century; fourthly, by 2010, double GNP as compared with 2000, control the population within 1.4 billion, enable people to have an easier life, and form the relatively perfect socialist market economic system. In 1997, the 15th National Congress of the CPC proposed the "New Three-step" strategy as: Step 1, in the first decade of the twenty-first century, double GDP as compared with 2000, enable people to have an easier life, and form the perfect socialist market economic system; Step 2, upon making efforts for another decade, to the 100th anniversary of CPC, develop further the national economy and perfect further all the systems; Step 3, by the mid-twenty-first century at the 100th anniversary of New China, basically actualize modernization and establish a prosperous and strong, democratic and civilized socialist country. In 2002, the 16th National Congress of the CPC proposed further that in the first two decades of the new century, based on optimizing the structure and increasing the benefits, GDP will be quadrupled over 2000 and comprehensively construct a well-off society at a higher level for the population of more than 1 billion by 2020. In 2007, the 17th National Congress of the CPC changed the target of "quadruple" from "aggregate" to "per capita" and proposed to quadruple GDP per capita over 2000 by 2020 on the basis of optimizing the structure, increasing benefits, reducing the consumption and protecting the environment. In 2012, the 18th National Congress of the CPC set forth a higher requirement for the economic and social development and comprehensive construction of a well-off society and proposed to double GDP and per capita income of urban-rural residents over 2010 on the basis of enhancing obviously the balance, harmony and sustainability of development. It is the first time to include, in the previous reports of CPC, doubling the income of urban-rural residents as the explicit strategic target for arrangement, reflecting the idea of scientific development, especially the human-oriented ideology as well as representing the new appeal for the balanced development of national wealth and people's wealth.

Reform must be carried for development. As Deng Xiaoping explicitly pointed out, all reforms have one common purpose: abolish those production relations and superstructures that cannot fit with the requirement of productivity development and clear away the barriers for productivity development by liberating the productivity. He also expounded profoundly the inherent contact between reform and development: reform is the direct power and solid foundation for development, only by reforming can barriers be eliminated for productivity development, while development is the purpose for all reforms and without development, reform will be meaningless.

Over the last three decades or so, with respect to the problems observed in the process of economic development, China has laid stress on reforming such aspects as micro economic base, market system construction, governmental administration system, especially macroeconomic management institution, distribution system and social security system, so as to widen the space for the economic development. (1) In terms of economic growth, GDP aggregate and GDP per capita increased remarkably. From 1978 to 2013, China's GDP aggregate increased from RMB 364.5 billion to RMB 56.8845 trillion (according to the primary calculation results published by National Bureau of Statistics, GDP amounted to RMB 63.6463 trillion in 2014), with a growth of 25 times as per comparable price; by GDP aggregate, China's ranking in the world rose from the 10th in 1978 to the 2nd in 2010; GDP per capita increased form RMB 381 to RMB 41,908, with a growth of 17 times as per comparable price. China actualized earlier the quadruple target of GNP and GNP per capita over 1980, respectively in 1995 and 1997, actualized in advance the double target of GNP over 2000 in 2007. (2) With respect to the adjustment of economic structure, industrialization and urbanization was advanced steadily. From 1978 to 2013, the added value and employment ratio decreased from 28.2 % and 70.5 % to 10 % and 31.4 % for the primary industry and increased from 23.9 % and 12.2 % to 46.1 % and 38.5 % for the tertiary industry, respectively (according to the primary calculation results published by National Bureau of Statistics, in 2014, the share of added value for the tertiary industry in GDP increased further to 48.2 %). In view of the circumstances from 1990 with the statistical records available, by the contribution rate and hauling rate for the national economy, the secondary industry ranked the first among the three industries and basically shared half and even more. From 1978 to 2013, the demographic urbanization rate rose from 17.92 % to 53.73 %, with an increase of 35.81 % points and an average annual increase of 1.02 % points. In view of the absolute figure, the urban population increased by 558.66 million, with an average annual increase of 15.96 million (according to the latest information disclosed by National Bureau of Statistics at Press Conference of National Economic Operation for 2014, the urban permanent population numbered to 749.16 million by the end of 2014, with an increase of 18.05 million as compared to the end of 2013; the proportion of urban population in the total population increased further to 54.77 %). (3) In terms of the welfare level for residents, income increased by doubling and living developed from inadequate food and clothing to well-off. From 1978 to 2013, the annual per capita disposable income for urban residents increased from RMB 343.4 to RMB 26,955.1 and the annual per capita net income for rural residents increased from RMB 133.6 to RMB 8,895.9, with a growth of 11.3 times and 11.9 times respectively as per comparable price (according to the latest information disclosed by National Bureau of Statistics at Press Conference of National Economic Operation for 2014, in 2014, the per capita disposable income for urban residents amounted to RMB 28,844, with an actual growth of 6.8 % upon exclusion of price factor; the per capita net income for rural residents amounted to RMB 9,892, with an actual growth of 9.2 % upon exclusion of price factor); Engel's coefficient for the rural residents and the urban residents decreased from 67.7 % and 57.5 % to 37.7 % and 35 %, respectively; while the (absolute) poverty line increased from RMB 100 to RMB 1,274 for annual net income per capita, the rural population of extreme poverty decreased from 250 million to 82.49 million, the incidence of poverty decreased from 30.7 % in 1978 to 8.5 % in 2013. Thus, the international community rated relatively high the effect of China's poverty reduction.

The successful mode of China for integration of economic transformation and economic development over the last three decades has gradually drawn the attention of the international media and academic circles. In 2004, the British famous think tank, London Foreign Policy Centre published the paper of Joshua Cooper Ramo, the Senior Advisor (Political Economy) of USA Goldman Sachs, in the title of "Beijing Consensus", with the attempt to outline and summarize the brand-new mode of China for advancing the economic development based on continuous reform over the last two decades for the purpose of distinguishing from the "Latin American Development Mode" based on the "Washington Consensus", "Shock Therapy" in the Russian transformation and part of "East Asian Development Mode". Such concept as "Beijing Consensus" still needs further discussion and more systematic promotion, but it was presented to, at least from one side, reflect the affirmation of such mode of China as "reform in line with economic development and advance development by economic transformation" by the international community.

## 6.2 The Evolution of Connotation of Development and the Sublimation of the New Reform Concept

In reform for the purpose of development, the denotation and connotation of "development" is continuously expanded and deepened along with the deepening understanding of the development theory and the changing practice of development. From the evolution of the development theory in the world, the following basic threads of thought may be observed:

### 6.2.1 *Economic Growth Theory*

Since the development economics emerging after "World War II" studied initially how the undeveloped countries could catch up with the developed countries, it mainly emphasized on the growth of economic aggregate and equated development to economic growth. In the works of early development economics such as The *Theory of Economic Growth* of Lewis (1955) and The *Stages of Economic Growth* of Rostow (1960), the growth of GNP and per capital national income was taken as the prime standard and even the only standard for judging the development. But in practice, the "growth without development" indicated the huge difference between development and growth. In 1966, Clower published his book in the title of "Growth without Development" regarding his research on Libyan economy. He found that the per capita income of Liberia increased sharply, but it mainly resulted from that the foreign companies invested and developed oil for exporting to Europe and America and Libyan technical standard, human capital accumulation and production of other sectors were not observed with any change accordingly. Furthermore, the increase of revenues resulting from oil export had not improved the living standard of its nationals, but enlarged wealth gap.[3] The *Human Development Report* published by UNDP in 1996 discussed collectively the relation between economic growth and human development and presented five circumstances of growth without human development, i.e.: (1) jobless growth—where the overall economy grows but does not expand opportunities for employment, and even worsens the situation of employment; (2) voiceless growth—where growth in the economy has not been accompanied by an extension of democracy or empowerment, political repression and authoritarian controls have silenced alternative voices and stifled demands for greater social and economic participation; (3) ruthless growth—where the fruits of economic growth mostly benefit the rich, leaving millions of people struggling in ever-deepening poverty; (4) rootless growth—where economic growth causes damages to cultural diversity and results in crisis of native cultures and incidence of national conflicts; (5) futureless growth—where economic growth causes destruction to ecology, resources and environment and affects the sustainability of economic growth.[4]

### 6.2.2 *Theory of Economic and Social Overall and Harmonious Development*

Around the 1960s, with social contradictions becoming prominent, the development theory was added with attention to "social structures and social problems", viewing that development is a systematic project for the economic and social overall and harmonious development in all aspect. In 1965, in his article titled as *Social*

[3] Clower (1966).

[4] United Nations Development Program (1996).

*Development: Key Growth Sector,* Singer proposed the concept on social development and laid stress on attention to all aspects of social development: education, health, nutrition and so on. In his opinion, "the problems observed in undeveloped countries include not only growth problem, but also development problem. Development is growth and change, and such change is not only in economy, but also in society and culture, and not only in quantity, but also in quality…Its main concept must be the improvement of people's living".[5] In their work *Society, Politics and Economic Development-A Quantitative Approach* (1967), Adelman and Morris proposed to understand the development from the angle of interaction of economic, social and political factors. By adopting the factor analysis approach rarely used by economists, they discovered the correlation between several key social and political variables and the level of economic development.[6] In his paper, the *Meaning of Development* (1969), Seers emphasized that the purpose of development is to reduce poverty, inequality and unemployment. In this paper submitted to the 11th World Conference of International Development Association, he said: "The questions to ask about a country's development are therefore: What has been happening to poverty? What has been happening to unemployment? What has been happening to inequality? If all three of these have declined from high levels, then beyond doubt this has been a period of development for the country concerned. If one or two of these central problems have been growing worse, especially if all three have, it would be strange to call the result 'development', even if per capita income doubled."[7] In 1970, in its important achievement *Contents and Measurements of Socioeconomic Development,* UNRISD claimed that development should be the integration of economic growth and social reform and has established the socioeconomic development indicator composed of 16 key factors.[8] In his book titled as *Economic Development in the Third World* (1977), Todro pointed out: "Development is not purely an economic phenomenon. In an ultimate sense, it must encompass more than the material and financial side of people's lives, to expand human freedoms. Development should therefore be perceived as a multidimensional process involving the reorganization and reorientation of entire economic and social systems."[9] Based on the foregoing new development theories, was undertaken worldwide during this period.

### 6.2.3 Theory of Sustainable Development

Around the 1970s, with the pressure of population, resources and environment increasing, the theory of development was added with "sustainable development", expanding to the idea of "coordination" to the relation between generations. In

[5] Singer (1965).

[6] Adelman and Morris (1967).

[7] Seers (1969).

[8] United Nations Research Institute on Social Development (1970).

[9] Todaro (1977).

1972, the research group composed by Meadows et al. from Massachusetts Institute of Technology submitted *The Limits to Growth*, the first research report after The Club of Rome was established, profoundly elaborating the viewpoint on the coordination between economic growth and resources environment, and harmonious development between man and nature. According to the report, since such five basic elements as the world population growth, food production, investment growth, environmental pollution and resource consumption operate in the mode of index growth rather than exponential growth, the limits to growth on this planet will be reached sometime within the next 100 years.. The best approach for avoiding the world collapse due to surpassing the natural ecological limit is control the growth, i.e., actualizing "non-growth".[10] The idea of "reasonable and lasting balanced development" elaborated in the report is the rudiment of the sustainable development ideology. In the book *Building a Sustainable Society* (1981), Director of Worldwatch Institute (USA), Brown further elaborated more systematically the "outlook on sustainable development".[11] In 1987, the research report of *Our Common Future*, WECD chaired by the former prime minister of Norway, Mrs. Brundland proposed, by starting with the "three-principle" of fairness, sustainability and generality for development, that sustainable development is the development that "can meet the demands of contemporary people and will not cause any harm to the capacity of the descendants to meet their demands". This interpretation has been widely recognized gradually by the international community. In 1992, the United Nations Conference on Environment and Development held in Rio de Janeiro, Brazil, with the delegates from 183 countries and regions present, adopted such two programmatic documents as *Rio Declaration on Environment and Development* and *Agenda 21*, indicating the outlook on sustainable development became the important guiding ideology for formulating the economic and social development strategies in the world.

### 6.2.4 People-oriented Development Theory

Around the 1980s, with the principle of ethics being gradually brought into the vision of development, the theory of development was added with more "humanitarian care", turning the focus of development from the mere growth of material wealth to the expansion of human freedom, improvement of human capacity and giving play to human potential. As early as in 1971, in the book *The Cruel Choice: A New Concept in the Theory of Development*, Goulet presented that the key value and basic factors of development should cover three aspects: life-sustenance, meaning to meet the basic living needs of man; self-esteem, meaning the self-possession and independence, eliminating the feeling of being controlled and dependent; freedom, meaning to extricate from such three evils as poverty,

[10] Meadows et al. (1972).

[11] Brown (1981).

ignorance and humbleness so that people can control their own fate.[12] In 1983, in the book *A New Concept of Development: Basic Tenets*, Perroux emphasized that development should be "overall", "comprehensive" and "inherent", the real development must be the comprehensive and coordinated co-advancing of economy, society, man and nature; and persisted in viewing "human comprehensive development" should be taken as the fundamental target and key value orientation of development; in other words, development should focus on human value, human needs and functioning of human potential, with the aim to meet the basic needs of man and promote the improvement of life and the comprehensive development of each member in the community.[13] In 1999, in the book *Development as Freedom*, the winner of Nobel Prize for Economics (1998), Sen emphasized that expansion of freedom is the prime purpose of development as well as its key means. Expansion of freedom is the prime purpose of development, which means that development can be regarded as a process for expanding the real freedom for people. Here, real freedom refers to the "feasible capacity" for a valuable life. Expansion of freedom is the key measure of development, mainly referring to five distinct types of freedom, seen in an "instrumental" perspective, these include political freedom (political rights and civic rights), economic freedom (economic facilities), social freedom (social opportunities), transparency freedom (transparency guarantees), and protective freedom (protective security). Such instrumental freedoms can help people to live more freely and improve their overall capacity.[14] With the foregoing latest meanings of development presented, since 1990 when the first *Human Development Report* was published, UNDP started to compile the human development index (HDI) including life expectancy at birth (LEB), adult literacy rate (ALR) and combined primary, secondary, and tertiary gross enrolment ratio (with one-third weighting) and GNI per capita (PPP US$), which was used to measure the achievements of human development and gradually drew the general attention of all the countries.

In view of that, over the last six decades or so, the understanding of the connotation of development has been continuously deepened from "material" centric to "man" centric, from economic development to social development, sustainable development, and human development.

Based on the continuous evolution of the theory of development in the world as well as the realistic conditions of the domestic development, in recent years, China has adjusted the previous ideas of development at the right time and laid stress on changing the mode of economic development, i.e., seeking the expansion from the unitary economic development to the "four-in-one" development including economic development, social development, harmonious development of man and nature and human comprehensive development, and the change in mode of economic development from extensive to intensive, from unbalancing to balancing and from under-sustainable to sustainable. Reform is carried out for the purpose of development means that as the denotation and connotation of development was

[12] Goulet (1971).

[13] Perroux (1983).

[14] Sen (1999).

extended and deepened, the contents of reform were also enriched accordingly and promoted the understanding of reform strategy. Such development and innovation in reform concept are particularly shown in the following two aspects:

1. Emphasis on the adjustment and general planning of social interest relationship. The essence of reform is to adjust the relationship of interests. In early reform, China adjusted the relationship of social interests so that absolutely most stakeholders would benefit from, to different extents. But due to the constraints of rooted institutional barriers and productivity development level, some in-depth structural contradictions and the pattern of interdependent interests had not been completely broken through; additionally, in the process of unbalanced economic growth and reform, due to inadequate general planning and consideration, some new contradictions were also observed in the relationship of interests, especially between urban and rural areas, between different regions and between different groups, and some non-coordinated and disharmonious problems were also observed between economic development and social development, between man and nature, and between internal development and opening up, and to some extent, "unbalance" was observed even in some aspects. If these problems were not resolved, they would hinder the establishment of a perfect socialist market economic system and influence the overall situation of economic development and social stability. The idea of "general planning" in the new reform concept was presented to coordinate properly the relationship of different interests in the process of reform, and was the starting point for defining the reform tasks in the new stage.
2. Emphasis on human comprehensive development. Marx explicitly pointed out the essence of a new society is "comprehensive development of human freedom". In the early stage of reform, China had not set forth the combined development of economy, society and man as an independent and integral guiding idea. The new reform concept guides, from a higher realm, the system innovation at a new stage. Such "innovation" focuses not only on the improvement of people's material and cultural living, but also on the promotion of human quality. It not only promotes institutionally the coordinated development of man and nature, but also promotes institutionally the public for participation in "democratic and perfect" construction of enterprises, community and state. The establishment of such idea has defined the fundamental target direction not only for deepening the reform of economic institution, but also for deepening the reform of cultural and social institution and even political institution.

## 6.3 How to Integrate Economic System Innovation and Development Model Innovation

In view of the development practice in China, the reform has powerfully promoted the economic development, but there are a number of contradictions in development mode and different structural distortions are serious, mainly manifested in: (1) in terms of the demand structure, economic growth was mainly driven by investment and export and relatively, the pulling effect of consumption and especially consumers appeared to be inadequate. (2) In terms of industrial structure, service industry was still undeveloped, especially the development of productive service industry lagged behind and industrial efficiency and competitiveness needed to be enhanced. (3) In terms of factor input structure, economic growth was actualized mainly by large-scale input of production factors (including natural resources), at the cost of environment, not by advancing the optimization of economic structure and allocation of resources and technical innovation. (4) In terms of urban-rural and regional structures, the urban-rural income gap was still relatively large; the urban-rural dualism system was ingrained, especially reflecting in the household registration system and corresponding welfare system and the identity difference of urban-rural residents on the rights of land. Additionally, the problem of unbalanced regional development was still observed and the eastern region was still in an absolutely advantageous position in view of the key indicators representing the regional economic strength, including the regional gross products, fixed asset investment, foreign trade and local fiscal revenues. (5) With respect to the social development, the gap of income distribution was still prominent; additionally, in a dynamic view, the inter-generational income liquidity tended to decline and was in the danger of falling into the solidification of the pattern for social ranks and classes and interests. (6) With respect to the sustainable development, the structural contradiction due to the constraint of resources and environment became increasingly prominent. All in all, the traditional development mode was non-coordinated, unbalanced and unsustainable. Thus, it is necessary to further deepen the reform, break through collectively the in-depth institutional barriers that handicap the change of development mode and provide the important institutional support for dissolving all the structural contradictions.

### 6.3.1 Advance Reform in Line with "Coordinated Development"

Firstly, improve the demand structure and expand further the consumption, especially the residents' consumption. Currently, in addition to such constraining factors as income distribution system in this aspect, the public service function of the government is still shortening, as has also affected the consumers' demands. The expenditures of the government in such fields of public services as education, medical and health, employment and social security is inadequate, causing a negative impact on residents' consumption in various aspects: (1) current consumption is reduced by intensifying the motive of residents for preventive savings; (2) the human capital accumulation unfavorable for residents restricted the "capacity" of laborers and their "negotiating ability" in the primary distribution; (3) the process is affected for employment of peasant workers in cities and relevant citizenship and consequently, the huge investment and consumption demands implied in urbanization is restrained. For this reason, it is necessary to enhance further the public service function of the government, give play to the external effect of public expenditures and promote private consumption by adjusting the expenditure structure of the government and increasing the social expenditures.

Secondly, optimize the industrial structure and advance the development of service, especially modern service. The non-development of service, especially the lagging development of productive service is closely associated with the industrial monopoly. For many service sectors, since the access barrier is serious, the market access environment is far from ease. Especially, the existing enterprises and new-coming enterprises are not in a state of impartial competition. As the existing monopoly enterprises dominating the market have the overwhelming first-move advantage over the new comers in competition as well as take some tactic actions to hinder the competition by their advantages (especially controlling the "bottleneck" segments and network infrastructures), it is hard to actualize effective competition. Under such background, it is fundamentally hard for private enterprises and private capital to access to many of the service sectors and eventually, it is still the state-owned economy that rules all the sectors or holds the position of monopoly. In view of the total investment of service industry (excluding rural households) in 2013, the state-owned holdings investment was up to 43.6 %. In the 14 major trades, except for such 7 trades as wholesale and retail (11.5 %), accommodation and catering (12.9 %), real estate (23.4 %), neighborhood service and repair and other services (29.5 %), lease and business service (29.5 %), scientific research and technical service (38.7 %), and culture, sports and entertainment (45.4 %), the state-owned investment in other 7 trades shared 50 % or more. The state-owned investment in water conservancy, environment and public facilities administration (77.7 %), transport, warehousing and postal service (76.9 %), education (74.1 %), public administration, social security and social organization (72.6 %), and health and social work (72 %) shared more than 70 %. To change thoroughly of the lagged development of service, it is necessary to advance the reform in the field of services: break through the sector monopoly and relax the industrial access restriction so that private capital can participate more in the development and market competition of services.

Finally, adjust the urban-rural and regional structures. The keynote of attention is to promote the high-quality urbanization, especially the urbanization of man. The biggest problem with the present urbanization is the incompleteness. In 2012, as per statistics of permanent residents, the urbanization rate was 52.57 %, while the share of the urban household registered population, i.e., the urbanization rate of household registered population was only 35.29 %. The gap between the urbanization rate of household registered population and the urbanization rate of permanent residents widened from 10.5 percentage points in 2000 to 17.3 percentage points. It indicates in 2012, 234 million persons sharing 17.28 % of the total population were permanent residents without urban household registration. Due to the barrier of the household registration system and especially the different welfare associated with the identity of household registration, the foregoing more than 200 million people are not equally entitled to different basic public services in cities.

Therefore, the future urbanization strategy shall turn from attaching importance merely to the increase of population ratio to the expansion of public service coverage and actualizing the urbanization of peasant workers by eliminating the gap between the urbanization rate of permanent residents and the non-agricultural household registered population. Currently, much resistance has been encountered locally in terms of easing the administration of household registration and gradually peeling off the unfair welfare benefits attached to the household registration, due to the problem with the fiscal input after all. It will be a test for the local governments to bear the higher pressure of public service with their available financial resources. Therefore, it is necessary to implement the fiscal reform in favor of strengthening the social services, rebuild the fiscal relation between the central and local governments, rationally classified the scope of power of office and rebuild the local main tax sources. Additionally, to enhance the support of state-owned enterprises' income to the public finance, used for expenditures of the people's livelihood and especially for social security.

### 6.3.2 *Advance Reform in Line with "Innovative Development"*

In our opinion, China's sustainable economic growth will eventually depend on changing from "exogenous growth" mode to "endogenous growth" mode. To realize such change, the fundamental approach is to drive by innovation. To make the technological innovation as the fundamental driving for sustainable development, in view of the institutional guarantee, two problems shall be resolved mainly: one is "getting incentives right" and the other is "getting prices right".

**On Getting Incentives Right**

As a whole, the incentive mechanism for innovation is obviously inadequate, mainly in the following two aspects:

1. The incentive function of the intellectual property system has not been given an adequate play. The intellectual property system is an important mean for protecting the technological innovation of enterprises. Without protection of intellectual property, the spillover effects of enterprises' technological innovation cannot be necessarily compensated for gains, leading to the problem of "thumb a lift", and thus constraining the innovation of enterprises and resulting in popular imitation and reproduction. After the mid-1980s, China enhanced the protection of intellectual property, but such protection has not been proper by now, resulting in the failure of such policy to play a full role.
2. The incentive mechanism for the remunerations and property distribution of human capital is not yet perfect. In technological innovation, since entrepreneurs, science and technology workers and other owners of human capital with great creative work undertake high risks and responsibilities, the remuneration and property distribution should reflect the adequate recognition of their value. Currently, however, China has not attached adequate attention to the value of

human capital in technological progress and has not taken adequate account of work complexity and contributions to enterprises in distribution, thus dampening the enthusiasm of human capital owners for innovating continuously and undertaking risks. It already becomes a material barrier for many enterprises in carrying out technological innovation.

In order to perfect the incentive mechanism for innovation, it is necessary to improve further the protection system for intellectual property and form the deterrence of confidence by strengthening punishment and increasing illegal cost. Additionally, the scientific evaluation and effective incentive mechanism should be established for the innovative activities of talents. For instance, the "technical capitalization" can be advanced encourage innovation of technological workers, by the system of technology investment and technical option.

**On Getting Prices Right**

Under the condition of market economy, prices have an important function for transmitting signals and playing an important interest-oriented role in regulating the allocation of resources. As the practice of development in Japan, South Korea, China Taiwan shows, with the effect of the normal market mechanism, due to the changes in the relative prices of different production factors in economic growth, the mode of economic growth will gradually turn from extensive to intensive. Currently, however, since the direct intervention of the government is still excessive for allocation of factors and pricing in the factors market, prices fail to truly reflect the scarcity and supply-demand relation of factors and the extent of environmental damages, thus resulting in the distortion of factor prices in certain sense. When the prices of land, capital and other factors tend to be underestimated, the market entities are directly stimulated for intensive use of relatively low-cost tangible factors and seldom have the motive and pressure for investing in independent innovation.

The key for correction of such situation is to make correct price signals and to form the effective pricing mechanism of factors by advancing continuously the development and perfection of factor market so that the factor prices can be "approximate" to the real balanced level decided by supply and demand. Based on this, micro enterprises are enabled to make rational decisions according to market signals. With correct price signals, guide all economic entities to predict and adjust the behaviors of micro entities and establish the mechanism for sustainable innovation.

In addition to the foregoing two key institutional guarantees, it is also necessary to clarify the function of the government in innovation. On the one hand, it should be admitted that some external effects cannot be considered completely by market in the process of innovation. For instance, the innovation promotion of enterprises will provide other enterprises with public knowledge and infrastructure construction will reduce the transaction cost of enterprises and increase the return on investment. Since such external effects cannot be resolved through market, the government is required to play a necessary role in industrial upgrading and technological innovation. However, it should be also noted that the government cannot intervene excessively in industrial selection and technological selection. In recent years, in the process of promoting the strategic emerging industries, the government often determine whether one industry is of the development prospects according to its assessment of market supply and demand and forecasting of the changes in future supply and demand, and formulate the planning for industrial development in accordance with the assessment and forecasting. Actually, however, due to the uncertainty and its limited rationality, the government may not be able to make relatively accurate assessment of economic situation. It is actually the coordination mechanism for replacing market as per assessment and control of the government, with certain planned economic color. The huge vibration experienced by some emerging industries represented by PV industry in recent years is associated with petting for wrong technical direction, under the government-leading background, and the large-scale overlapping investment. In our opinion, in the circumstance that it is necessary to implement the industrial policy, in order to overcome the governmental failure, it is necessary to distinguish the selective industrial policy and functional industrial policy (Lall 1994), direct-intervention and indirect-induction industrial policies. As the key essence here, industrial policy should be taken as the tool for rectifying the market failure, rather than substituting the market. In other words, in the process of implementing the industrial policy, the government shall not try to substitute market, but to intensify market signals and private activities.

### 6.3.3 Advance Reform in Line with "Sustainable Development"

To actualize the effective utilization and protection of resources and environment, it is necessary to undermine the functional space of market mechanism. For instance, resources environment property system is introduced and especially the definition and trading system for property rights and its improvement.

In terms of the definition for property rights, for a long period of time, no property right has been defined for natural resources, especially ecological environment. Due to the ideological misunderstanding: property right is understood merely as a thing in kind, i.e., the so-called "physical concept of property"; such intangible matters as ecological environment are deemed as a kind of "public premises", without economic value, and are inexhaustible, which can be obtained without cost or at a low cost. In reality, most of the ecological environment resources are used without compensation, the beneficiaries of external economy can benefit without payment, and the interests of the external benefit providers are damaged. As the unclear property definition causes barriers in trading, it consequently leads to the "tragedy of commons" between and within generations in line with natural resources and ecological environment.

In terms of property transaction and circulation, the major problem is the incomplete price composition. Taking mineral resources as an example, the cost deficiency is particularly reflected in four aspects: (1) cost for paid-use of mineral resources: over a long period of time, at the segment of obtaining the mining right, absolutely most mining enterprises, especially state-owned enterprises, have obtained the mining right without compensation. Additionally, at the segment of mining of mineral resources, the tax levied from mining enterprises is excessively low. In recent years, the reform has been carried out for the system of obtaining the exploring right and mining right with charges, and new levy standard for compensation fee and new levy measures for tax, of the mineral resources have been formulated, but the strength still needs to be enhanced. (2) Cost for environmental governance and ecological restoration: at present, without the necessary compensation standard for environmental protection, many mining enterprises fail to bring such input as for mine environmental governance and ecological restoration after closing the pits into the production cost, thus the internal cost to be borne by enterprises is externalized. (3) Safety cost: at present, the status is not yet completely established for mining enterprises as the entity of investment on safety, and the input for safety is still inadequate. (4) Manpower cost: with respect to the employees, especially the peasant workers of mining enterprises, the rights assurance mechanism is imperfect and salary and welfare cost is relatively low. Due to the foregoing incomplete pricing cost, the prices of mineral resources are generally on low side. Consequently, it leads to the excessive use of mineral resources and severely environmental destruction.

To this end, it is necessary to perfect the system of defining the ecological environment property according to the idea of "environment is valuable". In line with this system, it is necessary to insist on two basic principles: (1) all the regions, enterprises or individuals with contribution to environment should be given earnings of the environmental property. (2) all the regions, enterprises or individuals granted with external economy of environment shall pay relevant charges to the owners of environmental property rights. The key is to establish the relevant mechanism for interest compensation of environmental property, including the mechanism of horizontal interest compensation between contributors and beneficiaries of external economy of environment and the mechanism for indirect vertical interest compensation with the state as the subject. With respect to the former, mainly in the circumstance that the interest margin is relatively clear, the beneficiaries of the external economy of the environment shall compensate directly the contributors, i.e., the owners of environmental property. It is mostly a kind of market-oriented mechanism for actualization of returns on property. With respect to the latter, in the circumstance that the interest margin is relatively vague, environmental tax is levied by the government to raise the funds for compensation and compensate indirectly the overflow portion of property by transfer payment.

Additionally, it is necessary to make gradually the resource enterprises, especially mining enterprises, reasonably bear all the costs caused in the process of resource development, so as to form full-cost resource price by internalizing some external costs. Particularly, it is necessary to (1) expand further the range for obtaining the mining right with charges, deepen the reform of resource tax, increase properly the charge standard for the use fees of exploring right and mining right and the compensation rate for mineral resources; resolve such problems as soon as possible as unreasonable reduction/exemption and overdue payment of compensation fees of mineral resources and use fees and payment of exploring right and mining right, so as to gradually reduce the resource cost; (2) establish the responsibility mechanism for mining enterprises for environmental governance and ecological restoration, to force the enterprises to withdrew from the sales income a certain proportion of funds for restoration and ecological compensation for the mine environment; consider levying the environmental ecological tax and gradually reduce the environmental cost; (3) intensify the subject status of mining enterprises for safety input, force enterprises to withdraw the safety fees, increase safety input and gradually reduce the safety cost; (4) perfect the right assurance mechanism for the employees of mining enterprises to ensure the basic salary and welfare level of employees and gradually reduce manpower cost.

### 6.3.4 Advance Reform in Line with the "People-oriented" Development

Reform should essentially have a foothold in two emancipations: one is the emancipation of productivity so that it is emancipated from the fetter of the old system; the other is the emancipation of man so that it is emancipated from the state of being fettered. If the reform at the preceding stage mainly focused on emancipating productivity, the reform at the next stage should take the "human comprehensive development" as a more independent and integral idea for guiding the institutional innovation. Such "innovation" should not only improve people's survival rights and economic development rights by focusing on people's needs for material life, and improve people's cultural rights and social development rights by focusing on people's needs for spiritual life and improvement of their quality, but also improve people's political rights and social administration rights by focusing on people's needs for participation in political life and social life. Therefore, the "people-oriented" system innovation should be the comprehensive institutional innovation covering economic, social, cultural and political systems. With respect to economy, the innovation should be advanced mainly for all the "people's livelihood" systems.

1. Advance reform of income distribution system

At the preceding stage, certain progress has been made in the reform of distribution system in line with the combination of distribution as per labor and distribution as per factors and the combination of efficiency and fairness. At the next stage, it is necessary to advance further the reform by distribution as per contribution of different production factors, expansion of residents' income source, fair distribution of income and narrowing of the income gap of residents. As for the current stage, it is necessary to increase the proportion of the resident income in the national income distribution and proportion of labor remuneration in the primary distribution. It can be resolved at three stratums of "ensure", "regulate" and "expand".

The so-called "ensure" means to ensure the factor earnings of residents: on the one hand, it is to ensure the matching between contribution and remuneration of labor factors; on the other hand, it is ensure the rights and interests of peasants on land. The so-called "regulate" means to strengthen the regulating function of the government in macro income distribution: on the one hand, it is to continue to implement the reform of personal income tax; on the other hand, it is to perfect the re-distribution system of public property income. The so-called "expand" means to expand channels for increasing residents' income. It is necessary to eliminate all the institutional barriers for employment creation, especially lay stress on resolving such problems resulting from labor flow barriers and public service supply barriers as unequal opportunities for laborers to access to jobs, education and health service, so as to promote the laborers' capacity for economic participation, income and wealth creation.

2. Advance reform of social security system

The major contradiction for the present social security system is the deficient coverage. With the pension security system as an example, currently, not only rural resident pension security system and peasant worker pension security system still have the relatively big space for deepening, but the urban staff and workers endowment insurance implemented for years is also observed with such problem as deficient coverage. For this reason, it is necessary to take the lead in making up the system deficiency in the following reform of social security system, so as to expand further the coverage of social security, and especially lay stress on resolving the problem of urban-rural coverage. While improving all security systems in connection with urban staff and workers and urban residents, the process of extending from urban areas to rural areas and the construction of social security system for rural residents and peasant workers should be further accelerated.

While resolving, at the first priority, the problem of "developing from nothing" for the coverage of social security, it is also necessary to start to resolve the problem of social security level "from low to high". However, it is necessary to prevent falling into the trap of populism and welfarism, define the reasonable security level, and prevent the welfare expenditures from rigidly endangering the stability of the government's financial resources, and the negative incentive and ethic risk problems due to excessive security from weakening the vigor and competitiveness of economies.

In addition to the reform of income distribution and social security system, it is also necessary to advance the relevant institution innovation in employment, education, health and safety (especially production safety, food and drug safety and environmental safety) in close connection with people's livelihood. The basic point should be to establish the effective public service system and gradually realize the equalization of relevant basic public services.

## References

Adelman I, Morris CT (1967) Society, politics and economic development-A quantitative approach. Johns Hopkins University Press, Baltimore
Brown LR (1981) Building a sustainable society. Norton and Co, New York
Chen X (1999) The economic system reform in rural China. In: Wang M (ed) The 20 years of economic transition in China. Foreign Language Press, Beijing
Clower RW (1966) Growth without development: an economic survey of Liberia. Northwestern University Press, Evanston
Deng Xiaoping (1993) Selected works of Deng Xiaoping, vol 3. China People's Publishing House, Beijing
Frye T, Shleifer A (1997) The invisible hand and the grabbing hand. Am Econ Rev 87:354–358
Goulet D (1971) The cruel choice: a new concept in the theory of development. Atheneum Books, New York
Lall S (1994) Industrial policy: the role of government in promoting industrial and technological development. UNCTAD Review, pp 65–69
Lewis WA (1955) The theory of economic growth. George Allen & Unwin, London
Meadows DL et al (1972) The limits to growth. Universe Books, New York
Pei Changhong (2009) An empirical analysis on China's establishment of an open economy. Res Financ Econ Issues 2
Perroux F (1983) A new concept of development: basic tenets. Croom Helm, London
Rostow WW (1960) The stages of economic growth. Cambridge University Press, Cambridge
Seers D (1969) The meaning of development. Int Dev Rev 11(4):3–4
Sen A (1999) Development as freedom. Alfred A. Knopf, New York
Singer HW (1965) Social development: key growth sector. Int Dev Rev 7(1):5
Stiglitz J (1998) Whither reform? Ten years of the transition, research report of China's national condition analysis, 44
Todaro MP (1977) Economic development in the third world. Longman, London
United Nations Development Program (1996) Human development report. University Press, New York/Oxford
United Nations Research Institute on Social Development (1970) Contents and measurements of socioeconomic development. UNRISD, Geneva

# Chapter 7
# China's Reform Under the Global Perspective

From the very beginning, China's reform has drawn the attention of the whole world. With the great changes of the former Soviet Union and East European countries from the late 1980s to early 1990s, the research tide set off worldwide on comparison of reforms. By creating the growth miracle, China's reform was spoken highly as a successful example. However, looking forward, China's reform needs to throw away the existing achievements and find the problems and challenges brought by the gradual reform (or marginal reform and peripheral reform). Therefore, it is necessary to explore the reform logic in the deep water area and crucial period, by surpassing the debate on advancing gradually and radically, with problems as guide.

## 7.1 The Basic Experience of China's Gradual Reform

Gradual reform is the most important characteristics of China's economic reform and the treasured experience of China in the success. For more than three decades, due to the gradual reform, China has maintained a rapid economic growth and a stable political situation. Comparatively, the former Soviet Union and East European countries have implemented the radical transformation or Shock Therapy. The reasons for the failure of Shock Therapy is still under discussion and the debate on ways for reforming is still in process, but the reality of economic stagnation and even collapse caused by the Shock Therapy is unavoidable.

China's reform is not to break through the existing system firstly, but to develop the new system by or in the "side" or "gap" of the existing system. With such new system developing and its proportion in the whole economy expanding, the reform of the existing system is gradually deepened. Such reform is carried out and advanced prudently from easy to difficult and from outside to inside within the frame of the existing system. It possesses the gradual characteristics in terms of time, speed and sequence selection. Therefore the co-existence of new and old systems is an important characteristic of the gradual reform. On the one hand, the



X. Zhang, X. Chang, *The Logic of Economic Reform in China*, China Insights,
DOI 10.1007/978-3-662-47404-4_7

tolerance of the old system is the necessity for reducing the social resistance for the reform by maintaining appropriately the vested interest in the early period of reform; on the other hand, since the new system will not grow overnight, it is also the necessity for the smooth transition of the system.

The gradual reform is of rich contents, mainly summarized as double-track transition and trial promotion (or look before you leap).

The double-track transition includes the reform of off-system growth and increment. The so-called "off-system" growth means to develop, outside the planned economic system, a new market-leading sector to make it one of the basic powers for market-oriented reform. In the process of China's market-oriented reform, such off-system growth is mainly shown in the following aspects: off-system reform of property system, i.e., allowing the development of the non-state owned economy outside the state-owned economy; off-system reform of the pricing system, i.e., allowing free pricing for some new products; off-system reform of the market organization, i.e., allowing the development of free market outside the planned distribution institution; off-system reform of income distribution, i.e., recognizing the rationality of distribution as per factor outside the distribution as per labor, and etc. The "double-track system" was initially used in the price reform, i.e., the so-called "price double-track system". The experience of "double-track system" was later applied in the reform of many other fields, such as reform of foreign trade system, reform of labor employment system, reform of ownership structure, reform of social security system, housing reform and etc. In terms of the whole economy, for the advancement of reform and development of market mechanism, the most important, influential and profound "double-track system" is the "double-track system" in the ownership structure, i.e., the double-track system composed of state ownership and non-state ownership, public ownership and non-public ownership. Instead of starting from the re-allocation of assets in stock, the increment reform focuses on making the market mechanism play a role in allocation of asset increment, which will lead the increment expansion and the reduction of stock proportion of the planned economy. The particular practices include: state-owned enterprises or peasants are allowed to determine independently the price, sales mode and income distribution for the incremental portion upon fulfilling the obligation of rendering to the government; as for the workers of state-owned enterprises, "existing method for existing employees and new method for new employees" may be applied: existing workers are treated according to the implicit "contractual conditions" between state-owned enterprises and staff and workers under the planned system, and new workers are employed in the mode of contracting freedom.

Trial promotion means to limit the market-oriented reform within a certain range (such as region, industry and even enterprise) and promote in a wider range and even nationwide after gathering experience. Most of China's economic reforms have not been launched nationwide at the same time, but been started with a trial for each reform measure within a relatively small range. After the pilot reform has made certain achievements, accumulated certain experience and the people have been psychologically ready before being promoted: e.g., the implementing of the household contract responsibility system, pilot enterprise contracting system and establishment of special economic zones and the pilot work for urban–rural general development now in progress in Chengdu and Chongqing, all of which have followed such principle. The gradual reform starts with the partial experiment like opening a "skylight" and creates the "domino effect" of system change, by driving various reforms with the key reform, so that the reform is carried out from easy to difficult, from one point to one area and from shallow to deep. As the biggest benefit, this practice has avoided the possible huge resistance, pressure and risk resulting from the rash comprehensive implementation in lacking experience, and ensured that the reform can be steadily advanced as a whole.

## 7.2 The Radical Transformation of the Former Soviet Union and Eastern Europe Countries and the Consequences

The radical reform (i.e., the so-called Shock Therapy) of the former Soviet Union and Eastern Europe countries is opposite to China' gradual reform. The reform mode featured as attempting to destroy comprehensively and thoroughly all the institutional arrangements of the planned economic system within a short period of time and then establish rapidly the institutional framework of market economy with a set of radical transformation measures (such as liberalization of economy, privatization of properties and macro stabilization) for one-step leap-over from planned economy to market economy. Therefore, it is also known as "Big Bang" strategy.

### *7.2.1 Russian Shock Therapy*

In the 1980s, the economic growth rate of the Soviet Union already dropped to 3 % and below, with some industries observed with a negative growth. Under such circumstance, the Soviet Union started a large-scale reform of economic system. The reform included two stages: the first stage was from 1985 to 1991 during which the gradual reform was carried out, but failed; then the second stage started from 1992 when the Shock Therapy was implemented. Upon collapse of the Soviet Union, in order to extricate Russia from the political and economic dilemma, Russian decision-makers for the reform proposed successively different reform programs.[1] The "500 Days Program" proposed by Grigory Yavlinsky claimed to use the Shock Therapy for privatization of production, liberalization of price, and free convertibility of Ruble and transit to the market economy in three stages within 500 days. This program was supported by Yeltsin and others and the Russian Federation declared to start the implementation of "500 Days Program", the Shock Therapy implemented comprehensively thence.

[1] Guo Liancheng (2005).

#### 7.2.1.1 Liberalization of Price

The first content of the Shock Therapy is the liberalization of economy, which was carried out mainly in such three aspects as liberalization of price, trade liberalization and free convertibility of Ruble and of which the driving force was the liberalization of price. The liberalization of price was considered by the radical reformers as the line of demarcation for the reform from gradual to radical. The impact of the price formation mechanism on Russian economic development can be classified into two different stages. Under the conditions of the planned economy with the public ownership as the main part, the planned system was established for price formation, the prices of important commodities were under the general supervision of the state and the price level was maintained in a relatively stable status. The implementation of the liberalization reform policy changed fundamentally the original price pattern and status. Since enterprises pricing on the basis of contracts, the price fluctuation increased, inflation was everywhere and market system started to be established. Liberalization of price became the main means for the implementation of economic system reform and transformation to the market economy, but (within a short period) the market chaos and high inflation were the cost to be paid for liberalization of price.

#### 7.2.1.2 Privatization of Property

In order to advance the transition to free market economy as soon as possible, Russia started, in 1992, the large-scale campaign of privatization: at the first stage, from 1992 to 1994, securities were privatized; at the second stage, currency started to be privatized in July 1994.

Due to the privatization of securities, Russian economy ownership structure was observed with an essential change. The monopoly status of the state ownership in the national economy no longer existed, which laid the foundation for market economy with multiple ownerships to achieve the denationalization of economy fundamentally. However, since privatization of securities had not completely finished the task of transferring enterprises to effective operators, it could not ensure the energetic increase of production efficiency and could not achieve the target of attracting funds for Russian economy. At the stage of privatization of securities, the overall economic situation was observed with high inflation accompanying the consecutive decline of production and "fast privatization". The purpose of privatization of currency was to privatize the state shares, land and immovable properties in enterprises. At this stage, the major measures were to implement the *Law of Russian Federation for Privatization of State-owned Properties and Municipal Properties.* Consequently, most of the state-owned assets were separated from the directive administration of the state and entered the market for operation and the base was established for market allocation of immovable assets and other items. The stage for privatization of currency was featured as transition from free allocation of wealth to actual purchase of wealth in the "relatively slow" process of privatization. In order to attract the important investors with the intention of controlling enterprises, Russia stipulated that each enterprise should offer the bulk stocks, equivalent to at least 15–25 % of its registered capital, for auction and tendering. Privatization of currency caused the speed of privatization to slow down obviously, but as the relevant data showed, at this stage, the process of large-scale privatization was basically completed.

#### 7.2.1.3 Macro Stabilization

Privatization of economy and privatization of property unavoidably resulted in high inflation. In order to contain the economic decline and high inflation, the macro stabilization policy was published accordingly as the supporting measures of the radical reform.

Stage 1: when macro economy fluctuated sharply and vicious inflation and huge fiscal budget deficit was observed, it became the prime task at the primary stage of reform to ensure macro stability. In early 1992, as measures were taken for liberalization of national economy, Russia avoided the collapse of budget system, eliminated the huge “currency pressure”, as well as prevented inflation. By aggressively tightening total demand and containing investment, Russia restored the supply–demand balance. Due to the changing price level, the status of consumer market showed a sign of normalization. The implementation of tight monetary policy and fiscal policy created the necessary premises for controlling inflation.

Stage 2: it started from the stable financial policy and ended with the largest-scale financial crisis in its history in August 1998. During this period, the government was basically successful in controlling the inflation at a relatively low level and the financial situation obviously tended to be stable. However, the reformers were unable to resolve two problems in the fiscal and credit fields. One was the excessive budget expenditures of governments at all levels. The huge budget deficit put a huge pressure on expansion of tax revenues. The excessively high tax revenue restrained the lawful economic activities, stimulated the development of shadow economy, and shook the base for investment. The other one was the failure of economy to create currency for long-term stable use. In the period of economic prosperity, part of the short-term loans were frequently converted to long-term investment. The expansion of such conversion scale increased the vulnerability of the banking system. To some extent, the crisis in Russia was related to huge short-term loans converting to long-term assets. In order to eliminate the pay-off crisis of the whole credit-money system, the major tendency of monetary policy was to increase the money supply. With the money supply becoming a special indicator, the level of interest rates became a derivative indicator which could hardly controlled by the central bank. The huge demand of the state for financial capital was the major feature of the financial field at that time. After the trust of Russian financial system was lowered, in 1998, the central bank gradually turned to implementing the rigidly tight monetary policy and it was such abnormal monetary tightening that triggered the economic decline. Budget deficit and poor effect of the budget policy were the problems observed in Russian economy for long. Due to the excessively large expenditure scale of the national finance, the interest was determined almost merely according to the short-term bond market, while all other interest rates would keep in line with the state bond market and the central bank already lost the ability to regulate and control the interest rates. Such reasons eventually led to the complete collapse of the short-term state bond market, while the new round inflation rose rapidly and the policy for stabilizing finance ended with a failure.

Stage 3: macro stability policy was implemented to respond to the crisis. Due to the failure of the stable finance policy, it was required to re-valuate the strength and weakness of Russian credit monetary policy. Obviously, the prime problem in the monetary field is the huge budget deficit resulting from the invalid budget policy and thus the solution for public revenue became the important factor of the economic policy. For the purpose of limiting the rising speed of inflation and stabilizing the exchange rates of Ruble, in 1999, the Central Bank of Russian Federation implemented the tight monetary policy. In addition to intervening strongly the foreign exchange market, the central bank restricted the expansion of money issuance by slowing down the growth rate of the domestic net assets. In 2000, the inflation started to slow down. The process of inflation in Russian economy in 2000 was of obvious periodicity which was related to the process for Russia to pay back foreign debts. It was the primary target of the central bank of Russian Federation to gradually reduce the inflation. Due to the cut-down of budget deficit and slow-down of inflation, Russian economy was with the inkling for the possibility of smooth development in the future. In 2001, the national finance of Russia was observed with the surplus of 0.4 % and the annual inflation rate was about 18.6 %.

## *7.2.2 Radical Reform of the Central and Eastern European Countries*

The radical reform of the Central and Eastern European countries can be summarized as price reform, property rights reform and financial reform.

### 7.2.2.1 The Control over the Price of More than 90 % of Commodities and Labor Service Has Been Abandoned and the Market-oriented Pricing System Is Basically Established

Since 1990, Eastern Europe countries have successively realized the liberalization of prices in different modes. By now, except for the prices for a very few of products and labor services with special significance to the national economy and people's livelihood under the control of the government, the control over more than 90 % of the prices is already abandoned and the market-oriented price formation mechanism is basically established. Since the liberalization of foreign trade and exchange rate developed rapidly, the commodity prices are still affected by international market price. Since the market competition is primarily formed and the market order is relatively stable, the random rise in prices basically disappeared. It has also created a necessary base for the market mechanism to function.

#### 7.2.2.2 Ownership Structure and Property System Are Observed with Material Changes and the Problem of Market Entities Is Basically Resolved

The ownership in Eastern Europe countries was reformed basically in three approaches: privatization of state-owned enterprises, reform of the property system for state-owned enterprises and access of emerging private enterprises. According to the data by World Bank, since 1990, the ownership structure in Eastern Europe countries has been observed with a material change: in most of the Eastern Europe countries, the output of private enterprises (including the enterprises of which the staff and workers held the shares and the state-owned shares were less than 50 %) shared more than half of their GDP in 1995. Czech Republic developed at the fastest speed: mainly by privatizing "investment bond" certificates obtained equally, the output share of private economy increased to 69 %. While implementing the privatization and access of emerging enterprises, Eastern Europe countries also carried out the major reform for the remaining state-owned enterprises. The first step was to intensify the budget constraint and throw the enterprises to the market. The second step was to reform the property system by property separation and risk bearing by oneself. By reforming the management and property system, the state-owned enterprises started to become the behavior subjects adapting to the market economy.

#### 7.2.2.3 The Major Breakthrough Achieved in the Financial Reform Has Provided the Necessary Base for the Market Establishment and Development for Capital and Other Factors

The financial institution reform of Eastern Europe countries was mainly centralized in three aspects: firstly, reform the original state-owned banks and establish the two-level institution. In this aspect, the central bank already basically unhooked the connection to national finance and no longer provided the public finance with deficit loans. The central bank started to take on, independently, issuing currency and formulating and implementing the national monetary policy. Meanwhile, other banks except for the central bank were commercialized. However, different countries took different measures in clearing the bad debts and adjusting the capital, and developed in an unbalanced way. The progress of Hungary and Poland was relatively larger in this aspect. Secondly, implement the privatization of banks and access of new private banks. In this aspect, by privatizing the "Certificates", Czech Republic and Slovakia privatized five state-owned banks; by selling, Poland and Hungary privatized two and four state-owned banks, respectively. As a whole, however, the privatization of banks was very hard in the Eastern Europe countries. Certain progress has been made with respect to the access of new private banks and foreign banks. In 1994, Czech Republic and Poland had 16 private banks, join-venture and foreign-capital banks. The third content of financial reform is to develop the capital market, as is particularly represented in increasing the supply of securities, expanding the demand for securities and improving the institutional environment for transaction. In this aspect, the Eastern Europe countries started to make a move, but the progress was little.

### *7.2.3 Consequences of Radical Transform*

China is much successful because of gradual reform, while the Soviet Union and Eastern Europe countries paid a heavy cost because of Shock Therapy. European Bank for Reconstruction and Development has recently conducted a survey on 29 CIS and transformed countries and observed that upon transformation for 15 years, only 30 % of the people considered the present life better than before the transformation.

As Fig. 7.1 shows, as by 2004 (upon transformation for 15 years), GDP was restored to the level of 1989 for half of the countries only. It should be noted that Russia's GDP was slightly more than 80 % of 1989, while that of Ukraine was about 50 % only. Poland's economy recovery was the best, up to more than 140 %, followed by Slovakia, Slovenia and Hungary. With respect to the pace of economic

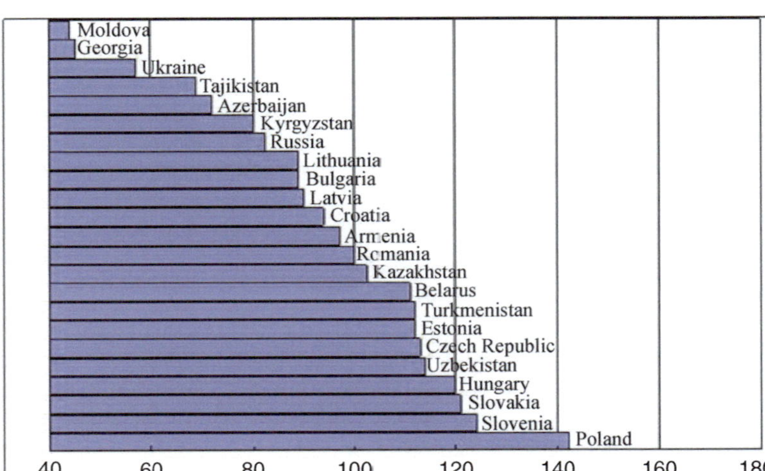


**Fig. 7.1** Percentage of GDP in the former Soviet Union and Eastern Europe Countries in 2004 Equivalent to GDP in 1989 (%) (Data Source: Popov (2007), "Shock Therapy Versus Gradualism Reconsidered", *CEFIR/NES Working Paper series No.68*)

recovery (see Fig. 7.2), Poland recovered earliest (as from around 1991); Hungary also recovered earlier (as from around 1993).

Besides, during the transformation, in addition to the declining GDP, the gap of income distribution in the former Soviet Union and Eastern Europe countries also expanded continuously (see Table 7.1). As comparison before and after transformation, the wealth gap (measured as per Gini Coefficient) worsened most in Ukraine, with Gini Coefficient rising by 0.24; Gini Coefficient of Kyrgyzstan, Russia and Estonia also rose relatively high, by 0.145, 0.142 and 0.124, respectively; Gini coefficient of Poland rose the least, being less than 0.03 only.

During the transformation, the economy of Poland and Hungary are in good conditions, which was not because they adopted the shock therapy for reforming, on the contrary, they actually adopted the tactics of gradual reform in many aspects. The Former First-ranked Vice Premier and Minister of Finance of Poland and famous scholar, G.W. Kolodko pointed out: "Poland succeeded by forsaking the Shock Therapy, but not otherwise. Without doubt, such policy as 'Shock Therapy' failed, and the accordingly thinking and action led to the sharp decline of production, so 'Shock Therapy' should be responsible for such miserable consequence."

For instance, for the reform of exchange rate, Poland selected the "gradual model". Within 10 years, the Polish government tried almost all the forms of exchange rate system: from pegging to dollar only to pegging to a basket of currency, from pegging to a basket of currency to crawling peg to a basket of currency and then to band float, before actualizing eventually the free-float exchange rate system. The Central Bank of Poland spent 5 years in implementing the relatively narrow crawling peg system so that the market could adapt to gradually; then spent

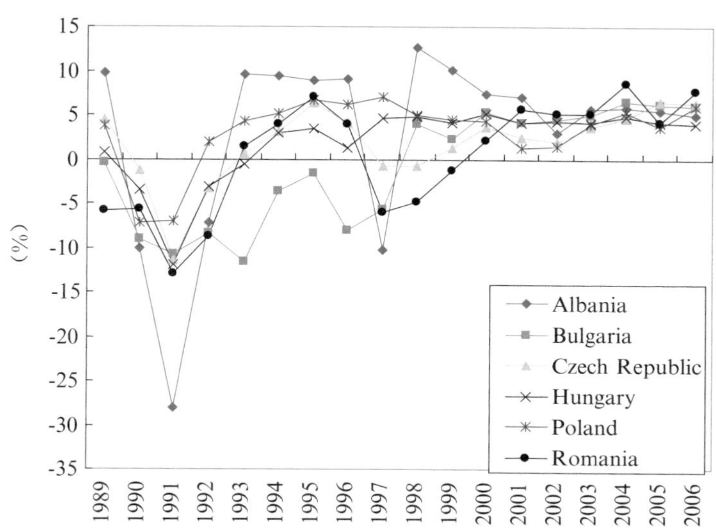


**Fig. 7.2** Changes of GDP growth rate in Eastern and Central Europe Countries before and after transformation (1989–2006) %. Note: The data for Albania after 2004 are the predicted data (Data Source: International Monetary Fund, *World Economic Outlook Database*, October 2007)

**Table 7.1** Changes of Gini coefficient in former Soviet Union and Eastern Europe Countries

| | Before transformation | After transformation | Gap |
|---|---|---|---|
| Poland | 0.272 | 0.301 | 0.029 |
| Slovakia Czech | 0.174 | 0.223 | 0.049 |
| Republic | 0.194 | 0.254 | 0.060 |
| Hungary | 0.248 | 0.308 | 0.060 |
| Romania | 0.233 | 0.280 | 0.047 |
| Estonia | 0.230 | 0.354 | 0.124 |
| Belarus | 0.228 | 0.288 | 0.060 |
| Kazakhstan | 0.257 | 0.354 | 0.097 |
| Bulgaria | 0.228 | 0.317 | 0.089 |
| Lithuania | 0.225 | 0.324 | 0.099 |
| Russia | 0.238 | 0.380 | 0.142 |
| Kyrgyzstan | 0.260 | 0.405 | 0.145 |
| Latvia | 0.225 | 0.320 | 0.095 |
| Ukraine | 0.233 | 0.473 | 0.240 |

Data Source: Keane and Prasad (2000)

another 5 years in expanding continuously the crawling float band and increasing gradually the flexibility of the exchange rate policy and the elasticity of exchange rate system. With the floating space of Zloty exchange rate expanding continuously, it was natural to implement the completely free float exchange rate system finally. Therefore, during the transition from fixed exchange rate system to floating exchange rate system, Poland was not observed any major fluctuation (Wang Yu 2004).

## 7.3 Why Didn't the Shock Therapy Work?

Why didn't the shock therapy work in some countries? The theoretical circles are still debating on this issue by now. Three major reasons should be noted: (1) Shock Therapy ignores the importance of institution underpinning; (2) Shock Therapy ignores the important function of the government in transformation; (3) The three items of Shock Therapy cannot be actualized simultaneously.

### *7.3.1 The Importance of Institution Underpinning Is Ignored*

If a nation lacks of liberalization, privatization and stabilization policies based on an appropriate institution, the nation cannot see the expected successful result by implementing comprehensively the liberalization of price and privatization of enterprises. The difficult point for the transformation of Russia and other countries was how to realize the institutional change smoothly and steadily without causing excessive economic and social chaos. More complexly, due to the huge amount of uncertainties and unexpected changes in the process of reforming, it is necessary to maintain the political support of people to transformation. The Russian scholar pointed out (Popov 2007) that the impact of a powerful institution cannot be ignored. The extent of liberalization is not so important in the early period of transformation, but on the contrary, the institutional capacity of the state is very important. Considering the different initial conditions, the dropping output after transformation is generally accompanied with the bad enterprise environment, while the latter is the result of institutional collapse. When liberalization itself is not complementary to the powerful institution, it is impossible to ensure the good economic performance. The institutional capacity depends largely on the rule of law and democracy. As data shows, authentic government and democratic system can both generate the powerful law assurance and effective institution. But in the circumstance that the rule of law is extremely weak, an authentic government is more capable than a democratic government system in maintaining the effective institution. However, within a relatively short period of time, one democratic government system without liberalization is the poorest in terms of institutional capacity and thus also generates the worst impact on the output.

### 7.3.2 *The Important Function of Government in Transformation Is Ignored*

The function of government in transformation has been a topic for debating endlessly for a long period of time. Nowadays, due to the successful transformation of China and the failure of Russia in transformation in the first 10 years as well as the problems of spontaneity, blindness and stagnation of growth observed in the market economy of Russia and other countries, all the countries in the world and economic circles have no choice but to reconsider the relationship between government and market in transformation. A number of scholars led by the famous economist Stiglitz presented that due to the inadequate information and incomplete competition, it is a normal for market to fail, so there must be the state intervention. "Transformation can be regarded as continuous pursuit (actually endless) for perfect cooperation between government and market". And, for a developing country and developing market economy, the problem of governmental intervention is that whether intervention is proper instead of the extent of intervention. During the transformation, the important function of government is mainly represented in four aspects: (1) eliminate the hindrance and resistance to reform; (2) establish all the infrastructures of the new system; (3) maintain the stable macroeconomic environment, intensify market and make up the market failure; (4) strive to maintain equal opportunities and social justice (Wu Jinglian 2004).

### 7.3.3 The Three Items of the Shock Therapy Cannot Be Actualized Simultaneously

According to one scholar (Lin Yifu 2007), since "Shock Therapy" ignores the endogeneity of institutional distortion, it is not aware that the three items of "Shock Therapy" (liberalization of price, privatization and governmental maintenance of fiscal balance and macro stability) cannot be actualized simultaneously. For instance, if liberalization of price or privatization is implemented separately, it will cause no problem, but if the two are implemented simultaneously, it will only lead to two results, in the circumstance that enterprises have no viability: the whole society collapses, triggering the huge unemployment; or the government subsidizes the enterprises without viability. This is because enterprises without viability would often engage many labors, and the reason for the government to subsidize them is not because of their state ownership, but because they have no viability. Upon implementation of "Shock Therapy", the original technologies and industries remain unchanged, but the government tries hard to avoid them from bankruptcy, and protect and subsidize them for the following two reasons: (1) these industries are very advanced and very important for the modernization of the country; (2) since these enterprises engage massive labor force, once becoming bankrupt, it will naturally trigger massive unemployment and thus lead to a unstable society. It should be pointed out that in the case of privatization, the protection and subsidy to be provided by the government is more than the amount to be provided in the case of state ownership. When the enterprises without viability are state-owned, their factory directors and managers will ask the government for protection and subsidies, but they cannot hold such subsidies personally. However, after these enterprises are privatized, the factory directors and managers can be right and proper to hold the surplus subsidies for themselves. Therefore, in the case of privatization, the owners of enterprises owners are more enthusiastic and have more reasons to ask the government for protection and subsidies. However, since the government does not own the capital, its enthusiasm remains unchanged for providing enterprises with protection and subsidies. Thus, the amount of protection and subsidies will not decrease, but will increase. In the early 1990s, most of the people had not believed it, but as the huge quantity of empirical studies (including the studies carried out by World Bank and Eastern Europe countries) indicate, the protective subsidies obtained by the large-scale enterprises upon privatization were more than when they were not privatized. In the meanwhile, however, the government receipts decreased to some extent upon reforming. This is because in the case of nationalization, the profits of state-owned enterprises have to be rendered to the national finance, but in the case of privatization, the government can obtain revenues only by collecting taxes from enterprises and tax collection is not an easy matter. Thus, the government can protect and subsidize enterprises only by issuing notes massively, but it will in turn trigger higher inflation. In 1993 and 1994, the inflation in Russia was more than 10,000 %, as a result of the misunderstanding at that time.

## 7.4 Exploration Beyond the Gradual Reform

While affirming the great achievements of gradual reform, it is also necessary to see that such mode is full of the "reformism" color, i.e., gradually introducing the market factors without denying thoroughly the old system. China's reform has basically followed a strategy of "peripheral propulsion", by resolving easy problems first before resolving the most difficult problems finally. This practice is steady, but has also brought about many challenges.

Firstly, it is the friction of dual system. Compared with the radical reform, the weakest point of the gradual reform is its incompleteness and duration. That is why it is said "better a finger off than aye wagging". Upon reforming and opening up for more than three decades, the market-oriented extent in China is already increased much, but the chronic illness of the old system is not yet cured thoroughly: such as non-separation of government and enterprises, soft budget constraint for investment and delay in development of financial market, which have caused overlapping barriers for the operation of the new system.

Secondly, coordinated advancement failed for the reforms in different fields. The "coordinated advancement" of reform means the different reforms are undertaken simultaneously and gradually, rather than reforming one after another. Furthermore, the reforms advanced in different fields spontaneously shall be coordinated and promoted with each other as much as possible, without hindering each other. If the reforms in different fields cannot be advanced coordinately, they will handicap each other and affect the efficiency of the whole system. With the economy becoming more market-oriented, some economic fields where reform is already implemented will face risks due to the lagging of reform in other fields. For instance, exchange rate control is more relaxed than 10 years ago. On the occasion when capital flows in, the large-scale intervention with the foreign exchange market may cause severe unbalance of the balance sheet within the financial system (even though such contradiction has dissolved to some extent in recent years with the international balance pattern changing and appreciation pressure on local currency being lowered as well as the central bank basically withdrawing from the normal intervention in the foreign exchange market). Similarly, with liberalization development, the risk of another-round bad debts to be undertaken by banking industry which is supported by the government will rise up. Furthermore, many constraining factors for the efficient operation of the financial system are co-related. Therefore, reform requires a comprehensive method. Within the three decades, China has made a great progress, but still has a long way to go. China should insist on the trial-and-error approach, but should make a bolder trial. As the two authors of IMF have claimed, "now, it is the time for going beyond crossing the river by feeling the stones and to make a bigger step in reforming."[2]

In terms of present China, financial reform and political reform should follow up timely.

---

[2] Martin Wolf (2006).

Thirdly, the problems brought about by the unbalance strategy: "gradual reform" selects the partial, unbalanced and from-point-to-area path. The selection of such path has, from the very beginning, determined the unbalance of economic development, "allowing some people to get prosperous first so that they can drive others to get prosperous before the common prosperity can be finally actualized". However, since the reform and opening up, "getting prosperous first" is mostly reflected, but there is still a long way from common prosperity. In view of the urban–rural development, the breakthrough point of reform started from the rural areas, but the strategy has been adopted for prior development of cities for the sake of advancing the industrialization. Consequently, the "dual economy" emerged in urban and rural areas, while the rural development has lagged behind for long and its gap with the urban development has expanded continuously. It is relaxed to some extent in recent years, but such gap is still huge. In view of the regional development, having a series of advantages, the coastal areas have been at the front of reform and become the biggest beneficiary of reform, but the central and western areas have been backward for long and the gap between the two is huge. China has implemented such strategies as the Western Development, Northeastern Revitalization and the Rising of Central China (recently added with Eastern Region First), but the unbalance of regional development cannot yet be resolved fundamentally within a short period of time. Furthermore, with the economic development, the problem of social income distribution and fairness also becomes increasingly prominent. All these will become the hindrance affecting the normal and orderly development of economy and society.

Fourthly, the paradox of governmental function transform and gradual reform: the gradual reform is essentially the reform implemented compulsively by the central government for the centralization mode. In this regard, a paradox is observed: i.e., the existing governmental institutions are the initiators and organizers of reform as well as the objects of reform. The dual-status of the government is beneficial for carrying out the relatively stable reform as well as will bring about unfavorable impacts on reform. Since the governmental departments at different levels are unlikely to be "selfless" completely beyond the secular world, they will consciously or unconsciously take into account their immediate or vital interests to influence the formulation and execution of policies. As expected, the gradual reform should be carried out without touching the existing pattern of power and interests, but at present, it seems to be increasingly hard.

The foregoing problems indicate that currently, China's reform is already in a critical period. The gradual reform has multiplied a number of vested interest groups, which become the resistance for advancing further reform. If it is desired to continue with the "gradual" reform and achieve the final victory, it is necessary to intensify the reform and resolve the in-depth problems left over by the traditional system thoroughly. In any circumstance, reform and opening up will require courage, determination, political desire and explicit aim. In the rapid-changing world, a nation is required to catch up as soon as possible. It means that China should advance the reforms in all the fields at the earliest and ensure the coordination and co-advancement of reforms in different fields.

## References

Guo Liancheng (2005) Russian economic transition and economic theory of transition period. The Commercial Press

Keane MP, Prasad ES (2000) Inequality, transfers and growth: new evidence from the economic transition in Poland. IMF working paper, WP/00/117

Lin Y (2007) Development and transition: trends, strategies and viability. www.nsd.edu.cn

Popov V (2007) Shock therapy versus gradualism reconsidered. CEFIR/NES working paper series, No 68

Wang Yu (2004) Classic progressive reform in exchange rate system in Poland. China Foreign Exch Adm 7

Wolf Martin (2006) China's reform: please surpass gradual development mode, Financial Times in UK, 12 June 2006

Wu Jinglian (2004) Roles of Chinese government in transition of market economy. Natl Econ Manag 9

# Chapter 8
# The Reform Has Dived in the Key Stage

The reform and opening up of more than three decades has observed with achievements as well as challenges. At present, the biggest challenge is that reform is already in the key stage and crucial period, with the pace slowing down and the hardship for advancing forward, showing a "deadlock" status: tangle between different interest groups and impact between different reform appeals. Like the cycle of economic operation, reform also seems to encounter such cycle, from the rapid advancement in the past to the present deadlock. In the key stage, the major challenge of the reform must respond to is how to face directly such problems as hindrance of interest groups, inadequate driving force of reform, common view of reform to be rebuilt and inadequate top design of reform.

## 8.1 The Reform Has Dived in the Key Stage and Crucial Period

China's exploration for reform has always been compared with crossing a river. The other shore is the target of reform, while this shore is the starting point of reform. Where to enter the water means where to reform first. From entering the river to reaching the other shore, in the circumstance of having no knowledge of the river width, the speed of water flow and the depth, it will be often the only way to "Look before You Leap". Today, in the circumstance that the reform encounters overlapping dilemmas and even falls into a deadlock and key reform can hardly be advanced forward, we again think of the metaphor of crossing a river and call this difficult stage as the entrance of reform into the key stage. Obviously, in the key stage, the circumstances to be faced are even more complex and the possibility of encountering dangers increases sharply. Then, higher requirements are set forth for decision-making capacity, courage and wisdom of the reformers.



X. Zhang, X. Chang, *The Logic of Economic Reform in China*, China Insights,
DOI 10.1007/978-3-662-47404-4_8

The reform has entered in the key stage. What's the particular meaning of this sentence in addition to the metaphor?

The entrance of reform into the key stage mainly means that the reform enters into such a stage that it faces mostly material problems and sensitive problems, of which many regard the in-depth social contradictions, involve the adjustment of interest relationship and affect the situation as a whole if a single move is made in one part, and some are the hard nuts for years though it has been the desire to crush them. Such circumstance is actually much associated with the approach of gradual reform selected.

The strategy of gradual reform is often taken by starting from outside the system, from the aspects easy to reform and from areas with less resistance so that the effect can be rapidly achieved and force can be aggregated for advancing the reform further. However, gradual reform will also create many problems: i.e., some easy aspects are improved, but the hard nuts are left behind. Furthermore, gradual reform may also easily cause the solidification of some group interests. As the experiences over the years prove, if the reform is not thorough, when advancing to certain specific stage, new vested interest groups will be often formed. When it is necessary to further break through the existing pattern, these interest groups will become the major resistance hindering the advancement of reform. Currently, the phenomena of interest solidification seem to be everywhere: the interests of governmental departments, industrial monopoly and various vested interest groups will all form a solid "fence". The so-called "fence of interest solidification" means the defending barrier set up for safeguarding the vested interests. The fence of interest solidification has two features: one is that interests are obtained by applying the public power; the other is that the profiting subjects are away from the public class that to be benefited from the reform. As for the vested interest class, the fence is the umbrella and amulet for their interests, but as for the public, the fence is a barrier for them to obtain interests. As a chronic illness in the institutional mechanism, the fence of interest solidification has by now penetrated widely in between urban and rural areas, among regions, among industries, between state-owned and private economies and among different social groups, which becomes a huge obstacle for further deepening the reform, restrains the economic and social creativity, lowers the efficiency in allocation of resources, limits the space for the social members to flow up and reduces the positive energy of reform. If the previous reform is mostly for the reform designers to study on adjusting the interests of others, the future reform will then start from the vested interest sectors within the system, from changing others to changing themselves and cutting down their own power and interests.

Currently, China's economy is in a new normal and appears "structural slowdown". This time, only by reforming can we positively fit with the new normal and move in the new stage of growth. Without deepening the reform, development can hardly have vitality and last long and even falls into the "middle income trap". In the early period of reform, "Pareto Improvement" environment of "everyone benefits" was exciting thus the resistance for reforming was less. Nowadays, when the reform enters into the key stage, the reform in a true sense can be hardly observed with the phenomenon of "not damage to the interests of anyone". Facing to the in-depth contradictions and problems in the social and economic development, it will not do to avoid and detour; there will be no way out without improvement and opportunities will be lost and more cost will be paid if being slow. Therefore, it is necessary to firmly advance the reform and storm the fortifications properly with the high sense of historical mission and responsibility and the prompt determination and courage.

## 8.2 The Political Economics of the Reform

Reform itself is a kind of learning. To advance the reform, it is necessary to master the political economics of reform, which involves such contents as rebuilding of common views for reforming, improvement of power mechanism for reforming and interest balancing and incentive compatibility of reforming.

### *8.2.1 Rebuild the Common Views for Reforming*

If the reform more than three decades ago was started by cohering the maximum common views of the whole society, for there would only one way—die, without reforming, today, it will be hard to form a common view for reform in the circumstances that there is still a way for survival, there are still some resources for spending freely and the economic system is profoundly transformed, social structure is profoundly changed, interest pattern is profound adjusted and ideology changes profoundly, so it is not easy to form common view. Without a common view for reforming, it will be hard to generate the power for reforming and advancement of reform will become flubdub.

"All the people up and down with one purpose will win". In a war, with one heart "up (the government)" and "down (the public)", it is possible to minimize the internal friction and get together forces. To advance the reform, the central and local governments and the government and the public are required to have the same cognition and achieve the coordinated pace in action accordingly. "Up and down with one purpose" forms a base of common views which can inspire the maximum positive energy for reforming and provide the strong assurance for the reform to storm fortifications and overcome difficulties.

The reform and opening up has been in process for more than three decades, why do we continue with reforming? It is the first question to reply. Theoretically, since it is a dynamic process for adjusting the production relation to adapt to the development of productivity, there will be naturally no end for adjusting the production relation by reforming. Practically, reform is also the fundamental approach for resolving the present realistic problem: all the particular problems with economy, society, culture, finance, state-owned enterprises, rural area, education, medical service, endowment and other fields shall be resolved only by advancing the comprehensive and in-depth reform.

It is undeniable that in the present China, the social structure is of multiple levels, interest pattern is of multiple elements, social psychology changes frequently and different regions, sectors and social groups have different expectations of their own for reforming, as is the basic national condition. Facing various reform appeals, it will be naturally a bigger challenge for further deepening the reform to handle the complex interest relation properly. At present, in the process of carrying out the reform measures, special attention shall be given to avoiding the preference of reforming if it suits or not reforming if it does not suit, and abolishing the mode of thinking that hinders the progress of reform.

It is impossible for the reform to satisfy all the people and all the groups without any dispute, but it is not meant that the reform losses the common view and falls into the narrow interest separation. Ideological unification is to find the greatest common divisor and seek common ground while reserving differences. Actually, such general appeals as "market economy", "democracy", "cultural power", "harmonious society" and "beautiful China" are still releasing the dividends continuously. There are still many other reforms that conform to the fundamental interests of the vast masses and conform to the long-term target of the overall development, which can become our biggest common views. The maximum common views for reform and the concern and support of people for reform will not depend on different voices, but on the response of most people triggered by the reform. Even in the chorus of agreeing with the reform, there may be an incompetent person pretending to play the Yu (a music instrument) or a person singing out of tune intentionally. The existence of such noise may not mean to prove the problems with the reform, but just indicates it is necessary to resolve such problem by reforming.[1]

Currently, the curtain is unveiled for deepening comprehensively the reform. To rebuild the common view for reforming, firstly, it is required to have the sense of historical responsibility. Without reforming now, one will undertake the historical responsibility thereof and shall be aware of the importance of reform for the development of China and the rejuvenation of the Chinese nation, today, tomorrow and in the future. Secondly, it is necessary to enhance the opportunity consciousness and progression consciousness of reform. Currently, since it is still the strategic stage of opportunity for China to develop and the window stage for reform, only by positive reform will it be possible to break through the difficulties and stride over the middle income trap. Thirdly, it is necessary to plan for all the works and carry out practically all the reform tasks with the reform as leading and with the concept of reform.

[1] Commentator from Guangming daily (2004).

### 8.2.2 *Improve the Power Mechanism for Reforming*

Each breakthrough and development of understanding and practice for the reform and opening up is sourced from the practice and wisdom of people. The driving forceof reform comes from the enthusiasm of local governments, grassroots and people. The local governments, grassroots and people should be encouraged to emancipate the mind and explore actively; different regions are encouraged to carry out the differential pilot work and to be good at finding the cutting point for reform from the focuses concerned by the public and the difficult points of people's daily life and it is necessary to advance the top design and grassroots exploration for positive interactions and proper integration.

However, the power mechanism for the present reform needs to be intensified. The remarkable feature of the current reform is that the central government first proposes the top design and then advancement is carried out from up down. Such path is of the benefit for operating from a strategically advantageous position, but shall be actively responded by the society at all levels before it may become effect. Nowadays, the enthusiasm of many local governments and public servants are not yet mobilized. Generally speaking, the provincial governments are mostly watching on and waiting; the governments at the city and county level naturally view that the reform is not yet brought into their agenda and will reach the grassroots at least 2 years after. The sectors at all levels mainly take a perfunctory attitude. The reform program for most of the ministries and commissions is not yet published and even if the program is drafted, it is mainly meant for relaxing the partial dilemma. In terms of the vast public, they generally feel the gap between the expectation and the actual progress of reform, so their enthusiasm for reform drops to some extent. Obviously, the reform will remain on paper at the meeting only with the design of the central government, without the participation of the local governments and the public.

Firstly, mobilize the people for active participation. The key to mobilize the enthusiasm for reform rests in enabling the participants to benefit from reform. The previous reforms could spread like the force of a prairie fire and advance further step by step for the fundamental reason of bringing the real interests to the people, bringing about the opportunities for fair participation and development and winning the support from the vast people. It is the fundament driving force of reform. The reform shall be comprehensively deepened with the starting point and foothold of promoting the social fairness and justice and enhancing the happiness and benefits of the people. Therefore, it is necessary to establish the fair and effective institutional mechanism so that the dividend of reform and achievements of development can be shared by the public. The present interest distribution is really observed with some unreasonable aspects and must be adjusted. However, the interests shall not be adjusted only with a static viewpoint. To cut the "cake" under the vested interest pattern, the dynamic and developing sight shall be deployed, focusing on incremental interest and cutting the "cake" reasonably while making the "cake" bigger. Even when adjusting the vested interest pattern, the practice of simple equalitarianism shall not be carried out either. First, it is necessary to safeguard and protect properly the interests of poverty-stricken groups as well as low-income people and enable them to get more opportunities from reform for development. It is necessary to expand gradually the middle-income classes and enable them to have a wider space for development. It is also necessary to protect the legal interests of the high-income people so that they can freely invest, develop and create a better environment for development. It is necessary to enable different social groups to show their respective capacity and play their proper role, enable the vitality of all labor, knowledge, technology, management and capital to burst forth and enable all the sources of creating social wealth to flow adequately, thus forming a situation for all the sectors at all levels to participate widely in and support the reform.

Secondly, advance the grassroots exploration for reform. Currently, the problem of inadequate power for some grassroots reforms shall be given high attention. Actually, the difficult points are often concentrated at the grassroots and the voice of the grassroots for reform is the highest as well as the most powerful. These difficult points include the problem of "the last one kilometer" for implementation and practice as well as the new circumstances and new problems emerging continuously in the process of development. With the grassroots exploration, it will often become "beyond the control" and "scratching an itch through the boot" to resolve such difficult problems. At present, the exploration for grassroots reform is observed with various barriers: some local government leaders—the "first hands" are still used to pursue the proper figure of GDP, are reluctant to leave the vested interests and are also limited by the capacity of "not knowing how to reform". But, the uppermost problem is that many local governments have no idea of where is the boundary of reform and are worried about different risks resulting from their "exploration" against law and regulations. In view of this, to advocate for grassroots exploration, it is also necessary to energetically create the atmosphere for reforming, rationalize the institutional mechanism, improve the examination system for the political performance of the local leaders, systematically "activate" the local vitality and enable the grassroots to be full of spirit for reform. For instance, for the places and grassroots which already develop at the head, it is necessary to further release the space for reform, grant the local governments with more authority and encourage them to provide more reform "samples" for resolving some difficult problems rather than rely merely on the top design. Additionally, it is necessary to study and stimulate, at the right time, some policies and measures for encouraging the grassroots reform exploration, encourage the grassroots reformers for success and tolerate with their failure, establish the mechanism for error tolerance and responsibility exemption and really get rid of their afterward worries about "making a bold trial and breaking through courageously" so that they have adequate confidence and power when "having a big go". Today, with the reform in the key stage, any reform will affect the situation as a whole if a single move is made in one part. If relying merely on the personal "courage" and "unafraid" of leaders, it will be hard to advance the reform effectively and the potential negative effect of reform should not be ignored. Today, the bigger test for the reformers should be how to ensure the participation of the public in reform for the sake of cohering the maximum common views and power for reform. Today, with the law being continuously perfected, the reform moving into the key stage, and the weighing and balancing of different interests becoming more complex, what the reformers should do most is obviously to listen to the public opinions, utilize the public support, and ensure the successful advancement of the reform in the set direction. After all, for the previous reform by breaking in laterally, not only the space becomes increasingly limited, but the marginal effect is also dropping continuously. Obviously, it is currently urgent for the reform to ensure the reform will be corrected from time to time in the process by following more the procedural justice, enabling the governmental act to really regress into the frame of rule of law—"no action without authorization by law" and involving more public forces in the process of reform. It will be well if promoting the rebuilding the reform evaluation and participation mechanism—to simulate the inherent power of officials for reform and innovation by the examination of power and equal power and responsibility, as is the one and only way for rousing the enthusiasm of officials for reform and innovation.

### *8.2.3 Interest Balance and Incentive Compatibility of Reform*

Power comes from inspiration. Only when considering they can benefit from a reform will the reform participants be empowered to appeal for the reform, participate in the reform, and promote the reform.

Since the reform involves interest relationship in various aspects, the practical road of reform is actually advanced slowly in the process of handling different complex interests' mechanisms. Therefore, the design for the further reform should take into account the interests of different parties as much as possible. In another word, in the process of promoting the reform, we cannot merely pay attention to the program, but must pay more attention to rebuilding the interest balanced pattern and shall consider the compensation for the interest losers in advances.

What is associated to rationalize the interest mechanism is actually the so-called incentive compatibility. What is the incentive compatibility? In the circumstance with ethic risk, how to ensure the party with advantages in information (known as the agent) will act according to the desire of the other party to the contract (the principal) so as to maximize the utility for both parties? Simply speaking, no one can maximize the interests of his or her own by damaging the collective interests. Since the individual interests and collective interests are consistent, everyone tries the best to work for realizing the target of their own interests and the result thereof is also to maximize the collective interests. As the modern economic theory and practice indicates, the contradiction and conflict between individual interests and collective interests can be effectively resolved by implementing the "incentive compatibility" principle so that the acting mode and results of the actors will comply with the target of maximizing the collective value: i.e., actualizing the consistence of such target functions as individual value and collective value. Since the tactics of the participants to rationally maximizing the individual interests are consistent with the tactics expected by the mechanism designer, the participants will voluntarily take action according to the tactics expected by the mechanism designer.

Now, the incentive compatibility of reform is looked into in view of the relationship between the central and local governments. One important item of the current reform is to rebuild the relationship between the central and local governments. Currently, such relationship is observed with the problems of asymmetric power and asymmetric interests (Hu Angang et al. 2014): including the prominent problems of excessive centralization and excessive concentration under "regulations" dictatorship as well as the prominent problems of excessive decentralization and excessive distribution under the "blocks" dictatorship; the problem of "superior and bureaucracy" as well as the problem "countermeasures are always found for the governmental policies". The interests are asymmetric. For instance, with the business tax changed to VAT, the local interests were damaged and therefore, they had no power for reform; the local governments complain about the non-matching of authority of office and financial resources. Especially in terms of long-term issues, overall issues and sustainable development, the starting point of interests is not completely consistent between the central and local governments. In order to give play to the enthusiasm of the central and local governments, make their "incentive compatible" and keep consistent and maximize the target functions, it is necessary to clarify the functions of the central and local governments and form, as a whole, the work-division and cooperation system and incentive compatibility mechanism for the CPC central committee to make decisions, the central government to plan, the ministries to guide, the provincial governments to take the general responsibility, the governments at the city and county levels to implement.

### *8.2.4 Mechanism Design of Reform*

In reforming, China currently encounters one biggest problem, i.e., the hindrance of departmental interest and vested interest. Upon recalling the reform over the last three decades, it may be observed that any reform of "changing oneself", i.e., the reform in the field dominated by the governmental department, will be deviated or stagnated for such reasons as "particularity" and "complexity", while the reforms led by the non-competent administrative authority are mostly successful with remarkable achievements. For instance, the reform in the industrial field is relatively thorough just because the direction for the reform of industrial system was not decided by the industrial sector itself. Consequently, the industrial administration of the government was cancelled, while the power of other governmental administrative authorities "changing themselves" has been intensified, such as NDRC and MOE. It actually runs in opposite directions for the market reform to reduce the governmental intervention. Therefore, to practically advance the reform and restrain the expansion of the power of the governmental sector during the process of reform, it is necessary to establish effective check and balance mechanism. In this regard, reference can be made to the assumption of "veil of ignorance": i.e., let the designer of reform program design the reform program without knowing their interest. In other words, it is the officials of the relevant administrative authority of the government are required to participate actively in reform and to give play to their advantages such as high quality, experiences and knowledge of facts as well as to disconnect the connection with the departmental interests when participating in the reform. To do so, it is necessary to require the reform program designers to carry out the reform program design without knowing where their interests are, i.e., without knowing in which department they will serve in the new system in the future. Actually, it is to build the "veil of ignorance" in the reform mechanism. The simplest way is: from the relevant administrative department, select the excellent officials to compose the reform institution together with the experts without any direct interest relation for formulating the reform program. Additionally, it is necessary to specify explicitly that after the reform program is completed and adopted, its designers will not return to the previous unit, but will be assigned by the Ministry of Organization for other important tasks. As the key meaning, it is to make uncertain the future status of the reform program designers so that the interest disturbance can be eliminated in terms of procedure. In this way, it is possible to give play to the advantages of the administrative authorities in human resources, service and information as well as to prevent the administrative authorities from protecting the interests of their own by making use of such advantages in the process of reform design.[2] The mechanism of reform shall be designed with consideration to interest check and balance as well as to the execution. Therefore, for the top reform and overall advance, it is also necessary to establish a high-level coordination committee to ensure the feedback of opinions from all sectors (especially the ministries/commission and local governments), and have adequate authority for coordinating properly and treating equally different opinions. At present, the general secretary of the Chinese Communist Party acts as the leader of the steering group for deepening the system reform, with the intention of playing a leading role, but it may not become a regular coordination mechanism.

## 8.3 Top-level Design and Promotion Is Valuable Experience for China's Reform

Reform is a very complex systematic project, including both "breaking" and "establishment". It is quite a long process and related to the vital interests of all walks of life, and bears relatively great risks. Reform cannot be smoothly carried out if there is no unified and strong political leadership, including the authoritative government with relatively strong executive force and credibility. Particularity and complexity of China's national conditions also determines the special importance of government roles during the process of reform. Planning and coordination roles of

---

[2] Bei (2013).

the leadership, the Communist Party of China and the government led by it, have been specifically reflected in the following three aspects over the last more than 30 years.

### 8.3.1 *Ensuring Political Desirability of Reform*

**First, Ensuring the Relatively Clear and Consistent Direction and Goals of Reform** Transition lessons of some countries indicate that political and economic shocks will be particularly intense and the transition period will be longer if there are too frequent political changes, any session of the leaders cannot implement a set of comprehensive strategies and policies, and the formulation of strategies and policies is swayed by the oligarchy. In China, leaders with relatively consistent goals and relatively clear strategic intent have always more successfully managed the process of reform by virtue of their wisdom and ability as well as the influence and firmness in upholding idea of the reform so as to prevent the process from deviation and make the process develop along with the established goals. This is the basis for ensuring the desirability of reform.

**Second, Ensuring the Effectiveness of Reform Path** It is reflected in the deployment and guidance as well as the stimulation and sublimation of China's leadership to reform from the top to the bottom. Deployment of the reform program, especially the selection of initial action, is mainly discretionarily determined and selected based on the major constraints or most urgent issues in reality as well as the timing for easing such constraints or solving such issues. Subsequent reform requirements will follow one after another after the initial reform is launched since reform is often "path dependence", and institutional changes will gradually evolve to another path along with some internal logic. Based on this, China's leadership pays attention to the trajectory of such endogeneity in the follow up actions and tries to ensure the fit of the speed and sequence of reform with the induced institutional changes as far as possible in the process of "consciously" guiding the reform. As seen afterwards, China's reform process is in line with some rational logical sequence precisely due to this although China does not seem to design the complete reform strategies in advance. Local reform experimentation and innovation which breaks through the existing institutional framework is allowed and even encouraged by China's leadership; successful part of reform practice and experience from the grassroots will be concluded and perfected in a timely manner, and deviated part will be promptly corrected and adjusted; on such basis, wisdom of the grassroots will be integrated and enhanced to the theoretical summary and institutional innovation, and promoted nationwide.

**Finally, Ensuring the Legitimacy of Decision-making Process** This is closely related to the appeal for perfecting the public governance. In recent years, China pays attention to introducing the process of public choice and gradually increases the social participation, and emphasizes more on organizing the social force by adopting a variety of ways in the reform decision-making, including joint discussion of reform program by experts, so as to enhance the public participation, transparency and scientificity of the reform decision-making process, ensure the stakeholders to participate in the decision-making to some extent and strive to make the reform decision-making take account of the interests of all aspects.

### 8.3.2 Ensuring Political Feasibility of Reform

First, focus on maintaining the unity of nation and social stability in the transition period. During the last more than 30 years, China has paid attention to giving play to the backbone role of the leadership in "centralizing the overall situation and coordinating all parties", gathered the strength of over a billion people and strived to maintain the orders in the reforming society. It can been seen from the practice of China's reform that the unified leadership can prevent the nation from falling into the state of disunity and disintegration in the process of promoting the reform with diversified economic subjects, which provides the fundamental condition for the smooth implementation of reform.

Second, focus on coordinating the interests of all aspects so as to reduce the frictional costs of reform. Reform is a profound revolution which is related to the economic base, superstructure and many fields, it will certainly change the inherent interest pattern of the older system and a variety of unreasonable interest patterns formed in the process of institutional transition, and will inevitably encounter various obstacles and challenges. In particular, China adopted some strategic selection during the process of accelerating the promotion of market orientation in the early stage of the economic transition, such as the strategic protection to some state-owned sectors, government departments and local government directly participated in the market competition as a "player" instead of a "referee". These strategic institutional arrangements may lead to the formation of endogeneity of interest groups. Such endogenous interest groups, different from the general interest groups generated due to fair competition during the process of market orientation, are often strongly stimulated to maintain the status quo and resist the introduction of reform policies with Pareto improvement characteristics. These special interest groups with the relatively stronger capacity to act than the general interest groups can apply the stronger political influence on the political decision-making process, therefore, such groups are more likely to interfere with the uncompleted transition of market orientation and enable the institutional arrangements to be locked under the state of low-efficiency equilibrium. In this pattern, interest adjustment has become the major factor which affects the crucial practical process of reform. The clear attitude of authoritative political force to the promotion of reform or the effective management capability of such political force to the process of reform can greatly amend the political influence of all parties subjectively, inhibit the expansion of special interest groups and promote the social state to move to the efficient equilibrium.[3] Exactly in this context, China focuses on giving play to the coordinating roles of political authority to the reform in the process of reform decision-making along with the gradual deepening of reform process in recent years so as to prevent certain vested interest groups, especially departments and local interests, from controlling the formation of reform program and reform progress as far as possible. Designing the reform program through setting higher-level inter-departmental reform coordination agencies with relatively transparent interests helps to get rid of the constraints by the special interest groups, ensures the continuity of reform and prevents the reform from deformation.

Last but not least, focus on building of governance capacity. International studies concerning the transition economy stressed the important roles of government transition in the economic transition, especially in order to achieve the transition of government to the type of market support and become the supporting and utilizing role of the market, effective public sectors and updating of human capital of government are essential. Some commentators have pointed out that "In both the economy and politics, the replacement of obsolete human capital may well be the central problem of transition".[4] In the process of reform during the last more than 30 years, China has paid attention to promoting the transition in the professionalism of officials and put forth efforts on cultivating the capabilities of formatting and implementing the proper reform strategies and policies. This is one of the important reasons that China's leadership has better performance in the process of maintaining and promoting the market orientation compared with the leadership of other nations in transition.

### *8.3.3 Ensuring Political Credibility of Reform*

First, ensuring the time consistency of basic reform policies. For example, the incentives of continuity and stability of the aforementioned land contracting policy to the continuing investment in land by farmers.

Second, ensuring the credible commitments of investment incentives. This is also mainly reflected in the booming of aforementioned investment policy environment and non-public economy which are relatively credible.

Finally, ensuring the credibility of reallocation commitment. In the adjustment process of interests related to reform, credible political commitments, especially the dynamic consistency of political game of reallocation, are the important factors for ensuring the successful reform. As seen from the reform practice in Latin American countries, exactly the uncertainty of individuals to the future policy results and the shortage of credible reallocation commitment increased the resistance to reform and weakened the reform consensus. However, leadership tries to make the credible

[3] For the related theoretical analysis, please see Tang Yugang and Zhao Daping (2007).

[4] (U.S.) Shleifer and Vishny (2004).

commitments to enhance the benefits of reform and compensates the interest-impaired parties through tax-transfer payment plan in the process of China's reform, thereby increasing the likelihood that the reform can be accepted.

## 8.4 Top-level Design Needs to be Combined with "Look before You Leap"

At the beginning of reform and opening up, Deng Xiaoping proposed the theory of "Look before You Leap", which is to call all the party members and the whole nation to free the mind and conduct bold exploration in essence. This theory also guided the early and mid-stage reform. At present, the reform has been promoted deeply. The practice of seeking the breakthrough point relying on perceptual knowledge has no longer been wise and turning to rational exploration is a must. It is the higher-level reform which depends more on confidence of theories and consciousness of road to guide the in-depth development of reform. Reform ways transfer from the bottom-to-top typical demonstration to the top-to-bottom top-level design. Demonstration effect of previous major reform was formed by the masses through the exploration at the grass-roots level and such reform was promoted nationwide after being found by the central government, it is the process of reform from the bottom to the top. Household contracting was approved by Deng Xiaoping and promoted nationwide after 18 families of farmers in Xiaogang Village, Fengyang County, Anhui Province allocating the farm land to families. Such significant reform initiated by masses solved the food issue of the whole nation, agricultural stabilization and development issues, and also triggered and promoted the reform of state-owned enterprises in the cities, and became the primary point of China's reform. Future reform will rely on the top-level design by the CPC Central Committee and the State Council to plan the reform program and promote the reform nationwide through the way from the top to the bottom. It is the new path, new way and new selection of reform.

Reform does need top-level design after reaching the current stage so as to ensure the correct direction of the reform and prevent from occurring significant issues in the major relationships and key links. China has accumulated relatively rich reform experience after years of exploration and practice and possessed the conditions for completing the top-level design. Top-level design and overall planning shall be elaborately conducted from the overall strategic situation, mutual matching and joining of different reform measures shall be completed, and the reform shall be promoted through the comprehensive coordination.

Modern market economy is a huge complex and sophisticated system. Construction of modern market economy cannot be implemented while designing, and it is also not a pair of humble straw sandals whose structure needs no design. Otherwise, all the subsystems cannot be mutually connected and coordinated. Market economy is a big system and each local government and department may often have the respective work convenience and interests in mind and make the institutional arrangements conducive to achieving the local interests. However, it is afraid that a system jointed by the independent local design from grassroots cannot be coordinated and operated.

The so-called top-level design is precisely to take the new characteristics of China's comprehensive reform into consideration, different from the reform model which depends on individual efforts. It is to make the coordinated plans to the economic, political, cultural, social and ecological systems, strengthen the studies and judgment of all the reform relevance, strive to achieve the matching between the overall and local situation, combination between the permanent curing with the temporary solution as well as the mutual promotion between the progress and breakthrough, adopt the reform strategy of holism and master the systematicness, relevance and supporting of the reform. Top-level design of reform involves the following three aspects:

First, strengthening the studies on reform and making full theoretical preparation. Objectively speaking, the Third Plenary Session of the 18th National Congress has portrayed the overall blue print of socialist market economy in theory, and roughly sketched the basic path for reaching such ideal state. However, on the one hand, reform is a great cause with the mass participation. Educating the masses by using this theory, widely absorbing the recommendations of the masses and further enriching this theoretical system is still the arduous task which needs completing; on the other hand, reform covers extremely wide fields, theoretical preparation for reform in some aspects is slightly insufficient. Therefore, strengthening the studies on reform through mobilizing the social force will continuously improve the theory and strategy of China's reform and find a more effective reform path. Such process can also enhance the public participation in the reform and mobilize the enthusiasm of public participation in the reform.

Second, the reform, systematic design and comprehensive promotion need mastering as a whole so as to avoid the fragmentation. The reform involves too wide aspects and has too strong practicality, and reform program in each field has the need for further improvement and refinement although the Third Plenary Session of the 18th National Congress has made the comprehensive and systematic deployment to the reform, especially the subsequent overall promotion planning which particularly needs the clear and detailed ideas. In the next step, the reform needs mastering as a whole so as to avoid the fragmentation, specific goals and roadmap need proposing for each reform in the meantime. Reform shall simplify the rules and reduce the cumbersome administrative procedures, improve the transparency and promote the rebuilding of social rules, and promote the implementation of reform under more public and transparent social rules. Progressive reform is conducted "one by one" "progressively". Insufficiency in collaborated promotion and systematicness will often lead to the mutual constraints among institutions. As pointed out by Masahiko Aoki in *Towards A Comparative Institutional Analysis*, various systems in one institution are strategically complementary, other systems may either accordingly change or keep unchanged which makes it hard to cooperate with the new systems and hinder the implementation of new systems if changes occur in a or several systems. Therefore, institutional reform shall be promoted as a whole in nature and can be conducted step by step in the implementation, otherwise, there will exist huge costs for the system operation. Reform and opening up is a profound and comprehensive social reform, each reform will have significant impacts on the other reforms and need to coordinate with other reforms. Reform and opening up is a systematic project, must adhere to the comprehensive reform and be promoted in the coordination of all the reforms. Without the top-level design, such reform will surely impracticable.

Third, strengthening the mechanism design o f the reform. A high-level authoritative institution which is detached from the local interest is needed in conducting the top-level program design of the reform to carry out the design planning from the top to the bottom and monitor the implementation of planning with the support of the grass-roots level innovation. It is sure that conducting top-level design needs the participation of more people, and needs to listen to the appeal of the public and political innovation by the grass-roots level government. The basic concept of mechanism design is that a watermelon will be fairly allocated if the person who cuts the watermelon is the last person who takes it. Top-level design of the reform shall also have such mechanism, that is, it shall not make the reform design become the cutting benefits of reform in advance, and it shall enable all the participants in the reform to see the hope of fairly sharing the benefits of reform and shall be the practical mechanism protection.

Of course, emphasizing top-level design does not mean to give up the theory of "Look before You Leap". China is a large country which must not appear the disruptive error on fundamental issues. It will be irrevocable and irreparable once such error occurs. Meanwhile, reform cannot be abandoned due to this. Therefore, experimental exploration shall be adopted to achieve the experience and reach the consensus, be promoted after being certain so as to accumulate small victories to big victories. China is vast in territory, local conditions vary widely, the current reform is very complex and many cases are hard to be expected in advance. For the major reform which must make a breakthrough but is not accurately mastered, prior experiment in qualified regions shall be encouraged and supported, or exploration shall be conducted in the experimental area of the reform. Such reform shall be promoted in a timely manner after being successful and promptly corrected after any problem occurs so as to maintain the risks and influence in the local area. This is the effective way to positively and steadily promote the smooth implementation of the reform. In the future process of reform, macro-economic thinking and top-level design shall be strengthened, the systematicness, integrity and collaboration of the reform shall be paid attention to, and grassroots innovation, bold experiment and bold breakthrough shall be continuously encouraged so as to gradually deepen the reform and opening up.

## 8.5 The Initiate of Overall Reform

The 18th National Congress of the CPC proposed the five-in-one overall layout, including economic, political, cultural, social and ecological construction exactly based on the background that the reform enters the key stage and the intertwined interest relationships needs the top-level design and systematic arrangements to break the deadlock. Accordingly, China's reform also enters the new stage, the "Five-in-one" comprehensive reform. It means that the reform will not be simply limited to the economic field, seeking the "vertical deepening" of economic system reform shall also breakthrough the unilateral economic system innovation and further integrate the economic system reform with the political, cultural, social and ecological system reform. This means to promote the economic system reform with the socialist market economy as the base point and accelerate the promotion of the political, cultural, social and ecological system reform respectively with democracy, advanced culture, harmonious society and sustainable development as the goals in the meantime so as to form the new pattern of system on the basis of the "Five-in-One" institutional innovation.

In 1994, China introduced the reform strategy of "overall promotion and key breakthrough". Then there form deployment after the 18th National Congress of the CPC is an upgraded version of the overall promotion strategy. The overall reform in 1994 was mainly limited to the economic field, but the comprehensive reform in the new era (mainly referring to the period after the 18th National Congress) covers the political, cultural, social and ecological system reform in addition to the economic reform. The other four major reforms which support and promote the economic reform will be stated one by one in the following.

### 8.5.1 *Steady Promotion of Political System Reform*

Political system reform needs to match with the economic system reform so as to adapt to the establishment of socialist market economy system and create the favorable political environment.

China began to place the democracy building on the relative important position, proposed the goal of building the high-level social democracy and started to conduct the in-depth studies on the issues of political system reform in the meantime of vigorously promoting economic system reform based on reflecting and re-recognizing the democracy issues after the Third Plenary Session of the 11th National Congress. As early as 1980 when the reform and opening up just started, Deng Xiaoping made a speech under the title of *Reform of Leading System of the Party and State* on an enlarged session of the CPC Central Committee Political Bureau, and systematically explained the guiding ideology and basic ideas of the political system reform. The speech can be regarded as the declaration that China set its mind to conduct the political system reform, and is the programmatic literature for guiding China's political system reform. In the speech, Deng Xiaoping proposed that power should not be too centralized, Party and government administration should be separated, government functions should not be substituted by the Party administration, and put forward many valuable opinions on the political system reform. He pointed out that in order to eliminating residual influence of feudalism, the key point is practically reforming and perfecting the systems of the Party and State, systemically ensuring the democratization of political life of the Party and State, the democratization of economic management and democratization of the overall social life, promoting the smooth development of modernization construction cause.

The 13th National Congress of the CPC deeply expounded the theory related to the political system reform, proposes that "the economic system reform cannot ultimately succeed without the political system reform", and determined to adopt a series of reform measures, including: separation of Party and government administration; further decentralization of power; reforming the government institutions; reforming the cadre and personnel system and establishing the system of national civil servants; establishing the system of social consultation and dialogue; improving several systems of socialist democracy, including improving the system of people's congress, improving the CPPCC and implementing the competitive election, etc.; strengthening the building of socialist legal system. In the subsequent national congresses of the CPC representatives, promotion of political system reform was covered to some extent. The 14th National Congress of the CPC put forward to "adapt to the economic system reform and economic development" and "actively promote the political system reform in accordance with the requirements of the close combination of democratization and legislation". The 15th National Congress of the CPC pointed out to "continuously promote the political system reform" and defined the goal of "constructing the socialist country under the rule by law". The 16th National Congress of the CPC clearly stated to "learn from the beneficial achievements of human political civilization", and identified the construction of socialist political civilization, material civilization and spiritual civilization as the three basic goals for the construction of socialist modernization. The 17th National Congress of the CPC proposed to "deepen the political system reform" and made deployment for expanding the inner-party democracy, developing the grass-roots level democracy, implementing the rule by law, strengthening the power control and supervision as well as the administrative system reform.

The 18th National Congress of the CPC listed the political system reform separately and explained it as an important part of the report, which sufficiently shows the cognition and consensus of the CPC Central Committee to the importance and urgency of political system reform. The report placed institutional building in a prominent position, proposed to "pay more attention to improving the leadership and governance styles of the CPC", "perfecting the democratic system and enriching the democratic form" and "giving play to the important roles of rule by law in the national governance and social administration".

The Third Plenary Session of the 18th National Congress proposed to strengthen the construction of socialist democratic political system. Regarding the measures, the first is to promote the people's congress system to advance with times, especially improve the legislative drafting, demonstration, coordination and review mechanism, enhance the quality of legislation and prevent the local protection and departmental interest legislation; improve the system that the "people's government, people's court and people's procuratorate" are generated by the people's congress, responsible for the people's congress and supervised by the people's congress; improve the system that the people's congress discusses and determines major issues, and government at all levels reports to the people's congress at its level before the major issues are introduced; strengthen the functions of examining and supervising the budgeting and final account of the people's congress, and supervising the state-owned assets. The second is to promote the wide multilayer institutional development of deliberative democracy. Deliberative democracy is the specific form and unique advantage of China's socialist democracy, and the important reflection of the CPC's mass line in the political field. It is to carry out the extensive consultations in the whole society under the leadership of the CPC with the major issues of economic and social development as well as actual issues related to the vital interests of the masses as the contents, and stick to the consultations before the decision-making and in the implementation of decision-making. The third is to develop the democracy at grass-roots level, smooth the democratic channels and improve the election, discussion, publicity, debriefing and accountability mechanism at the grass-roots level, carry out various democratic consultations at the grass-roots level, promote the institutionalization of consultations at the grass-roots level, establish and improve the resident and villager supervision mechanism, promote the self-management, self-service, self-education and self-supervision of the masses in the urban and rural community governance, public affairs at the grass-roots level and public welfare undertakings, improve the democratic management system of the enterprises and institutions with the congress of employees as the basic form, strengthen the construction of democratic mechanism of social organizations and safeguard the employees' democratic rights of participation in the management and supervision.

The Fourth Plenary Session of the 18th National Congress took the "ruling by law" as the theme for the first time, and conducted the top-level design and strategic deployment for accelerating the construction of socialist country under the rule by law, precisely, under the leadership of the CPC, it is to adhere to the socialist system with Chinese characteristics, implement the socialist theory of rule by law with Chinese characteristics, form the complete normative legal system, efficient implementation system of rule by law, rigorous supervision system of rule by law, vigorous protection system of rule by law, form the perfect inner-party system of laws and regulations, uphold the joint promotion of rule, governing and administration by law, stick to the integrated construction of country, government and society of rule by law, achieve the scientific legislation, strict law enforcement, judicial justice and abidance of all the people by law, and promote the modernization of national governance system and governance capacity.

China's political system reform has made certain progress after the efforts of more than 30 years: introduced the inner-party democracy, develop the systems of people's congress and political consultations, and reformed the administrative institutions several times in constructing the systems of the ruling party and regime; improved the self-governance of urban residents, develop the self-governance of rural villagers and democracy at the grass-roots level in the democracy construction; abolish the life tenure of cadres and leading posts to implement the tenure system, and promote the system of national civil servants in the cadre and personnel system; amend the constitution, formulate and revise a series of important laws and regulations in the legal system construction.

China not only enhances the democracy construction to the strategic height of socialist modernization construction but also pays attention to proceeding from the reality, promoting steadily and focusing on the actual effect on the overall guiding ideology in the process of promoting the political system reform. Proceeding from the reality is to be in line with the national conditions of China in the current stage without blind advancing, especially from the actual needs of economic system reform, to combine the democracy construction of economic system reform and development of socialist market economy, strive to establish all the systems which are conducive to improving the efficiency and enhancing the vitality, and may mobilize the enthusiasm of all the aspects. Steady promotion takes account that socialist democracy construction cannot be conducted in an isolated manner and will be inevitably subject to the constraints of the economic and cultural development levels, and socialist democracy construction as well as the construction of material and spiritual civilization are mutually conditioned and promoted. Focusing on the actual effect is that whether the democracy construction has the actual achievement will be finally inspected by the results of practice, depending on whether political situation of the nation is stable, whether the living conditions of residents are improved and whether the productivity is developed in a sustained manner. As seen from the current conditions in China, maintaining the proper coordination and matching of political system reform and economic system reform after the economic system reform achieves significant progress shall be the important content for continuously implementing the aforementioned guiding ideology.

### 8.5.2 *Gradual Promotion of Cultural System Reform*

Gradually promoting the cultural system reform is mainly to continuously meet the people's increasingly growing spiritual and cultural needs, and form the theoretical guidance, public opinion force, values and cultural conditions which are conducive to the reform and opening up.

At the beginning of the reform and opening up, China clearly divided the concepts of material civilization and spiritual civilization, and regarded the socialist spiritual civilization as an importance performance of the significant characteristics and advantages of socialism on the basis of summarizing the historical experience, thus emphasizing that the socialist spiritual civilization must be constructed in the meantime of constructing the material civilization. This is an important contribution made to the Marxism. Prior to this, no Marxist literature had explicitly divided the human civilization to the material civilization and spiritual civilization, or generalized the civilization phenomenon, such as education, science, culture, ideas, ideal, morality and discipline, etc. by using such brief concept of spiritual civilization. Moreover, the past discussion had not taken the spiritual civilization as the goal of struggle for the construction, therefore, socialist spiritual civilization cannot be enhanced to the height as characteristics of socialism.

China continuously deepened the cognition to the construction of spiritual civilization, including the rules of cultural construction along with the practice development of constructing the socialism with Chinese characteristics after establishing the goal of fighting for the construction of socialist spiritual civilization. Over the years, China has strived to develop the advanced socialist culture, construct the harmonious culture and constantly deepen the cultural system reform in order to meet the requirements of socialist market economy. There are two key points in this aspect: the first is the reform in the overall value system, which is to promote the cultural diversity based on constructing the socialist core value system. It aims at resulting in the widespread social identity through the construction of knowledge system, values, ideas and beliefs as well as code of conduct, cohere and motivate the social members, and maintain the social coordination and stability. The second is to deepen the reform in the cultural institutions, the focus is to draw a line between the public cultural undertakings and market cultural industries, and form the respectively different operational mechanism. The former is leaded by the government (reflected in the supply responsibility, especially the investment responsibility, or payment and purchase responsibility), aiming at providing the overall social members with the public cultural services and safeguarding their cultural rights and interests; the latter is market-oriented so as to meet the spiritual and cultural needs of social members in various aspects at various levels.

### 8.5.3 Accelerating Promotion of Social System Reform

China's social structures and interest patterns have accordingly had the unprecedented and profound changes with the development of market economy. Meanwhile, independence and diversity of people's thinking becomes increasingly stronger with the promotion of political system reform as well as the enhancement of the public in the awareness of democracy and the improvement in the political participation enthusiasm. In recent years, China has constantly deepened the cognition to the social harmony and strived to explore the new mechanism of social operation and social service in front of the unprecedented social reform so as to form a set of new social governance models which adapt to the economic marketization, political democratization and cultural diversity.

China has focused on handling three sets of relationships in the process of promoting the social system innovation: the first is the relationship between wealthy country and people's livelihood, which is to enable the economic development achievements to reflect more on the improvement in the people's livelihood through the institutional construction in the meantime of the rapid economic growth and continuous enhancement in the comprehensive national strength so as to create the favorable social environment and conditions for the reform and opening up. The key points of this aspect center on the employment, revenue distribution, social security, education, medical care and other most direct and realistic interest issues which are concerned by the public, promotion of government transition, establishment and perfection of public fiscal system, and achievement of equalization of public services. The second is the relationship between vitality and order. On the one hand, it is to pay attention to the stimulation of the social vitality and give play to the creativity of social organizations and social members. On the other hand, it is to strive to construct the social order which adapts to the marketization, focus on the promoting the "separation of government administration from the management of social organizations", cultivate and develop all types of non-governmental organizations, give play to the coordinating roles of the public in the social construction and management, and construct the institutional arrangements of coordination and distribution of responsibilities as well as joint governance of the government and society. The third is the relationship between the diversity and balancing. It is to comply with the trend of diversity of economic sectors and diversity of social force, and pay attention to balancing the interest relationships among the diversified force, focus on the social equity and justice, establish and improve the institutional mechanism which coordinates the interest relationships.

### 8.5.4 Commencing Promotion of Ecological Civilization System Reform

The report of the 18th National Congress stressed that ecological civilization was closely related to the outstanding difficulties and issues faced in constructing the road of socialism with Chinese characteristics, from the "excessive resource and environmental costs of economic growth" pointed out in the report of the 17th National Congress to the "intensified resource and environmental constraints" warned for a second time in the report of the 18th National Congress. China gross energy and resources are rich, but the per capita consumption is low, such energy and resources are unevenly distributed, and constraints of land and other scarce resources are strengthening. China's ecological environment is very fragile, national forest coverage is low, desertificated land, water and soil erosion, and degradation area of natural grassland is large, quality of surface water and offshore environment is not optimistic, biodiversity is decreasing and functions of some important ecological function areas are seriously degraded. China's emissions of major pollutants are huge, the environmental pollution is serious and people are facing with the relatively bad living environment. Therefore, solving the resource and environmental constraints in China has reached a crucial period. Exactly in this context, ecological civilization is placed on such a very important position.

As seen from the perspective of institutional construction of ecological civilization, the core goal is the pursuit of sustainable development, which is not only to meet the needs of contemporary people but also develop without constituting any hazards to the future generations. This involves the vertical fair allocation of wealth, especially the natural wealth, between the contemporary people and future generations. It is also the practical issue of sustainable development.

For China, the increasingly prominent resource and environmental constraints need the countermeasures from many aspects, and institutional innovation is the key point. The first is to deepen the reform and innovation in the field of ecological environmental protection, accelerate the reform in natural resources and their prices, establish and improve the paid use systems of resources and ecological compensation systems which reflect the market supply and demand, degree of resource scarcity, ecological value and intergenerational compensation. It is to vigorously develop the environmental protection market, promote the third-party control of environmental pollution, and give play to the incentive and restraining roles of market mechanism. The second is to grasp the key links and work in key areas, strictly promote the development in accordance with the positioning of main functional areas, accelerate the designation of the red line for ecological protection, make efforts to solve the air, water and soil pollution as well as other outstanding environmental issues; optimize the space development pattern of state-owned land, scientifically deploy the production space, living space and ecological space, and leave more repair space to nature; and give full play to the leading and guiding roles of the government. The third is to increase the strength in ecological and environmental protection, establish and improve the legal system of property rights of natural resources, economical and intensive use systems of energy, water and land, pollution prevention systems of water, air and soil, practically pay attention to the implementation of the amendment of the *Environmental Protection Law*, and give fully play to the normative and protective roles of environmental law.

## References

Bei J (2013) Build the veil of ignorance for the reform mechanism. Chin Bus J

Commentator from "Guangming daily (2004) cohering reform consensus: comprehensively deepening reform series I". Guangming Daily, 24 Mar 2014

Hu Angang et al (2014) Modernization of national governance in China. China Renmin University Press, Beijing

Shleifer A, Vishny R (2004) The grabbing hand (trans: Zhao Hongjun). China CITIC Press, Beijing

Tang Yugang, Zhao Daping (2007) Discussion on short-term decisions of government supply preference: political equilibrium and economic efficiency. Econ Res J 1:29–40

# Chapter 9
# Better Play the Role of the Government: Reconstruction of the Government Functions

China's in-depth promotion of economic system reform needs to achieve the coordination and balance among the relationships of enterprises, market and government. As seen from the progress of current overall economic system reform, reforms in enterprises and market have achieved relatively large progress but government administration system reform has lagged far behind and become the largest weakness through the formation of micro-basis and construction of market system in the previous reforms. Such lag and containment has led to the sticky situation of reform in the monopolizing industries, market reforms in land, capital and other elements, reform in revenue distribution system as well as the reforms in other key areas and important links, and some reforms are even in the state of "progress or regression". This needs to "offset the weakness" as soon as possible and seek the breakthrough progress in the administration system reform. The core of government administration system reform is the transformation of government functions, which is to achieve the transformation of government function orientation from the economic construction to public services. Currently, government at all levels is still relatively prominent in the constructive characteristics and faces many institutional obstacles in the transformation to the service-oriented government. In the next stage, only conducting deeper institutional reform may achieve the breakthrough in the transformation of government functions.

## 9.1 The Distortion of Government Behavior

In term of the distortion of government behavior, unauthorized, absent and mal-positioned behavior coexists, and un-authorization is particularly prominent. At present, the economic development model leaded by government has not completely changed, and government departments still directly interfere in the macro-control activities of enterprises through the investment project approval, market access, price control and other means. In recent years, government, in the



X. Zhang, X. Chang, *The Logic of Economic Reform in China*, China Insights,
DOI 10.1007/978-3-662-47404-4_9

name of macro-control, has further strengthened the interference in the micro-economic activities. In particular, government at all levels has still input relatively great energy in the production and operation field, and undertaken a large number of economic construction functions, therefore, such government still has the characteristics of construction-oriented government. It seems that local government has excessively penetrated the micro field, especially the strong impulse in the investment promotion and land operation, which shows the distinct characteristics of corporatization behavior. Professor Jean Oi from department of politics in Stanford University has ever used the concept of "local state corporatism"[1] to more directly analyze the corporatized behavior by the local government in China. Currently speaking, such "local state corporatism" or characteristics of "development-oriented government" of the local government is still widespread.

It needs to be noted that the emergence of "bad market economy", that is, the conspiracy of power and capital, exchange of power and interests as well as other market-oriented trend of power generated in the process of the aggressive interference by the government, shall be prevented in the context of the microcosmic, corporatized and interest-oriented government behavior caused by the economic development model leaded by government. This may result in that the deeply interfered government power cannot quit in good time along with the changes in the stage of economic development and market maturity, and then the institutional arrangement is locked under the state of low-efficiency equilibrium in a long term. For us, hazards of some countries in the world (such as some countries in the Latin America and Southeast Asia) brought by the omnipresent and strong interest-oriented government are the lessons. Such countries of market economy dominated and led by power and wealth fell into the trap hindering development in succession, and the lessons that such countries cannot smoothly achieve the modernization are worth being profoundly taken by us.

With respect to the prominent position of economic construction functions, the public service functions of government are still too few and weak. Compared with the national standards, the input remains low although greater support by the fiscal expenditure has been offered to education, medical care, social security and other public service fields in accordance with the new concept of development and the idea of constructing the public finance since the "11th Five-year Plan".

The first is government expenditure in education. The weight of public education expenditure in GDP fluctuated at the level of 2–3 % and reached 4 % for the first time until 2012, finally achieving the goal of "achieving the proportion of national fiscal expenditure in education of 4 % in GNP in 2000" committed in the Chinese Education Reform and Development Outline issued by the Chinese government in 1993, however the proportion dropped to less than 4 % again in 2013.[2] Such proportion was also at a relatively low level in international comparison: the world average

[1] Oi (1992).

[2] The judgement is made based on the weight of national finance used for educational expenditure in GDP. The weight of national finance used for educational expenses (mainly including public finance budget for educational expenditure, taxes collected by government at all levels for education,

level in 2010 was 4.9 %; such levels in the low-income countries, middle-income countries and high- income OECD countries were respectively 4.1 %, 4.8 % and 5.4 % (in 2011).

The second is government expenditure in medical care. The weight of public medical care expenditure in GDP has sustained at the level of less than 1 % over the years and slightly increased in recent years, and such weight in 2013 was 1.5 %. According to the statistical caliber by the World Bank, the world average level and the level in high-income OECD countries were respectively 6.1 % and 7.9 % in 2012, but such weight in China was only 3 %, being at a relatively low level. The weight of public medical expenditure in GDP in China was 56 % in 2012, less than high-income OECD countries (61.4 %) and the world average level (59.8 %).

The last is government expenditure in social security. The weight of fiscal employment and social security expenditure in the fiscal expenditure and GDP of the current year has respectively reached the levels of about 10 % and 2 %. However, the weight of social security employment expenditure in GDP has risen relatively slow in recent years; and the proportion of social security employment expenditure in fiscal expenditure has fluctuated at the level of 10–11 % in recent years. The goal of "gradually increasing the weight of social security expenditure in fiscal expenditure to 15–20 %" was proposed when the "10th Five-year" planning of labor and social security undertakings was formulated at the beginning of this century. Meanwhile, it should be noted that the current weights of social security expenditure respectively in fiscal expenditure and GDP are also significantly lower even compared with the world level in the 1990s, with these two proportions were respectively 27.5 % and 12.2 % in the high-income countries, and respectively 15.7 % and 4.6 % in the middle-income countries. Currently speaking, public consumption in social security and welfare is the uppermost expenditure item in the public finance system of some countries, generally reaching about 40 %.

## 9.2 Adjusting Finance and Taxation Incentives, and Modifying the Micro-orientation Behaviors of Local Governments

Given the profound impacts of financial and taxation system on the behavior of local government, promotion of transformation in government behavior needs to start from adjusting the financial and taxation system. The core of such adjustment is trying to change the direction of incentives to behavior of local government, i.e. cutting the highly related link between the growth in local fiscal revenue and the attention of government in production and operation, and enabling the growth in local fiscal revenue to more directly connect with the effective provision of public services by the government. Specifically speaking, the following measures can be taken:

---

enterprise appropriation in the enterprise-run schools, school-run industries and social service revenue used for educational expenses) in GDP was 4.3 % in 2013, slightly exceeding 4 %.

The first is to reduce the weight of indirect taxes and weaken the distorted incentives to local government for purely pursuing the output growth.

Generally speaking, the capability of tax collection and management is also relatively limited in the stage of underdeveloped economic level due to the relatively low national revenue level per capita. Therefore, source of revenue tax, property tax and other direct taxes is insufficient, and the collection of various commodity turnover taxes can be comparatively easier to be achieved. Accordingly, the formation is of certain inevitability in taxation arrangement with indirect taxes as the primary taxes. According to statistics, the weight of direct taxes to indirect taxes in high-income countries, middle-income countries and low-income countries are respectively 2:1, 1:1 and 0.4:1 in general. This means that expanding direct taxes and reducing indirect taxes (especially in the local perspective, establishing the taxation system with property tax, revenue tax and other direct taxes as the main body, and accordingly reducing the weight of value-added tax, corporate tax and other commodity turnover taxes) will have more solid basis in reality, with China changing from the lower-middle-income country to the upper-middle-income country and the accompanying enhancement in national revenue level as well as in the capability of tax collection and management. The weight of indirect taxes in the overall tax revenue can be more actively reduced properly through the re-design of taxation system in the meantime that such internal system works. For example, further reform and perfect the system of value-added tax, reduce the tax rate of value-added tax and expand the scope of deduction on the basis of the reform in value-added tax transforming from production-orientated to consumption-orientated, and change the status quo that the tax burden level of value-added tax is relatively too high. The goal of adjusting the weight of indirect taxes in the next few years may be roughly set between 40 % and 50 %, and to be further adjusted discretionarily in the future.

In the process of adjusting the weight of indirect taxes, the system shall be explored and reformed of collecting some taxes from enterprise production at the place of production to the system of collection such taxes from the sales links as the place of final consumption under the circumstances of suitable conditions. This can weaken the direct interest relationship between the local government and expansion of production scale, and reduce the incentives to the direct participation in the production and operating activities; and on the other hand can also strengthen the direct correlation between the increase in the local fiscal revenue and the enhancement in the revenue and consumption levels of the local residents, and urge the local government to pay more attention to the improvement in the welfare level of the local residents.

The second is to adjust the existing fiscal revenue system related to land and housing, and curb the impulse of local government for land operation.

Unified real estate tax integrated by the land rent collection in a single time and taxes centralized at the development and sales links can be considered, unified collection of property tax or real estate tax (especially to the housing property of residents) with the value of real estate as the tax base at the retaining link of real estate can be explored, and such taxes can be taken as the large stable source of local fiscal income. Thereby, transform the local short-term land finance to the long-term land finance, i.e. to transform from paying excessive attention to the operation of city to making great efforts to provide the public services. Local attraction will be gradually enhanced and local real estate will continuously appreciate as long as the local government focuses on optimizing the provision of local public services, thus accordingly expanding the local tax revenue source. Cultivation of local tax revenue resource will be directly connected with local residents' peaceful and content life and work when the value of property tax as the future main local tax greatly depends on the governance environment created by the local government, thus introducing the local government behavior to the more standardized and rational direction which is more suitable to the functional positioning.

Prior to the official launch of property tax, land revenue administration shall be further standardized. It is to incorporate the full amount of land-transferring fees into the local budget and implement the management of "separation between revenue and expenditure", establish local "reserve fund of state-owned land revenue", and increase the input intensity in land requisition compensation, land occupation and compensation balance, low-rent housing construction and housing subsidies for low-income families. Meanwhile, it may also consider changing the system of land lease in batches to annual land lease system, which is to change the collection of land-transferring fees of several decades in a single time to the annual collection of yearly land rent (land-use fees), thereby weakening the internal driving force for the local government to blindly transfer the land.

The third is to rationally allocate the fiscal powers and authority of government at all levels, and to change the derivative financing pressure and distorted behavioral pattern of the local government on the premise of adhering to the principle of decentralization of powers.

The most critical content of promoting the transformation of government behavior through the adjustment in the fiscal and taxation system is the adjustment in the fiscal relationship between the central and local government. The core of relationship between the central and local finance is to solve the proper centralization on the allocation of financial resource and government functions, and it is also the issue of proper decentralization. In this regard, our basic view is to comply with the trend of international decentralization reform and continue to stick to the principles of decentralization. Moreover, such decentralization is reflected not only in the expenditure perspective but also in the revenue perspective.

1. Continuing to give full play to the roles of local government in the division of authority; and properly strengthening the expenditure responsibility of central government in the meantime.

   (1) Paying attention to the roles of local government in the provision of public services is conducive to solving the problem of asymmetric information and strengthening the public participation. According to the theory of decentralization, huge differences between regions will inevitably lead to the heterogeneous preference of local users to the public services; and government at grass-roots level with relatively small range of area under administration can

more accurately make response and decisions to the local needs by using the information advantages, more effectively provide the public services which comply with the local preference and specific local conditions, and thus better satisfy the users and ensuring the government at grass-roots level to achieve higher efficiency in the provision of public services. Moreover, government at grass-roots level can better supervise the quality of services and take the responsibilities in a more easy way. Studies on the theory of public choice show that the "small collective" with relatively small number of members has higher public service efficiency compared with the "large collective" with relatively larger number of members. Decentralization of expenditure responsibility to the local government is conducive to incorporating the fiscal decision-making into the general process of public choice and strengthening the characteristic of public participation of the fiscal decision-making procedures.

(2) Attaching importance to the roles of local government does not mean that the central government can thereby cast off the burden. The general principle in determining the boundary of expenditure responsibility between the central and local government is to take account of the beneficial scope of public services. For the national public services with the nationwide beneficial scope, significant scale effect and overflow effect, the central government shall assume the major expenditure responsibility. In recent years, some local public goods have produced the trans-regional and even nationwide overflow effect with the gradual expansion in the size of population movement, such as public medical care and basic medical care, compulsory education, pension insurance and unemployment insurance, etc. Take basic pension insurance as an example, the general practice of some countries in the world is that the planning funds are raised and managed by the central government, thus making the pension account become portable. The integration of national pension system is conducive to the free flow of labor force in the country, and also enable pension standard to tend to equalization among the different regions. China belongs to the few countries in the world which implement the local management of pension insurance. Under the fragmented management pattern, it is hard to transfer the pension account across provinces or cities, which forms the negative impacts on the liquidity of labor market and industry transfer among regions. In the next stage, it may consider to moderately transfer the expenditure responsibilities to the central government in pension, compulsory education of migrant children, justice, food and drug administration, cross-basin control of rivers and cross-region pollution, in order to construct the rational pattern of function division between the central and local government, thereby reducing the weight of special transfer payment, weakening the power of fiscal department in free administration of funds and preventing the abnormal phenomenon of "visiting departments in Beijing". It should be noted that giving full play to the roles of local government in the provision of public services and properly strengthening the expenditure responsibility of central government can be

accomplished without coming into conflict under some circumstances. This actually involves in the separation of financing and services of public services. For example, basic education is a typical type of public service which in some countries in the world that the service is provided by the government at grass-roots level and the related funds are provided by the government at high level. This may not only let the decision-maker understand the needs as much as possible in the provision of services, but also implement the equal standard in the process of public expenditure, achieving the general coverage and ensuring the fairness among the regions.

2. Taking the increase in local autonomous fiscal revenue as the core goal in the division of fiscal power, perfecting the local main taxes, rationally dividing the shared taxes and reforming the system of excessively centralized taxation power.

   Results of international studies on fiscal decentralization show that most expenditure of the government shall come from its own source of revenue in order to better achieve the accountability, and it is more conducive to making the local government assume the responsibility for the residents within the area under administration (taxable objects) so as to provide the desirable public goods to the region. For this purpose, decentralization reform shall be more actively implemented in the revenue perspective so as to correct the asymmetric decentralization between expenditure responsibility and revenue power as well as the pattern that local finance highly depends on the transfer payment.

   (1) Rationally dividing the taxes of government at all levels. Many fiscal scholars pointed out their respective theories in the world for the division principle of taxes between government at all levels, especially between the central and local government. The more famous is the theory of seven principles by Musgrave, the American fiscal expert.[3] The main points are: First, progressive

[3] In addition, some other scholars also conducted the studies on the principles of taxation division. Such as: Mintz proposed five principles, including efficiency (taxation division shall minimize the impacts on resource optimization allocation), simplicity (taxation system shall be simplified to facilitate the understanding and implementation of the public), flexibility (taxation division shall be conducive to the flexible application of budgetary expenditure, tax subsidies and a series policy instruments by government at all levels so as to achieve the adaptability of taxation and authority), responsibility (expenditure and taxation responsibility of government at all levels shall be coordinated) and fairness (tax structure, tax base and tax rate across the country shall be balanced, namely, the tax bearing of residents nationwide shall be balanced). Boadway et al. proposed six principles, that is, revenue tax is related to the fairness of the whole society and shall be put under the administration by the central government; related capital tax, property transfer tax and other taxes shall be put under the administration by the central government in order to ensure the formation of the national unified market as well as the free flow and optimization allocation of resources nationwide; the weighing between goals of fairness and efficiency related to resource taxation shall be shared by the central and local government; non-liquidity taxation is the ideal source of revenue by municipal government administrated by regions; social security tax, as the beneficial tax, can be jointly collected and administrated by the central and local government; value-added tax and sales tax which are collected in many links shall be put under the administration by the central government, but single sales tax and retail sales tax are more appropriate to be put under the administration by the local government. Seligman proposed three principles: the first is the principle of

tax which takes revenue redistribution as the goal shall be put under the administration by the central government since social equity concerns all citizens; taxes collected from individuals by adopting the progressive tax rate shall be collected by the government at the level which is most capable of adopting the comprehensive tax base. Second, taxation which is taken as the mean to stabilize the economy shall be put under the administration by the central government since the macroeconomic stability requires the central government to conduct the adjustment in the country, while taxation which is cyclically stable and has small fluctuation in the revenue shall be put under the administration by the local government. Third, the unevenly distributed tax source among the regions shall be put under the administration by the central government; otherwise, it may result in the imbalance in the tax revenue among the regions. Fourth, taxation which is imposed to the liquidity factors of production shall be best put under the administration by the central government; otherwise, it will distort the optimization allocation of resources among the regions. Fifth, taxation which is attached to the place of residence (such as sales tax and consumption tax) shall be more suitably put under the administration by the local government. Sixth, taxation which is imposed to non-liquidity factors of production shall be best put under the administration by the local government since the difference in tax rate will not change the regional distribution of production factors and the efficiency loss of resource allocation due to the local taxation competition may be avoided. Seventh, beneficial taxation and charges are applicable to government at all levels. Taxes which are more suitably put under the administration by the local government as the main local financial resources shall possess the following characteristics based on the results of research by Musgrave et al.: (1) tax source has clear locality and non-liquidity; (2) taking the place of residence as the basis can be of effective collection in accordance with the principle of benefit; (3) information requirements are more detailed, and local collection and administration are more efficient. Property tax, especially the property tax imposed on the real estate, is considered as the tax that is more suitably put under the administration by the central government and has the excellent potential to become the main local taxes if measured based on this characteristic. Firstly, real estate cannot be moved and has the characteristic of non-liquidity, and such tax source is relatively stable. Secondly, the public goods borne and provided by the real estate tax have clear beneficial area and scope of beneficiary, and can reflect the principle of beneficial tax collection. Finally, real estate is featured with

efficiency, that is, the division of inter-governmental revenue shall take taxation efficiency as the standard; the second is the principle of adaptation, that is, the division of inter-governmental revenue shall take width of tax base as the standard, taxes with wide tax base and narrow tax base can be respectively allocated to the central and local government; and the third is the principle of appropriateness, that is, division of inter-governmental revenue shall take fairness of tax burden as the standard.

significant difference, and large demand of tax information, so local government has administrative advantages.

From an international point of view, property tax in many countries is put under the administration by the local government and becomes the major financial source of government at lower level (mainly county and city-level) in the countries which implement the system of tax distribution. For example, the United States has the three levels of government, namely, the federal, state and local levels. Local government, including cities, counties, towns, school districts and special districts, collects property tax, and such property tax occupies the absolute weight in the local tax revenue. As the major source of funds of the local government, the property tax supports the public administration activities of the local government. For the property tax, since local government owns the partial legislative power and full legal enforcement power, it can more independently determine the tax base and tax rate of the property tax, and conduct the tax collection, daily management, supervision and inspection as well as a series of other work. In some developed countries, the property tax scale of local government is generally large, and property tax has become the important integral part of the local financial revenue and even the main tax in the local taxation system.

In China's taxation structure, current revenue from property tax which is mainly imposed on real estate is basically put under the administration by the local government, and such property tax occupies certain share in the local tax revenue; but on the whole, the scale of revenue from property tax is relatively small and still does not take up the position of main local tax or main local financial source. Commodity tax is the main tax revenue of government, and government mainly depends on value-added tax and sales tax, yet the weight of property tax in the total local financial revenue is very small. Objectively speaking, different stages of economic development, especially different levels of industrialization and urbanization, will result in the different tax structure, so the local government in China is not comparable to the local government in developed countries. Scale of property tax in China in the local perspective is also systematically lower than that in the developed countries even if the difference in development levels is taken into consideration. Structure of financial revenue of government at grass-roots level whose urbanization has reached a certain level has no essential change.

In view of this, it is believed that local tax structure shall be optimized by combining with the aforementioned land and housing tax reform through the collection of property tax or real estate tax so as to gradually cultivate such taxes into the main tax source of local government and the main tax of the local tax, thus to enhance the self-sufficiency rate of the local finance. In addition to property tax, it can be seen from the general characteristics of local tax system in the world that resource taxes as well as taxes of purposes and behavior are the main form of the local tax. Therefore, resource tax reform shall be accelerated and environmental taxes, carbon tax shall be collected as early as possible so as to achieve the important supplement to the main source of local revenue.

In the meantime of developing the pillar financial resource of government at grass-roots level, it may also consider to appropriately reduce the weight of shared tax, adjust the revenue proportion of local and central finance, and properly enhance the sharing standard of shared tax of government at grass-roots level. In particular, sharing based on types of taxes or proportion and other regulatory measures shall be adopted for the division of financial revenue among governments below provincial level so as to rationally define the revenue source of government at all levels and scientifically divide the levels of revenue and sharing proportion of the shared revenue.

(2) Rationally dividing the taxation power of government at all levels. In order to change currently too centralized situation of taxation power, more deep decentralization reform shall be conducted so as to properly increase the taxation administration authority of the local government and enable them to own more autonomous rights of financial revenue. Specifically speaking, tax items, tax rate, tax base and other elements of tax system of taxes which do not have relatively significant national influence may be allowed to be properly provided and adjusted within the certain limit by the local government based on the respective actual conditions on the premise that the central government formulates the unified taxation regulations. For example, the central government may set the unified floating scope of tax rate and allow the local government to make autonomous choice within such scope. For some local taxes whose collection effect is obviously regional, right to choice by local government regarding tax items shall be expanded, and local government shall be allowed to collect the respective local taxes through the legislative procedures of the local people's congress under the necessary constraints by the central government.

3. Seeking new path of competition mechanism among local governments

It is also necessary to conduct in-depth analysis to the completion among local governments due to the decentralization of fiscal power while talking about the adjustment in fiscal and tax system as well as the correction of government behavior. Strong decentralization incentives by the local government in China and competition among local governments have been considered as the important driving force for promoting the economic growth for a long time. The assumption of "Federalism, Chinese style"[4] emphasizes that Chinese government decentralization is conducive to enhancing the credibility of decentralization commitment of the central government and reducing the soft budget constraints of the local government. The theory believes that the decentralization arrangement in China brings the changes in the incentive structure to the local government, making them have strong incentive to keep and maintain the marketization process and promote the local economic

[4] See Montinola et al. (1995); Qian and Weingast (1997); Qian and Roland (1998); Jin et al. (2005).

growth. In recent years, some scholars further investigated the special experience of decentralization in China on the basis of such theories, especially the governance pattern with the Chinese characteristics to stimulate the local officials to promote the local economic development, i.e. "promotion championship" model conducted among local officials centered on GDP growth. In such model, government performance assessment mechanism centered on GDP achieves the compatibility between the political incentives and incentives for promotion of economic growth faced by the local government officials.[5]

How to transform the competition among local governments from purely promoting the economic growth to the promotion of improvement in public services is the issue that needs our consideration, under the context of more integration of "humane care" to the development vision and the call of the transformation of government functions, which differs from the past stages when economic growth is the only development goal.

Inter-governmental fiscal competition (surely including the information advantages of local government) shall be conducive to the improvement in the provision of public goods and enhancing the welfare level of residents in turn, based on the traditional theory of fiscal decentralization, especially the general views of fiscal federalism theory. Rational residents compare the earnings of enjoying the public services at the place of residence and the costs of fulfilling the obligations of tax payment; and local government has the most effective driving force for providing the public goods under the constraint of such comparison.

It is believed that the specific future local practice may consider forming the competition among local governments with the help of introducing property tax through the migration under free movement of population and the mechanism of "voting by feet" (quitting threat of liquidity factors). Which means, residents may greatly influence the local economic capacity, especially the value of real estate through changing the place of residence to choose the public services (such as education), thus substantially impacting the real estate tax based on the value of local real estate, and local government will have the incentives to make efforts to improve the public services.

It should be noted that the fiscal competition held here is the competition of tax source of property tax brought by the inflow of population factors, which can accordingly enhance the welfare level of residents and is a type of benign competition. However, the current fiscal competition generally adopted around China is the competition of tax deduction and exemption which attracts the capital factors and industry inflow, which is mainly for the purpose of investment attraction and promotion of production; such competition in some places has gradually evolved to the strategy of "racing to the bottom" with the suspicion of vicious competition. These two types of fiscal competition, though based on attracting the inflow of liquidity factors, are essentially different.

---

[5] See Zhou Li'an (2007).

## 9.3 Overcoming Local Government's Profit-seeking Behaviors by Abolishing Land Finance

Currently speaking, strong preference of local government to the "operation of city" is still closely related to the overlarge allocation power of land resource. Therefore, marketization reform of land allocation and price formation shall be accelerated, proportion of land allocation shall be further reduced, establishment of paid use system of operational infrastructure land shall be accelerated, and application scope of bidding, auction, listing and other ways of market competitive resource transfer shall be expanded. For existing "dual-track system" for price of resource, the merging shall be achieved as early as possible. In order to reflect the price support to the non-profit goals, scope of application and intensity of application shall be strictly controlled, and the tight isolation mechanism shall be constructed between the marketization price and non-marketization price when the non-marketization price is unavoidable; meanwhile, the formation of non-marketization price does not mean the unpaid use of resources, and paid use system of resources shall be established so as to reflect the most basic costs and values, and diminish the gap of "dual-track". In fact, price support shall be more reflected in the form of front-end support, and non-profit goals may be achieved through the backward shift (price subsidy) of the support link, thus fundamentally eliminating the existential place of "dual-track system".

From the perspective of appeal for correction of government behavior, land system reform is to fundamentally cut the pipeline by which the government can obtain the benefits through the monopoly operation of land resources. The key point here is to clarify the role and positioning of the government, and roles of government as land trader and direct operator shall be gradually weakened while the roles as service provider and supervisor shall be strengthened.

On the one hand, administrative mandatory transactions shall be reformed for voluntary marketization transactions: government shall no longer directly get involved in the transactions of land resources by virtue of compelling force; the negotiations and transactions shall be conducted between the current user of land and potential demander in accordance with the principles of "abidance by law, voluntariness and paid use"; and government, as the third party, shall only formulate the rules of transactions, supervise the transaction behavior, provide the transaction services, and maintain the favorable environment and order. On the other hand, separating the government system from the administration and operation system of state-owned land assets shall be taken into account, and functions of owners shall be implemented by the independent administration system (similar to the state-owned land assets supervision and administration commission) of state-owned land assets, which shall obtain the deserved resource transaction earnings as the owner of the resource, while government shall only receive the related tax revenue generated during the process of resource transaction. Government shall no longer directly administrate the state-owned land assets, while the operating system of state-owned land assets (similar to the operation company of state-owned land assets) shall achieve the authorized exclusive operation. Under such second best arrangement for the monopoly operation of resources, the role of government as the supervisor shall be strengthened, and monopoly pricing and excessive profit shall be prevented through the price supervision. Where necessary and feasible, establishment of several operation companies of state-owned land shall be considered and market pattern with proper competition shall be formed so as to avoid the extremely high monopoly price.

The pipeline by which the government can obtain the benefits through the monopoly operation of land resources shall be fundamentally cut off through the reform of the aforementioned transaction systems and the "dual-separation".

In the land system reform, a very important aspect is the reform in land expropriation system. According to the land system arrangement in the world, land expropriation system is a major mean for the government to solve the land use for the significant non-profit projects. In the aspect of land expropriation system, although specific national status is different, three basic principles are generally followed, namely, complying with public benefit or public use, ensuring just compensation and proper legal procedure.

In the next stage, criterion problems of collective land expropriation shall be further considered on the basis of the Ordinance for Housing Expropriation and Compensation on State-owned Land that has been introduced. Following three points shall be adhered to:

(1) Government shall not recover the land use rights (including changing the land use direction) of farmers at will, and shall strictly restrict the behavior of recovering land use right by using state power within the public benefit.[6] However, the non-profit change in land use direction and transfer of land use right does not need to be expropriated by the government and changed to be state-owned in principle, and shall be directly handled by the land transferor and transferee through independent decisions within the scope permitted by laws.

It should be noted that principle method and listing method shall be combined when the related laws define the public purposes, in order to prevent the generalization of land expropriation power and make the definition of public benefits become more explicit. That is: in addition to listing the general principles of land expropriation due to public purposes, specific scope of the public purposes shall be also listed. From an international point of view, specific scope of public interest generally involves in six aspects, namely: transportation construction, public building construction, military application, needs of public utility, land reform and other public facilities.

---

[6] In fact, government does not necessarily adopt the way of expropriation if the government needs to use the non-state-owned land even if for the needs of public benefits. In some countries, such as Australia, the government may also use the non-state-owned land through the ways of leasing (with the leasing period from 1 to 100 years) and agreement, etc. For the sequence and frequency of different ways in use, lease is the generally preferred way; land expropriation by force is only the last approach for the government to acquire the non-state-owned land and seldom used in reality (see Dou Hong 2006).

(2) It is also inappropriate for government to recover the land use right by force with non-economic means even if the government does need to recover such right, and the government shall recover the right by the way of purchase, namely, implementation of expropriation by purchase. In this process, current user of land shall be entitled to receiving reasonable economic compensation (the so-called reasonable economic compensation is that the economic interests or economic losses of current user of land shall not increase due to the land expropriation. The economic losses here include not only the direct losses due to the land expropriation behavior but also some indirect losses and opportunity costs, especially the expected loss in revenue), and compensation standard must be fairly determined by referring to the market value of land[7]; moreover, compensation fees shall be directly issued to the famer whose land is expropriated under the general circumstance for the land whose right has been verified.
(3) Government shall perfect the related procedures if the government needs to recover the land use right, and shall safeguard the full rights for knowledge, participation and decision-making of the current user of land by using announcement, consultation, complaint, arbitration and other mechanisms.

From an international point of view, some countries with relatively sound rule of law have the relatively perfect land expropriation procedures. For example, enabling the land holder who is affected by the land expropriation to directly participate in the whole process of land expropriation (including whether to expropriate the land, how to expropriate the land, how to compensate and how to implement, etc.), thus enhancing the right of speech of the opposite interest bodies in the compensation for land expropriation. Take another example, some countries and regions also establish the professional arbitration institution (such as the institutions in the neighboring region of East Asia, there is expropriation commission in Japan, the land expropriation committee in South Korea, appeal committee in Singapore, and land arbitration office in Hong Kong, etc.), which is independent from the approval authority of land expropriation in addition to the check-and-balance role and effective relief mechanism respectively played and provided by the independent judicial authority, in order to ensure the justice of complaint and arbitration mechanisms. The land holder whose land is expropriated may lodge a complaint to such institutions if there is objection in the land expropriation so as to obtain the corresponding ruling. Such international experience is worth learning.

---

[7] Currently, a viewpoint believes that a part of market value of land is brought by the infrastructure of government. Therefore, taking market value as the standard for compensation is unreasonable. In fact, it is also the belonging issue of land value-added revenue due to the external factors (including the economic and social development as well as the change in land use), namely, "the belonging of appreciation" to the public or the private. In this regard, at least two points shall be clarified: first, government may regulate the adjustment in value of land brought by the construction of infrastructure through the taxation instrument instead of directly participating in the allocation of appreciation earnings. Second, government shall follow the principle of "taking from the people, giving back to the people", if the government does need to use such earnings, mainly for the public purposes but not for satisfying its own interests.

## 9.4 Improving Public Governance and Making the Government Prioritize toward the Public Interest

An important issue involved in the proposition for further strengthening the public service function of government is how to ensure that the government truly represents the social public benefits and rationally gets involved, or how to avoid the alienation of public power. To address this problem, international theories and practice development show that perfection of governance structure of government is an important point of strength. The key point of reform in governance structure of government is to establish the bottom-up decision-making procedures in public matters so as to enable the government to understand the real needs of residents and make the positive response.

The first is to strengthen the characteristics of openness, transparency and public participation of the decision-making procedures. In the decision-making process of public service supply, effective demand and interest expression mechanism shall be formed on the basis of ensuring the related stakeholders to acquire full information through introducing formal and a series informal procedures (such as hearings, decision-making consultation and citizen survey, etc.) in order to reveal the true preference of the respective stakeholders. It should be noted that non-profit and autonomous social organizations at grass-roots level shall be actively developed for the purpose of better integrating the decentralized resident interests to reflect the true interest appeal as well as rights and interests on behalf of the residents.

The second is to fundamentally solve the conferring way of local government power. In order to guarantee that the public services provided by government are public in the direction and ensure that the government makes timely response to the public needs, the conferring way of power by the Party Committee and government at the higher level shall be gradually reformed so as to achieve that power is truly conferred by citizens, that is, administrative leaders shall be directly elected by the local residents. In relation to this, reform in the performance assessment mechanism of government shall also actively introduce the bottom-to-top performance evaluation mechanism with the participation of citizens in addition to perfect the up-bottom evaluation mechanism of government at higher level, so as to measure the satisfaction with the provision of public services,[8] thus forming the result-oriented accountability mechanism, thereby changing the stimulation and restriction conditions to the government officials at the grass-roots level, and making them transform from pursuing the maximum support by the government at higher level to the maximum support by the residents within the administrative region. It is believed that only the behavior of government produced by such democratic authorization can furthest comply with the interests of the clients (citizens) and enhance the satisfaction and

[8] From an international point of view, many countries introduced the measurement and evaluation mechanism to the satisfaction with public services to evaluate the quality of services by the public sectors in order to establish the government with the orientation of meeting the public needs, in emerging government re-construction movement.

social welfare level of residents through constantly perfecting the public services provided by government.

In the improvement of public governance, it is very important to implement the reform in the democratic fiscal administration system. Budget capital of government is from the people and shall be truly used for the people, since the public transfer their property rights to the government and designate the government to use the fiscal capital collected to provide the public services. Fiscal democratization shall be promoted so as to ensure that the handling of fiscal affairs are conducted in accordance with the democratic procedures, public needs of social members are fully reflected, opinions of citizens on the fiscal affairs are responded by the government, and fiscal behavior of government is supervised by the citizens. In a word, it is to construct the formulation and decision-making mechanism of public budget with the general participation of the citizens as well as the supervision mechanism to the budget implementation and results of decision-making.

For this reason, public participation shall be strengthened and fiscal decision-making shall be incorporated into the general process of public choice in the process of public budget, final account and financial management, so as to ensure that the stakeholders may participate in the decision-making to some extent, the government may better master the demand preference of public goods of the residents within the administrative region, and enable the decision-making take the interests of all the aspects into account as far as possible. Meanwhile, public and transparent management mechanism of budgeting and final accounting shall be implemented so as to enhance the transparency of public resource use, and comprehensively publish the financial balance, deficit position, assets and liabilities of government as well as the inter-government transfer payment to the public in a detailed and timely manner as far as possible. On this basis, introduction of result-oriented budgeting system (or target-based budgeting) shall be considered to improve the democratic supervision to the government budgeting and constraining force to the government behavior, conduct the performance evaluation to the implementation of fiscal budget through the social evaluation and supervision force composing of the public independent experts and non-governmental organizations, and accordingly establish the government accountability mechanism. It should be mentioned that the bottom-to-top fiscal supervision system based on the residents within the administrative region is more conducive to the supervision to the use of fiscal capital compared with the existing top-to-bottom administrative supervision system; it evaluates the direction and efficiency, thus ensuring that the fiscal expenditure can truly meet the needs of the public and achieve the expected goal of public budget, and ensuring to maximize the social interests with the minimum expenditure costs.

## 9.5 Exploring the Diversification of Public Service Providers

In fact, it is the limit problem of government responsibility. It is believed that emphasizing the basic responsibilities of government in the public service field does not mean to advocate returning to the situation that the government takes on all things, and it only stresses the payment responsibility of government in the basic public services. It is partly because China, as a developing country, faces the financial constraints of government; more importantly, China also needs to avoid the negative incentives and moral hazard issues brought by the excessive protection. Lessons of insufficient economic vitality and slow economic growth of some high-welfare countries are worth learning, and the hazards of Latin American populism are also the lessons drawn from the mistakes.

Another important issue related to the limit of government responsibility is the rational choice of supply model of public services. In this aspect, both theoretical development and practice has shown that private sectors relying on market mechanism and third sector (including community organization) relying on the voluntary mechanism are both supply force of public services that can be fully utilized. In other words, it shall not excessively emphasize the supply responsibility of government but shall stress more about the roles of competition, private participation and other marketization operation mechanism, and the government only needs to strengthen the corresponding regulatory responsibility.

1. Participation of Private Sectors

The first is the participation purely in the production perspective. In theory,[9] public production or private production depends on the nature of products or services. Private sectors have sufficient incentives to reduce the costs of production. Therefore, organizing the production through the market is more effective when it is relatively easy to supervise the quality of goods or services. However, producers in the private sectors may reduce the costs by sacrificing the quality in organizing the production through the market when it is very hard to supervise the quality of goods or services, when the government will be more efficient to produce such products or services here.[10] This means entry of private sectors to all the suitable field through service contract outsourcing or government procurement contracts (contracting out), service management contract (contracting in) and franchise contract shall be allowed in principle except for the fields which is relatively difficult to measure and enter into a contract, thus roles of private sectors in the service supply will be fully mobilized, and government shall strengthen the corresponding regulatory responsibility in the meantime.[11] This also means that some production and service links of the fields even invested by the government may be outsourced to private sectors through the auction and bidding systems of right of management, contracting, entrusted operation and other forms.

---

[9] For the related theoretical analysis, see Hart et al. (1997); Harding and Preker (2003).

[10] In addition, public institutions are generally more suitable to meet the needs with relatively high homogeneity, while non-government profit institutions have relative large advantages in suiting the needs of heterogeneity.

[11] In addition to contract supervision mechanism, it also needs to work with the price regulation and the regulation which ensures the effective and fair competition under necessary circumstances. In particular, for the incomplete information and information asymmetry, it is also necessary to strengthen the social regulation in some field and link, such as the regulation to quality of services.

The second is the participation in the investment perspective. For the non-profit and public fields which private capital is unwilling to enter, it may lever and attract the investment by private sectors through the policy design, such as government guarantee, tax reduction and exemption or material object support on the basis of weighing the investment risks and moral hazards. In particular, it may make the private participation meet some social goals through mechanism design which complies with the market rules and relies on the market force[12]; fiscal subsidy as well as the public auction and competition mechanism of subsidy based on the introduction of performance is very important in this aspect.[13]

2. Participation of Third Sector

Judging from international experience, third sectors in countries with relatively mature civil society, including industry autonomous organizations, social organizations with altruism characteristics (not-for-profit organization, NPOs, such as welfare agencies, volunteer organization and charitable organizations, etc.) and community organizations, play unique roles in the public service supply and promote the favorable fit between fairness and efficiency by relying on the characteristics of spontaneity, autonomy, innovativeness, flexibility and responsiveness (namely, make better response to the service needs). Moreover, governments of these countries mostly adopt the encouraging and supportive policies to the participation of third sector in the public services, and establish cooperative and interactive relationship through the contract outsourcing, government procurement, financial support and tax incentives, etc.

It should be noted that provision of public services at the rural grass-roots level shall pay attention to the self-supply and management models of rural community, or it may also said as the way of independent joint supply of consumers. Obviously, the community organization shall be the new autonomous community which reflects the social characters of citizens, but not the traditional community with non-separation of government administration and community management. In essence, such organization is the social coordination network established based on the trust and mutual benefit, as well as the independent and autonomous network management based on the cooperation of partnership. It mainly benefits from three factors that social supply mechanism can play the roles and facilitate the collective action. First, community members have the strong desire for consistent action for the public community affairs which relates to respective interests, and have internal driving force of the participation in supply for the public goods of relatively clear beneficial scope and nature of club. Second, community members are familiar with each other, fully

[12]Theories and practice show that private participation is conducive to promoting the general services on the whole, including expanding the coverage scope of service supply, reducing the service costs and price (in the mid and long-term) through innovating the supply technology, service models and enhancement in efficiency, changing the quality of services and improving the response ability of users to different needs, etc.

[13]Object of competition can be the minimum subsidy required for the provision of services; and the government supervises the specific service standards, or carries out the bidding for some service standards under the circumstance of fixed subsidies.

trust each other and communicate very well, which reduces the transaction costs of collective action; community reputation mechanism constitutes the powerful restriction to the inconsistency of individual behavior, all this making the rural community have good foundation for cooperation in the self-supply of public goods with the nature of club. Third, the financing way of self-apportionment becomes possible with the enhancement in income level of residents. Moreover, that farmers construct and maintain the materials and equipment required in the public goods may also save the capital input. Rural community members may employ all the social relations and mobilize the non-community members to participate in the raising of funds, which is similar to the voluntary donation of supply mechanism of the third sector under some circumstances. As a result, self-supply of public community services can be effectively conducted through equal consultations among the internal members within the interest community as well as some sponsors who have relatively strong organizational skills and certain authority prestige.

## References

Dou Hong (2006) Land use and administration in Australia. Chin Land 6:42–44
Harding A, Preker A (2003) Private participation in health services. The World Bank, Washington, DC
Hart O, Shleifer A, Vishny RW (1997) The proper scope of government: theory and an application to prisons. Q J Econ 112(4):1127–1161
Jin H, Qian Y, Weingast B (2005) Regional decentralization and fiscal incentives: federalism, Chinese style. J Public Econ 89(9–10):1719–1742
Montinola G, Qian Y, Weingast B (1995) Federalism, Chinese style: the political basis for economic success in China. World Polit 48(1):50–81
Oi J (1992) Fiscal reform and the economic foundations of local state corporatism in China. World Polit 45(1):99–126
Qian Y, Roland G (1998) Federalism and the soft budget constraint. Am Econ Rev 88(5):1143–1162
Qian Y, Weingast B (1997) Federalism as a commitment to preserving market incentives. J Econ Perspect 11(4):83–92
Zhou Li'an (2007) Studies on promotion championship of China's local officials. Econ Res J 7:36–50

# Chapter 10
# Playing the Decisive Role of the Market: Reform in Key Sectors

The Third Plenary Session of the 18th National Congress of the CPC made the strategic deployment for the comprehensive deepening of reform. Economic system reform is the key point of the comprehensive deepening of reform, the core issue is to well handle the relationship between the government and market, make the market play the decisive role in the resource allocation and better give play to the roles of government. In the aforementioned chapters, we fully stated how to correct the distortion of government behavior and make the government better play the roles. And in this chapter we will continue around how to give play to the decisive roles of market in the resource allocation. Meanwhile, reforms in several key fields will be discussed, thereby demonstrating the decisive roles of market.

## 10.1 Three Leaps of the Role of the Market

China's reform is the market-oriented reform at the very beginning. In the traditional planned economy, gradually introducing more and more market factors and making the market play more and more important roles can be said as the basic main line of China's economic reform. However, how well to give play to the roles of market has experienced the constant twists and turns as well as the ideological emancipation.

### *10.1.1 Market Regulation*

The understanding to roles of market had been gradually deepened from the convening of the Third Plenary Session of the 11th National Congress to 1992. The overall direction is to give play to the regulatory roles of market. The wording of socialist market economy had not emerged before the speech of Deng Xiaoping in the southern inspection tour.



X. Zhang, X. Chang, *The Logic of Economic Reform in China*, China Insights,
DOI 10.1007/978-3-662-47404-4_10

On December 18, 1978, the Third Plenary Session of the 11th National Congress of the CPC proposed to "work in accordance with the law of economy and pay attention to the roles of the law of value". Law of value plays the roles through market, attaching importance to the roles of the law of value is to pay attention to giving play to the role of market. Deng Xiaoping clearly proposed in his speech of *Current Situation and Tasks* in February 1980 that China's economic construction should implement the policy of "combination of planned regulation and market regulation". Report of the 12th National Congress of the CPC in September, 1982 proposed that "central issue of economic system reform was to adhere to the principle of planed economy orientation and market regulation assistance", and proposed to admit the roles of market regulation to a limited extent on the premise of sticking to the system of planned economy.

The Third Plenary Session of the 12th National Congress of the CPC convened in October 1984 proposed to "adhere to the planned reform direction of commodity economy, gradually realize the organic combination of planned economy and commodity economy as well as planned regulation and market regulation" and other new inferences. In October of the same year, report of the 13th National Congress of the CPC clearly proposed the new economic operation mechanism of "state regulating market and market guiding enterprises". Compared with the previous period, market roles are expanded in scope and content, from the limited and small scope to the mass and large scope, from the plan auxiliary to keeping pace with plan and showing the respective specialization. Since then, the understanding change of reform from the planned economy to the market orientation is achieved in the decision-making perspective.

### 10.1.2 Fundamental Role of Market

In early 1992, Deng Xiaoping pointed out in the speech of the southern inspection tour that: "Both planning and market forces are means of controlling economic activity." At the critical moment, Deng Xiaoping once again cleaned up some myth of major issues in theory. Market has been not only the regulatory measure for expansion of scope, but also the choice of path combined with the socialism in the value perspective. Giving play to the fundamental role of market in the resource allocation has become the essential requirement for the development of socialist market economy.

In October, 1992, the report of the 14th National Congress of the CPC formally proposed that China's goal of economic system reform was to establish the socialist market economy system and "enables the market to play the fundamental role in the resource allocation under the macro-control of socialist country". Fundamental role of market to the resource allocation is to allocate the resources to the links with better benefits through the functions of price lever and competition mechanism, and put pressure on and drive force to enterprises so as to achieve the survival of the fittest. In March, 1993, the First Plenary Session of the 18th National People's Congress adopted the *Amendments to Constitution of the People's Republic of China* and changed the "implementation of planned economy" to the "implementation of socialist market economy" in the preface. This is an historic step forward.

In September, 1997, the 15th National Congress of the CPC put forward to accelerate the marketization process of national economy, reform in the ownership and other basic institutional perspectives must be accelerated in order to "further give play to the fundamental role of market in the resource allocation", and clearly proposed that "the basic economic system in primary stage of socialism was the joint development of diverse forms of ownership with the public ownership as the dominant", "non-public ownership economy is an important integral part of socialist market economy" and other important inferences. On December 11, 2001, *Protocol on Accession of the People's Republic of China to WTO* entered into force, and Chinese government undertook to comply with international rules and open markets. The diversified market subject which adapt to the requirements of socialist market economy has formed so far, prices of most goods have been determined by market and the comprehensive multi-level opening up pattern has preliminarily taken shape. In November, 2002, the report of the 16th National Congress of the CPC formed announced that China's socialist market economy system had been preliminarily established.

In order to institutionally better give play to the fundamental role of market in the resource allocation, the report of the 17th National Congress of the CPC in October, 2007 proposed to deepen the understanding to the law of socialist market economy, promote the fair entry and break the institutional barriers; and develop the economy of mixed-ownership based on the modern property right system. In October, 2012, the 18th National Congress of the CPC proposed to accelerate the perfection of socialist market economy system, comprehensively deepening the economic system reform and "more greatly give play to the fundamental role of market in the resource allocation within the broader range".

Different from giving play to the regulatory role of market in the resource allocation, the process of giving play to the fundamental role of market in the resource allocation is the process of the establishment and perfection of socialist market economy system, and the process of transformation from the traditional single public ownership economy to the mutual containment and joint development of diversified ownership economy with the public ownership as the dominant. This process is reflected as the strategic restructuring of state-owned economy and stock reform of state-owned enterprises in a centralized manner, and gradually forms the national economy with the coordinated development of state-owned economy, private economy and foreign-funded economy, achieves the economic diversity with the diversified property rights as the core through the reform of ownership, and lay the general institutional foundation for giving play to the fundamental role of market in the resource allocation.

### 10.1.3 Decisive Role of Market

The *Decision* of Third Plenary Session of the 18th National People's Congress pointed out that: "both theory and practice had proved that allocating resources by market was the most efficient form. Market determining the resource allocation is the general law of market economy and market economy was the economy with market determining the resource allocation in nature. Improvement of socialist market economy system must comply with such law, spare no effort to solve the imperfection of market system, excessive government interference and lacking of regulation". This new positioning is another deepening and leap forward of understanding to the roles of market, and it is the landmark of theoretical innovation in the historical process of China's reform and opening up.

Giving play to the decisive role of market in the resource allocation must further perfect China's basic economic system. This is the basis of ownership. How to achieve the joint development of diversified ownership economy is not very clear although the report of the 15th National Congress of the CPC in 1997 established China's basic economic institutions in the primary stage of socialism, namely, the joint development of diversified ownership economy with the public ownership as the dominant. The *Decision* of the Third Plenary Session of the 18th National Congress of the CPC made the clear provision that: "the mixed-ownership economy with cross shareholding and mutual integration of state-owned capital, collective capital and non-public capital was the important realization form of the basic economic system". Mixed-ownership economy is the mutually containment and joint development of economic factors of different nature. Development of mixed-ownership economy is to enable the economic property rights of diversified ownership to obtain the equal protection, enable diversified production factors to freely flow among different ownership economy and enable the diversified ownership economy to carry out the fair and free competition through the institutional provisions so as to select the fittest and eliminate the inferior, and achieve the optimized allocation of resources.

Giving play to the decisive role of market in the resource allocation must further perfect the modern market system and promote the reform in the marketization of factor price. This is the basis of price mechanism and market system. Forming the price through market demand and supply as well as competition, guiding the direction of resource flow through the price fluctuations and achieving the optimized allocation is the basic requirements of the role of the law of value and it is also the centralized reflection of giving play to the decisive role of market. At present, the most important things for China are to accelerate the promotion of price reform in the resource products, further release the price of petroleum, natural gas, water, transportation, electricity, telecommunications and other fields; standardize the market price of land, enable the collective construction land and state-owned land to have the equal position in the property power, market entry, price formulation and revenue distribution, and gradually achieve the equal market entry as well as the equal rights and prices.

Currently, the core of economic system reform lies in the implementation of the strategy deployment made in the Third Plenary Session of the 18th National Congress concerning giving play to the decisive role of market in the resource allocation, continuing to promote the marketization reform, fully giving play to the leverage of reform in price, fiscal and financial fields, and releasing the bonus of reform, specifically including eliminating all the distortions of commodity market and factor market, breaking the monopoly by industry departments, loosening the government control, ensuring the fair and favorable competitive environment of microscopic subject, taking market incentives—especially price signals—as the guidance, clarifying the costs and benefits, actively and consciously promoting the transformation of economic structure and change in the development mode. Meanwhile, defining the boundary between government and market, delivering the issues that shall not be controlled by government or cannot be well controlled by government to market on the premise of fully respecting and giving play to the decisive role of market in the resource allocation. In particular, decisions of investment, saving, consumption, employment, research and development and other economic behavior shall be more made by enterprises, individuals and other market subject autonomously. Government shall better play the roles under the market failure, imperfect competition, existence of externality and other conditions, and behavior of market subject shall be standardized and regulated mainly through the establishment of judicial system and management system instead of the path of administrative orders.

## 10.2 Reform of the Administrative Approval System

The *Decision* of the Third Plenary Session of the 18th National Congress involved over 330 reforms, including nearly 120 reforms in the economic system and ecological civilization system. Due to the limited length of the article, it is impossible to specifically explain all the economic reforms, and it is only to interpret the reforms in several key fields. Administrative approval system is to be primarily discussed since only the reform of government can guide and drive the reforms in other fields.

Reform in the administrative approval system is the key point for the transformation of government functions, and also the prerequisite for market to play the decisive roles. On September 24, 2001, General Office of the State Council issued the *Notice on Establishment of Leading Group by State Council for Reform in Administrative Approval System*, and the reform in administrative approval system was comprehensively launched.

The State Council totally cancelled and adjusted 2,497 administration approval items in six batches from 2002 to 2012, accounting for 69.3 % of the original total items. The new government has vigorously promoted the reform in administrative approval system, cancelled and decentralized overall 600 administrative approval items since the establishment, and promoted the reform in commercial affairs system in 2014. The threshold for the entry of enterprises is lowered and the "inhibition" is loosened, thus greatly mobilizing the entrepreneurship and business promotion in the whole society. In the first three quarters of 2014, the number of newly registered market subjects was 9.2 million in China, the growth in number of new enterprises increased over 60 % compared with that in the previous year which appeared the growth spurt and drove over 10 million employments.

Reform in the administrative approval system has achieved certain success over the more than 10 years of reform practice and exploration, but there are also many problems: (1) Only a few high "gold-content" approval items have been cancelled or decentralized in some local government and departments; the problems of complicated or slow administrative approval procedures are still existing; opinions reflected by the mass on the approval established to the enterprises and a variety of professional qualification approval, project investment approval as well as verification are also very centralized. Some local government even specially set up the "model" and "show case" of reform to report to the authority at the higher level for the "nice appearance", but there are still a lot of difficulties for people to start a business. (2) The State Council decided to keep some non-administrative approval items after the implementation of the laws of administrative approval in 2004 in accordance with the needs for effective administration at that time. But some departments successively set up a batch of non-administrative approval items in the meantime that the State Council are cancelling and adjusting such items in succession, which is not conducive to stimulating the market vitality and enhancing the motive force for development. (3) Pre-approval problems. Pre-approval items are set before the business registration of enterprises, such as health permits, business certificate, safety production license and the others, involving education, culture, health and tourism as well as many other industries and fields, including the pre-approval items defined by the laws, administrative regulations and the State Council, and orders of approval and registration not clearly defined by the laws, administrative regulations and the State Council but are actually implemented in the real work. Some pre-approval items before the establishment registration of enterprises are large in quantity and have relatively high threshold, an enterprise needs to handle several approval items if it proposes to engage in various business activities, therefore, it is hard for the enterprises handle the establishment registration, and production and operating activities of such enterprises are also affected. (4) Supervision in the middle of and after the approval needs to be strengthened after the pre-approval items are cancelled. In the actual operation, pre-approval and subsequent supervision are out of line; some local market regulatory departments have the pre-approval and post-approval, cross department supervision and duplicate law enforcement, etc.; government departments still pay more attention to approval but less attention to supervision, and still take the approval as supervision. (5) Technical evaluation by intermediary institutions is an important link of administrative approval, but it has been one of the important factors which restrict the efficiency of approval. According to the statistics, Guangzhou "Long March Map" reveals the overall 779 day process of the enterprise investment project, including 214 days of approval as well as over 560 days of review and technical evaluation by the intermediary institutions. A few intermediary institutions have problems in qualification, service standards, service procedure, efficiency, monopolies and unreasonable fees, etc.

Direction of deepening reform in administrative approval in the next step has been clear, i.e. keeping a foothold at the convenience for investment and operation of enterprises, continuing to reduce the administrative approval items, the key point is to firmly clear and abolish the non-administrative approval items, and eliminate the "grey area"; lower the threshold for access; clear the commended projects by appraisal, professional qualification, qualification approval and affirmation items as well as public, transparent, strict and standardized setting and implementation of administrative approval items. (1) Enhancing the "gold-content" of streamline administration and institute decentralization. It is to continuously reduce the approval scope of investment projects, further revise the Catalogue of Investment Projects Approved by the Government; cancel the approval to the economic action which can be effectively regulated by the market mechanism, and try to cancel the functions that can be cancelled instead of decentralizing such functions as early as possible. The ultimate goal of streamline administration and institute decentralization is to stimulate the market vitality and corporate innovation power, decentralize the administrative approval items to the local government at the provincial level or below. It is still the adjustment of authority within the administrative system. The effectiveness of streamline administration and institute decentralization will be greatly reduced if the local government reform fails to follow up in a timely manner, carry on and administrate the authority decentralized by the central government. (2) Clearing the existing non-administrative approval items. It is to forbid the setting of administrative approval in the disguised forms of filing, register, registration, annual inspection, supervision and manufacture, affirmation, authentication, validation, designation, numbering and changing certificates as well as in the name of non-administrative approval, and prevent it from transforming to internal approval by violating the regulations. In the meantime, it is to prohibit recovering and centralizing the administrative approval items which have been cancelled and decentralized in the name of strengthening the supervision in the middle of and after the approval. (3) Reforming the business registration system. It is to promote the convenience in the business registration system, vigorously reduce the pre-approval or changing from pre-approval items to post-approval, and implement the "license before certificate"; encourage to explore the "three-in-one" registration system of business license, organization code certificate and tax registration; cancel some professional qualification and affirmation items, strengthen the supervision in the middle of and after the approval, innovate the regulatory ways and enhance the regulatory capacity. (4) Clearing the intermediary services in the pre-approval of administrative approval. Local government and departments shall comprehensive clear the technical examination, evaluation, authentication, consultation and other paid intermediary service items in the pre-approval of administrative approval, and cancel the items that can be canceled as early as possible; standardize the time limit and charges of items that needs retaining, and publicize to the public; it is prohibited to charge in disguised form or set up charging items illegally by making use of implementing administrative approval; it is prohibited to change the administrative approval items to the intermediary service items to conduct the disguised approval as well as paid services. (5) Promoting standardization of administrative approval. It is to simplify the procedures of administrative approval items which are retained, and provide the time limit for the completion of handling so as to achieve the equality, fairness and openness. Local government shall establish and improve the government affairs center and online affair handling platform to centralize the handling of administrative approval, implement the one window of one department to the public and "one-stop" service of a level of local government. (6) Standardizing the positive list of authority. It is to sort out the administrative authority of government and departments at all levels, scientifically define the scope and classification of administrative approval as well as other administrative behavior, administrative law enforcement, public administration, guidance services and other administrative authority, standardize the administrative discretionary power, publicize and optimize the operational procedures of authority, and promote the authority list institution of local government and departments on the basis of improving the authority list institution of administrative approval (Ren Jin 2014).

Basic ideas of reform in administrative approval system can be further summarized as the "three lists": first, "list of authority", defining what the government should do so as to achieve that "nothing can be done without authorization by laws"; second, "negative list", defining what enterprises should not do so as to achieve that "anything can be done if it is not prohibited by laws"; and third, "list of responsibilities", defining how the government to conduct the regulation after the cancellation of administrative approval items so as to achieve that "legal responsibilities must be assumed". It is to restrain the improper intervention by the government to microeconomic activities, decentralize the authority to the market and society and stimulate the creativity of all kinds of subjects through the aforementioned "three lists"; optimize the micro-regulatory functions of government and achieve the effective micro-governance in the meantime of reducing the approval.

The core of reform in administrative approval system is the streamline administration and institute decentralization. The streamline administration and institute decentralization has three roles: the first role is to reduce the government intervention, stimulate and release the market vitality. The second role is to reduce the intervention and public power, namely, reducing the opportunity of rent-seeking and corruption in the meantime. The third role is to reduce the administrative expenses. Administrative expenses will be reduced due to the reduction in the number of related public employees after the cancellation and merger of institutions. Certainly, the most important role of reform in administrative approval system is to clear the space for the decisive role of market in the allocation of resources.

## 10.3 Reform of the Mixed-Ownership System and State-owned Enterprises

Concept of mixed-ownership economy was proposed in the Decision of the Third Plenary Session of the 14th National Congress of the CPC over 20 years ago. Mixed-ownership economy has rapidly developed over the years. By the end of 2011, the number of total central enterprises and incorporated enterprises was respectively 20,624 and 14, 912, the restructured coverage is 72.3 %, increasing over 40 % compared with the 30.4 % in 2002. Central enterprises actively introduced the private capital and foreign capital, promoted the diversified investment source and ownership, and vigorously developed the mixed-ownership economy in the restructuring. For example, the average state-owned equity in the 34 second-level and third-level enterprises under CNOOC is 40–65 %, and most such enterprises are basically enterprises of mixed-ownership. From the perspective of public listed companies, by the end of 2011, the number of public listed companies held by central enterprises was 368 in total, including 260 purely domestic listed companies and 78 purely foreign listed companies as well as 30 companies which are both listing at home and abroad. Over 40 central enterprises achieved the overall listing of the primary business among the public listed companies, and the central enterprises engaging in petroleum and petrochemical, aviation, shipping, telecommunications, metallurgy, construction and other industries basically achieved the overall listing of the primary business. With the constant development of mixed-ownership enterprises, the dominant position of public ownership has been gradually consolidated. About 915.75 billion was raised from the capital market at home and abroad through the restructuring of central public listed enterprises from 2007 to the third quarter of 2012. For the perspective of overall development of the state-owned enterprises, operating income of state-owned and state-held enterprises (excluding financial enterprises) increased from 10.73 trillion to 39.25 trillion with the annual increase of 17.6 % from 2003 to 2011; total assets and owner's equity were 85.37 trillion and 29.17 trillion, respectively 4.3 times and 3.5 times compared with those in 2003. This reflects the superiority of mixed-ownership as an important realization form of the basic economic system (Huang Qunhui 2013).

In China, both ownership reform and reform in the state-owned enterprises are the very important directional reforms. Mixed-ownership economy with the cross shareholding and mutual integration of state-owned capital, collective capital and non-public capital is the important realization form of the basic economic system, and it is conducive to the function enlargement, maintenance and appreciation, and competitiveness enhancement of state-owned capital as well as to making the best of capital of various ownership, the mutual promotion and joint development. The Third Plenary Session of the 18th National Congress proposed to promote the mixed-ownership and state-owned enterprise reforms. It is not to carry out the "privatization", "denationalization" or "elimination of state-owned enterprises", but a good opportunity for state-owned enterprises to promote the national industrial upgrading, optimize the industrial structure and enhance the control in the key fields as well as the reversed transmission mechanism for the state-owned enterprises to establish and improve the good modern management system and become the health market subjects.

The new round of state-owned enterprise reform adheres to the direction of mixed-ownership, and will be conducive to: optimizing the layout of state-owned economy, further give play to the driving form of state-owned capital; improving the corporate governance structure and achieving the separation of government functions from enterprise management; benign interaction of public and non-public economy, and enhancing the national competitiveness. Future mixed-ownership and state-owned enterprise reforms shall focus on the following six aspects:

First, promoting the corporate shareholding reform of state-owned enterprises, especially promoting the mixed-ownership reform of large enterprises, including central enterprises. Currently, most of the over 50 super large central enterprises are still implementing the general manager responsibility system and have not carried out the transformation to the corporation system; strategic investors have not been introduced and the enterprises are still solely owned by the state even such enterprises have implemented the corporation system. Among the over 110 central enterprises supervised by the SASAC, only China Unicom, Shanghai Bell, China Southern Power Grid, the State Nuclear Power Technology Corporation, Commercial Aircraft Corporation of China and a few other enterprises (shareholders are mostly state-owned institutions, local government and social security fund but not private capital) have achieved the diversified equity at the parent company level, the rest enterprises are basically solely owned by the state. Therefore, overall listing of qualified large state-owned enterprises shall be promoted; and unqualified large state-owned enterprises shall accelerate the diversified reform of equity, non-state-owned capital shall be encouraged to participated in the investment in the central enterprises in the financial, petroleum, electricity, railway, telecommunications, resource development, public utilities and other field, and mixed-ownership reform shall be promoted; for the large state-owned enterprises which need to keep the sole ownership by the state, corporation reform shall be accelerated and corporate governance structure shall be improved.

Second, striving to eliminate the policy barriers which restrain the non-public enterprises to participate in the state-owned enterprise reform, ensuring the openness and fairness, and enhancing the participation enthusiasm of non-state-owned economy in the reform. Encouraging non-public enterprises to participate in the state-owned enterprise reform needs to start from the basic requirement of being conducive to the corporate competitiveness and overall economic efficiency, eliminate existing policy barriers which restrain the non-public enterprises to participate in the state-owned enterprise reform, create the conditions for deepening the reform and form the powerful driving force for the deepening of reform. At present, participation of non-public enterprises in the state-owned enterprise reform also faces many policy and market barriers. The first is that government has not provide the timetable for loosening the fields which private capital shows relatively high willingness of entry, including energy, transportation, medical care, education and telecommunications, etc., and also has not provided the “negative list” of fields that can be entered if there is not prohibition. It is hard and costly for private capital to enter such fields through the participation in the mixed-ownership reform. The second is that private enterprises are facing “glass door”, “spring door”, “revolving door” and a variety of other hidden barriers. State-owned enterprises have “policy bonus” in the project approval, land, taxation and household settlement. The third is that state-owned enterprises with monopoly power and good financial performance are lack of driving force for the introduction of private capital; government and internal management group of enterprise are lack of enthusiasm in promoting the mixed-ownership reform. The fourth is that some local government formulates the "special provisions" for the business scope and geographical layout of mixed-ownership enterprises in the introduction of non-public enterprises, which affects the commercialization degree and independence of the mixed-ownership enterprises, results in the actual dissymmetry of equity and control of non-public capital as well as the hidden danger of subsequent power struggle among shareholding companies. The fifth is that identity transformation and settlement barriers are the worries for the participation of non-public enterprises in the state-owned enterprise reform.

Third, trying and exploring the introduction of employee shareholding system in the promotion of mixed-ownership reform. Introduction of employee shareholding system by state-owned enterprises in the promotion of mixed-ownership is conducive to both the mixed-ownership reform and perfection of corporation governance of state-owned enterprises, and the establishment of long-term employee incentive mechanism so as to make the employees and enterprise to form the interest community. The key point for the employee shareholding system to effectively play the dual effect for enhancing the economic incentive and improving the social governance depends on the design of specific program. Improper program design will not give play to the role of incentive and will also result in the loss of state-owned assets, rent-seeking and interest transfer. Successfully promoting the introduction of employee shareholding system in the mixed-ownership reform shall adhere to three principles, including incentive compatibility, incremental share and long-term orientation.

Fourth, accelerating the opening of competitive market and creating the conditions for the promotion of mixed-ownership by state-owned monopolies. State-owned enterprises reform in the monopoly industries shall be based on the functional positioning of enterprise with broadened access, diversified investment, effective competition, rational allocation and independent supervision as the key directions so as to enhance the market opening and competition, create the conditions for state-owned enterprises to promote the mixed-ownership through the gradually opened competitive market, and achieve the synchronous enhancement in competition efficiency and scale economy.

The first is to solve the closed operation of business activities and bidding system of state-owned enterprises in the monopoly industries which are insufficiently open to the public. It is to promote the opening of bidding in the telecommunications, electricity, oil and gas, public utilities and other fields to the public, and encourage private enterprises to apply for the qualifications in survey and design, construction, supervision, consultation, information network system integration, network construction and project bidding agencies, etc.

The second is to strengthen and improve the supervision to monopoly business, and prevent the related enterprises from crowding out the competitors by relying on the network facilities. For the monopoly business which requires physical and operational integrality in technological economy according to the industry characteristics, the monopoly operation can be authorized to one or a few state-owned enterprises, non-state-owned capital can enter in the form of equity investment, but it shall prevent the related enterprises from crowding out competitors by relying on the network facilities and abusing the dominant position in the market. With the maturity of socialist market economy system and growth of private economy, dependence on state-owned economy in the aforementioned field shall be gradually reduced so as to achieve the transformation from the single-large shareholder to the social enterprises with diversified equity. For the import and export of resource products and services, market access shall be broadened and more operators shall be permitted so as to form certain competitive pressure on the domestic monopoly enterprises.

The third is to construct the competitive market structure and better give play to the role of competitive mechanism. In the upstream field of oil and gas industry, the focus is to solve the excessively centralized exploration and mining rights of oil and gas as well as the problem of the single-large shareholder, and introduce a group of qualified and capable enterprises engaging in the shale gas, shale oil, coal bed methane, tight gas and other unconventional development of oil and gas resources; in the downstream field, the focus is to strengthen the refining business of qualified enterprises, change the crude oil and refined oil import control, increase the entities engaging in the import business of crude oil and refined oil, cancel the "hidden policy" that crude oil imported by non-state-owned business must be delivered to the two major oil company for the processing, broaden the free domestic trading of imported crude oil and allow the non-state-owned enterprises to organize the import based on the market needs. Telecommunications industry shall perfect the related provisions on code number resource and management of market competitive behavior, safeguard the rights and interests of consumers, and make more detailed provisions on the exit mechanism of enterprises, individual privacy protection, service quality guarantee and other aspects. Electricity industry shall focus on solving the insufficient competition in the electricity generation side as well as the excessive monopoly over the electricity purchase and sales, give the electricity generation plant and users the respective rights to choose and bargain in the sales and purchase of electricity, broaden the limit for electricity generation enterprise to directly sell electricity, allow the all the distributed electricity generation for self-use or directly sales of electricity to terminal users, allow all the industrial enterprises above the designated size as well as large and middle-sized electricity users in other industries to directly and independently choose the electricity supply, greatly increase the number of direct electricity purchase users, and change the pattern of exclusive electricity purchase of power grid enterprises, solve the not transparent powers in the dispatch and trading as well as grid access approval of electricity generation plant and users, unfair settlement of electricity charges and difficult grid access approval.

Fifth, perfecting the administration system of state-owned assets by centering on the administration of capital. The first is to establish the administration system of state-owned assets with the full coverage. Currently, there is no institution which is defined and established to represent the state to fulfill the duties of contributors for the state-owned financial assets, natural resource assets and non-operating assets, so it needs to establish and improve the administration system for the state-owned assets except the state-owned assets of industrial and commercial enterprises.

Integration of government administration with enterprise management as well as government with capital still exists even in the field of non-financial operating assets. For example, over 80 departments at the central government level conduct the direct management to the thousands of subordinate enterprises instead of incorporating them to the centralized and unified supervision system of state-owned assets. Such situation must be changed. The second is to improve the administration system of state-owned assets. Regulation of state-owned assets shall be strengthened by centering on the administration of capital, reform the authorization and operation system of state-owned capital, organize several operation companies of state-owned capital, and transform some state-owned enterprises to the investment companies of state-owned capital. In this regard, successful cases of similar foreign companies (such as Temasek in Singapore) can be learnt and used for reference. The last is to perfect the operational budgeting system of state-owned capital. Proportion of earnings from state-owned capital turned into the public finance shall be further increased to 30 % in 2020; and such earnings shall be more used for the protection and improvement of people's livelihood, especially for enriching the social security fund so as to alleviate the debts of social security fund instead of keeping such earnings in the state-owned enterprises for the use of their capital expenditures and cost expenditures.

Sixth, strategically adjusting the layout and structure of state-owned capital. Currently, state-owned enterprises are still too large in quantity and the transformation progress of state-owned central industrial and commercial enterprises is not ideal. SASAC has envisaged adjusting and restructuring the 196 enterprises established in 2003 whose duty of contributors is fulfilled by SASAC to 80–100 enterprises in 2010. However, there were still 116 state-owned central industrial and commercial enterprises by the end of 2012. In the meantime, the layout of state-owned economy is not rational and the distributional fields are still too broad. At present, state-owned economy respectively involves in 94 types and 380 industries among the 95 major types of national economy and 396 national economic industries. Such a broad distribution, especially the pattern of large distribution in the downstream competitive fields, is not conducive to better give play to the roles of state-owned capital in achieving the national strategic goals and maximizing the social interests. Therefore, functional positioning of state-owned capital shall be further defined so as to promote the state-owned capital to more invest in the important industries and key fields related to national security and national economic lifeline, focus on the provision of public services, development of important forward-looking strategic industries, protection of ecological environment, support of scientific and technological progress as well as safeguarding of national security, and exit from the general competitive industries as soon as possible.

Certainly, reform in mixed-ownership economy needs to comply with the market rules, adjust the measures based on the local conditions and combine with the respective conditions of state-owned enterprises, and the mixture of mixed-ownership economy shall be determined by the enterprises. State-owned enterprises shall grasp the opportunities for the development of mixed-ownership economy, get rid of the malpractice of substituting enterprise management by government administration, achieve the independent operation, realize the "separation of government administration and enterprise management", and enhance the efficiency and competitiveness.

## 10.4 Reform of Fiscal and Taxation System

On the basis of the reform of tax distribution system in 1994, the fiscal and taxation system is gradually improved and developed to the system as it is today. Over the years, fiscal revenue has greatly increased and control capability of government has significantly enhanced. However, with the development and changes in the situation, the existing fiscal and taxation system has become increasingly inadaptable and incomplete. Which reflects in: (1) irrational distribution between the central and local government and asymmetry of administrative authority and fiscal power. Central government shares a large proportion of taxation while the local finance is relatively tight, the main cause for the land finance. (2) Ineffective budget enforcement. Currently, there are approximately 1/3 government departments disclose the bills of "three public expenditures", but the disclosed budget is too brief to be understood. The expenditure structure focuses too much on the economic construction but less on medical care, education, social security and other social expenditures, which deviates from service-oriented government. (3) Land finance. Proportion of land revenue in the local fiscal revenue is abnormally high, which is also the mean for local financing platform to get the bank leverage. Land finance directly leads local government to be kidnapped by the real estate and banks are also involved, forming the huge potential systematic risks. (4) Irrational taxation structure. Under the pressure of sales tax and value-added tax, the individual marginal tax rate is high. It suppresses the profitability of enterprises on the one hand, and is not conducive to the expansion of personal consumption on the other hand. Therefore, reform must be conducted.

Deepening reform of fiscal and taxation system aims at establishing the sustainable modern fiscal and taxation system, which is unified, complete, legal, standardized, public, transparent and high-efficient, and conducive to optimizing the resource allocation, safeguarding the unity of market, promoting the social justice and achieving the stability of the state. It focuses on promoting the reform in the following three aspects:

The first is to promote the budget openness and standardize the fiscal expenditures. Government budget revenue is from the public, so the public has the right to supervise the expenditure. China's financial fund is observed with non-standard usage, inefficiency and precipitation, in addition, borrowing behaviors of some local governments lack restriction for a long time, which is inseparable from low transparency of budget and weak supervision and inspection. Budget system reform is to strengthen the full-covered budget management, improve the transparency of budget, innovate in the budget preparation technology and strengthen the supervision by National People's Congress. (1) The budget openness shall be further strengthened and the scope shall be expanded. Budget and final accounts of governments at all levels shall be open to the society, and all the "three public expenditures" of financial allocation shall be even more open. Except for the pubic budget, budgets for governmental funds, state-owned capital operation and social security funds shall be open to the society. Fiscal transfer payments at all levels shall be gradually open and transparent. (2) The opened contents shall be detailed. Departmental budget for basic expenditures and project expenditures shall be opened as soon as possible. The system of revenue and expenditure budgetary accounting items of government shall be improved and open items shall be specified, so as to make the accounting items clear enough to be understood by ordinary people and supervised by the society. (3) Supervision and inspection of budget openness shall be strengthened, and accountability mechanism of budget openness shall be established. It is to make the budget preparation and implementation more transparent, and make the use of fiscal capital more efficient by increasing the transparency and strengthening the supervision and restraint, so as to reduce the opportunities for rent-seeking and corruption.

The second is to promote the taxation reform to improve the government revenue system. It is to deepen the taxation reform, optimize the taxation structure, perfect the taxation functions, stabilize the macro tax burden, manage the tax in accordance with the law, establish the taxation system which is conducive to the scientific development, social equity and market unity, and give full play to the functional role of taxation in raising fiscal revenue, adjusting allocation and promoting structure optimization. Government revenue system shall adapt to the realistic trend of obtaining the revenue from individuals and families instead of from enterprises. The specific practice includes: taxation structure shall gradually transform from the orientation of indirect tax to direct tax; "transformation from sales tax to value-added tax" shall be steadily promoted on the basis of reconstruction of value-added tax system; consumption and social development will be respectively promoted with the decrease and increase in consumption tax; some taxation systems for the special purposes shall be combined or cancelled; reform of individual income tax shall be implemented for enhancing the national competitiveness; reform of real estate tax must take prudent measures; reform of administrative charges and governmental fund system shall be accelerated; legislation for government revenue shall be strengthened.

The third is to divide the administrative authority and expenditure responsibility, and adjust the fiscal relationship between the central and local government. Division of administrative authority and expenditure responsibility between central and local government and between governments at all levels has been unclear, unreasonable and nonstandard for a long time. In general, the central government departments failed to manage many affairs. Central government surely needs to strengthen the administrative authority and expenditure responsibility. With the purpose of ensuring the central and local government to find their proper positions, take their own responsibilities and coordinate and cooperate with each other, so as to promote the maximization of the overall efficiency of government governance, reform shall be implemented, relative systems of administrative authority and expenditure responsibility shall be improved, stable financial pattern of the central and local government shall be kept, and revenue division of the central and local government shall be specified. To build a more stable fiscal relationship between the central and local government, in accordance with the requirement for mobilizing the enthusiasm of the central and local government, with keeping the reform orientation for fiscal administration of system of tax distribution. The practices include clearly dividing the administrative authority and fiscal expenditure responsibility of governments at all levels, speeding up the technical breakthrough, further improving the tax distribution system and establishing the fiscal revenue division system with the combination of distribution of tax, rent and interest, further improving the policy goal system for equalization of public services, reconstructing the fiscal transfer payment system, further improving the management system of local debts and enhancing the hard budget constraints for local government finance.

The debt management system of local government which has drawn public attentions will be analyzed emphatically. The basic idea can be summarized as "blocking the illegal channels and building the open channels", i.e. closing the channels for local government borrowing through enterprises and public institutions, especially giving the local government certain authority for debt financing while stripping the government financing functions of financing platform companies, so as to form the debt financing mechanism of local government with the government bonds as the subject. For the general debt financing by government for the development of public undertakings without revenue, local government shall finance by issuing general bonds and repay by the general public budget revenue. For the special debt financing by government for the development of public undertakings with certain revenue, local government shall finance through issuing the special bonds and repay with the corresponding governmental fund or special revenue. Furthermore, the investment and financing model of public-private partnership (PPP) shall be used to strengthen the cooperation between the government public investment and private investment. Participating through franchising in the investment and operation of public undertakings with certain revenue, such as urban infrastructure, is especially encouraged. Agreed revenue rules, such as franchise, reasonable pricing and fiscal subsidies, disclosed in advance by government can ensure the stable long-term revenue of investors. Investors contribute according to the marketization principles, to establish the cooperation projects independently or jointly with the government for construction and operation of companies for special purposes, in accordance with the agreed rules. Investors or companies for special purposes can borrow and assume the repayment responsibility through the bank loans, corporate bonds, project revenue bonds, asset securitization. Government undertakes responsibilities related to the franchise, reasonable pricing, fiscal subsidies, in accordance with the agreed rules, but is not responsible for repayment which should be taken by the investors or companies for special purposes. As a consequence, the responsibilities of government and enterprises are defined. Government and enterprises will repay the respective borrowings and take the respective risks. In order to further harden the budget constraints and prevent the moral hazards, the following steps shall be taken: (1) incorporating the local government debts into the overall budget management, and incorporating the governmental debt as a fixed target into the government performance examination; (2) establishing the comprehensive financial reporting system of government for the accrual basis and disclosure system of local governmental debts, and establishing the credit rating system of local government; (3) central government will not help the local government for repayment of debts, the local government shall repay the debts of borrowing by its own. In short, it is to gradually enhance the transparency of debt risks of local government by promoting the financing system of local government, effectively supervise the borrowing of local government in the way of marketization, thus enhancing the liability constraints of local finance, putting an end to the fiscal opportunism and preventing the impulse borrowing.

## 10.5 Reform of Financial System

China is a country with high saving rate. Total saving rate of domestic sectors has been close to or over 50 % for years. However, due to the low efficiency, the financial system of China cannot functions properly as the financial intermediaries and fails to fully transform the saving into the domestic investment, thus resulting in the constant existence of gap between saving and investment. In recent years, China has given the domestic savings to foreign countries. For example, China purchases US treasury bonds, which is a safe investment way with low yields. And it indicates that American financial institutions fully play the intermediary roles to transform China's domestic saving to investment. A scholar has ever vividly described this phenomenon by "parking theory". He believes that some excess savings are forced to be "parked" in a foreign country due to the ineffective capital allocation of the financial system of China. People will transfer the investment abroad to home only when the efficiency of domestic capital allocation is improved to a certain level (Corden 2007). In order to smoothly transform the domestic saving to domestic investment and accelerate the development of domestic financial market, reform of the financial system shall be further deepened in accordance with the directions of the following "five points" in the future.

1. Marketization of interest rate

As an importance price in the factor market, interest rate is the decisive factor for the effective allocation of capital. In order to construct the formation mechanism of interest rate determined by market demand and supply, contents of the reform shall involve the following three aspects:

The first is to promote and achieve the marketization of deposit interest rate. For this purpose, the upward floating range of deposit interest rate shall be further widened, the scale of interbank large certificates of deposits shall be expanded, the marketization pricing scope of debt products of financial institutions shall be gradually expanded and finally relaxing the upper control of deposit interest rate so as to achieve the free floating. As the supporting measures for the marketization of deposit interest rate, the deposit insurance system shall be established as soon as possible to cover all the financial institutions of deposit, and the mechanism of limited compensation and differential rate based on risks shall be implemented so as to strengthen the market constraints and prevent the moral hazards. In addition, the exit mechanism for the marketization of financial institutions shall be improved to strengthen the protection of depositors and prevent the bank run by clarifying the exit rules for financial institutions in the failure of operation, including risk compensation and sharing mechanism.

The second is to prefect the market interest rate system, and improve the macro-control mechanism of marketization interest rate. The measures shall include: improving the self-discipline mechanism for pricing of market interest rate and promoting the formation of benchmark interest rate of borrowing so as to enhance the self-pricing capabilities of financial institutions and provide the reference for the pricing of credit products; further giving play to the roles of Shanghai Interbank Offered Rate (shibor) and cultivating the target interest rate of the central bank's monetary policy; accelerating the cultivation of treasury bond market, enhancing the depth and liquidity of market, and promoting the risk-free yield curve constituted by the rate of return of treasury bonds with different time limit to be the benchmark for the asset pricing of middle and long-term financial products.

The last is to correct the dual structure of interest rate. The "dual structure" includes not only the difference between the interest rates of traditional banks and shadow banks but also the difference between the financing costs of large state-owned enterprises and the medium, small and micro-sized non-state-owned enterprises.

Shadow banks is actually the product of innovative alienation under financial repression, which reflects the existence of regulatory arbitrage, that is, the financial institutions try to avoid the administrative financial regulation, including credit rationing and restrictions on credit growth (loan restrictions on the financing platform of local government and real estate industry), capital constraints, liquidity constraints of loan-to-deposit ratio, and pursue the arbitrage opportunity created by the control of deposit interest rate. In order to effectively respond to the unlimited sprawl of shadow banking business with regulatory arbitrage as the main purpose, it shall further loosen the control of the formal banking industry, especially loosen the control of credit rationing and direction of loans to the banking system (by the management of a variety of regulatory indicators, and control the credits by marketing tools); promote the marketization of deposit interest rate in the meantime. And then, promote the transfer of off-balance sheet assets to balance sheet assets so as to achieve the convergence of capital cost inside and outside the system.

Differential pricing of interest rates among enterprises mainly reflects the distorted impacts of hidden guarantee on the interest rates. Under the current system environment, large enterprises, especially large state-owned enterprises, are often regarded as the high quality customer resource by banks due to the existence of government credit endorsement. Such enterprises can obtain the low-cost capital (according to the statistics, about 65 % bank credit pricing are higher than the benchmark interest rate, about 25 % loan interest rate are the benchmark rate, and only about 10 % loan interest rate are lower than the benchmark interest rate. The scope of customers which enjoy the lowest interest rate is very limited, mainly the large state-owned enterprises), and lend such capital for higher earnings through the entrusted loans, credit loans and other channels. Part of the credit capital does not flow to the real economy in the process that large enterprises act as the "financial profiteers", but "idle" within the financial system. Meanwhile, in order to ensure the overall revenue, banking sector tends to raise the interest rate of loans for medium-sized and small enterprises to achieve cross subsidy under the downward floating of interest rate of loans for large enterprises. Consequently, financing will be more difficult for medium-and small-sized enterprises which need large amount of capital, and such enterprises will bear the higher costs of interest rates. In such a condition, in order to reduce interest rate spreads brought by the dual system of interest rates, reform shall be implemented to make banks and state-owned enterprises the market subjects constrained by disciplines to ensure the equal participation of all the enterprises in the competition and enable the level of interest rate to truly reflect the market demand and supply by explicating market risks.

2. Commercialization of bank

State-owned commercial banks in China have made certain progress in commercialization reform in recent years, especially after the shareholding reform and public listing. In general, the basic property right pattern of state-owned commercial banks does not change too much, and the state-owned banks still undertake certain quasi-fiscal responsibilities. Basic market pattern led by large commercial banks has not materially changed since entering the new century although there are certain changes in the market shares of asset size of banking financial institutions. Under the aforementioned structure of property right and market, the moral hazards formed by "non-bankruptcy of state-owned banks" and "non-bankruptcy of large banks" show that China's banking system needs more thoroughly commercialization transformation so as to truly change the operational mechanism and operating mode, and promote the allocation of financial resources to change from administration-oriented to the market-oriented.

Changing the financial system with the orientation of large state-owned banks shall be based on a set of fair, open and transparent market rules, adopt the access model of "negative list", constantly loosen the market access for the private capital entering the field of financial services, allow the qualified private capital to establish small and medium-sized banks and other financial institutions by laws, allow such capital to participate in the restructuring, increase in capital and shares of state-owned financial institutions, promote the diversified equity of financial institutions and expand the competition in the banking industry. In particular, the way of "blocking" shall not be taken to the internet finance largely emerged in recent years and unnecessary administrative control shall be relaxed so as to make the internet finance provide better financial services to the real economy, especially the small and medium-sized enterprises under the free market environment.

3. Direct financing

From the perspective of financial structure, China has maintained the pattern with the orientation of indirect financing, which brings the mismatching of capital structure. In order to disperse the risks caused by the over-reliance on debt financing, China's change in financial structure from debt financing to the equity financing shall be promoted, and the social financing structure shall be optimized. It needs to actively develop the direct financing, establish the multi-level capital market system, create the mechanism which is conducive to the formation of equity capital and increase the weight of equity investment through multiple channels.

Currently speaking, there are relatively obvious administrative factors in the capital market which is taken as the platform for direct financing. There is also intervention by administrative power in the industry access, security issuance, business development and other aspects. In the meantime, the market operation is vulnerable to the administrative regulation. Vigorous development of capital market shall further simplify the approval procedure, reduce the administrative controlling factors, depend more on the adjusting role of market mechanism in the issuance, pricing, transaction and other segments, and fully mobilize the enthusiasm of all the market participants. In particular, it shall promote the reform in the share issuance registration system. With the core of information disclosure, to reduce the material review and value judgment by the regulatory departments of securities to the qualifications of issuers in the process of share issuance, to weaken the administrative approval, to enhance the elasticity and flexibility of issuance system, to decrease the costs of share issuance and to improve the financing efficiency. In addition, to strengthen regulation in and after the process, and to strengthen the market and integrity constraints to the public listed companies, intermediary institutions and other market participants.

In order to promote the equity financing through multiple channels, it shall also accelerate the development of the curb market on the basis of continuously perfecting the mainboard, SME board and GEM, including National Equities Exchange and Quotations (the "new third board market") and various regional equity exchange markets (called as "the fourth board market"). Meanwhile, it is to attract more private equity investment funds, venture capital funds and equity financing for the support to innovative and growing enterprises. In addition, it shall encourage the financial innovation of changing the debt capital to the equity capital, especially promote the securitization process of public utility projects, so as to solve the long-term capital financing problem for the provisions for the construction of urban infrastructure, medical care, education and other public services. It is also conducive to solving the maturity mismatching (short-term borrowing for long-term investment and short-term borrowings for long-term usage) in the balance sheet through the provision of stable and continuous middle and long-term capital.

It also shall attach importance to the development of bond market in order to achieve the goal of significantly enhancing the weight of direct financing. Currently, China's development of corporate bonds and other fixed-earnings products is still lagging behind, and cannot meet the different risk preference of investors and needs for conducting the effective portfolio. In the development of bond market, it shall also strive to reduce the unnecessary administrative control, further develop to the marketized registration system especially in the issuance of corporate bonds, and strengthen the regulation to the transaction segments of corporate bonds in the meantime.

4. Flexibility of exchange rate

China abandoned the 7 year exchange rate system of pegging to the US dollars, started to implement the managed floating exchange rate system on the basis of market demand and supply with the adjustment by referring to a basket of currencies, and officially launched the flexibility reform of the exchange rate mechanism of Renminbi in July, 2005. However, formation mechanism of exchange rate of Renminbi has not achieved the full marketization with the needs of export-oriented strategy, and the flexibility of exchange rate is still insufficient. It not only artificially expands the trade surplus, but also brings huge challenges to the macro-control. In particular, the misaligned exchange rate of Renminbi caused by stimulating exports is the direct reason for the excess liquidity, write-off pressure of central bank, constant inflow of hot money and "The Impossible Trinity".

China's international balance of payments has changed in recent 2 years, current account surplus has obviously dropped, the expectation of the Renminbi's exchange rate has been changed from unilateral appreciation to the two-way volatility and the expectation of the prices increasing of domestic assets has been weakened. All of these changes shall be taken as a chance to consolidate the pattern that the central bank basically exits the normal intervention to the foreign exchange market, deepen the marketization reform in the formation mechanism of exchange rate of Renminbi, further expand the floating range of exchange rate of Renminbi, enlarge the flexibility of exchange rate and make it the floating exchange rate which truly reflects the market changes.

5. Liberalization of capital account

China started to successively open the transactions of capital items and steadily promote the convertibility process of capital items after achieving the complete convertibility of Renminbi in the current account in 1996. In particular, China's reform in capital items has speeded up, the "two-way" inflow and outflow of capital has been further strengthened in recent years. However, overall speaking, China's degree of capital control is still relatively high, which still has relatively large distance from the opening of capital account. According to the previous evaluation of convertibility to 40 items in 7 major categories of capital items in China by the IMF, there are 4 inconvertible items, accounting for 10 %, mainly participation of non-residents in domestic monetary market and fund trust market as well as the derivative instruments of buying and selling; there are 22 partially convertible items, accounting for 55 %, mainly in the four general categories of bond market transactions, stock market transactions, real estate transactions and individual capital transactions; and there are 14 basic convertible items, mainly in the credit instrument transactions, direct investment and liquidation of direct investment, etc.

Therefore, it shall further promote the convertibility of capital items of Renminbi, promote the convenient trading and investment, create the favorable conditions for expanding the external investment of enterprises and individuals as well as defining the external investment subject position of enterprises and individuals, and meet the requirements of the strategy of "going out" as well as the acceleration of economic structure adjustment and industry transformation upgrading.

The next step is to promote the convertibility of capital items and raise the openness of external finance. Since the convertibility of Renminbi in the direct investment business, credit business and securities business is relatively high, mediate and low respectively from the perspective of current business distribution, the key point is to promote the opening of securities market, whose process should be orderly and controllable.

In this regard, it may firstly promote the external openness of bond market with relatively low risks. Continuously promoting the related overseas institutions to invest in the interbank market with Renminbi is an important measure to open the domestic bond market. It may broaden the channel for overseas investment of Renminbi to inflow to the domestic places, and provide the certain opportunity for maintaining and appreciation of the value of Renminbi obtained from abroad, and it is conducive to enhancing the wishes of overseas economic subjects to hold Renminbi. In the future, it may also take account of expanding the bonds issued by overseas institutions in China with the valuation in Renminbi, namely, the issuance scale of "panda bond", and relaxing the qualification restrictions on overseas institutions for the issuance of bonds in Renminbi. This is also an important measure for promoting the external opening of bond market of Renminbi.

On the basis of opening the bond market, it may also prudently promote the opening of stock market (even in the market of financial derivatives). In this regard, it may also develop the market of international board in addition to continuously promoting the system of Renminbi Qualified Foreign Institutional Investors (RQFII), i.e. to allow the qualified foreign enterprises to issue the shares in Renminbi in the domestic market. To attract the overseas investors to hold more Renminbi by providing them with more financial products valued in Renminbi. In addition, interconnecting mechanism of domestic and overseas stock markets shall be further expanded on the basis of the Shanghai—Hong Kong Stock Connect to make the domestic capital outflow through such legal and controllable channel and invest in the steady capital market with high earnings so as to open the new channel for the limited opening of capital items.

As the transitional arrangement before the complete opening of capital items, it may establish the offshore financial center of Renminbi with Hong Kong as the base to explore the liquidity and transaction mechanism of overseas capital in Renminbi and expand the overseas investment channels of Renminbi. In recent years, Hong Kong has vigorously promoted the development of bond market with valuation in Renminbi (offshore bond in Renminbi is also called as the dim sum bond). In the future, it may take advantage of the strengthen of Hong Kong international financial center to constantly expand the scale of financial assets with the valuation in Renminbi, promote the domestic financial institutions to issue the bonds in Renminbi in Hong Kong and other countries (regions) and provide the overseas investors who hold Renminbi with more Renminbi investment and hedging instruments, so as to enhance the attraction of Renminbi to the overseas investors and promote the cross-border use of Renminbi. Of course, promoting the development of international and offshore markets of Renminbi eventually also needs the more open capital account to promote the international investors to increase the use of Renminbi as the investment currency.

## 10.6 Reform of Land System

The crux of land problem lies in the artificial divided and solidified right to use. The same land enjoys different right. Under the current system, ownership and right to use of urban land belong to the state, ownership of land in the rural and suburban areas belongs to the collective, but collective contractual right of land belongs to the farmers, and the right to use of rural residence land and collective construction land respectively belongs to farmers and the collective enterprises. Government can nationalize the collective land through the levy, confiscation, requisition and expropriation. Meanwhile, government firmly controls the right of land to participate in the industrialization and commercialization in hand through the strict land use planning as well as the highly centralized administrative approval. In fact, farmers are completely isolated from the industrialization and commercialization process of land factor, but only own the contractual right of farmland and the right to circulate within the collective, namely, the so-called same land enjoying different right. Recently, Guangdong conducted the trial of internal township circulation of rural homestead, but it was only the internal circulation within the town and collective, the right of farmers to benefit from land is severely suppressed.

In fact, right of use farmland is the most core assets of farmers, but the existing land system greatly suppresses the farmers to enjoy the right to benefit from such asset; homestead and construction land cannot directly enter the market but only through the approach of expropriation by the government. However, farmers can only receive the extremely limited compensation and fail to benefit from the industrialization and commercialization of land factor after the expropriation by the government; land management right can only be circulated within the collective, which suppress the intensive and scale development of agriculture.

Therefore, it shall further deepen the reform in land system, give farmers more land property rights, safeguard the equal land rights of farmers and urban residents, fully protect the related land property rights of farmers and enable the farmers to achieve more property revenue in the earnings from land appreciation. On the one hand, it is to protect the rights and interests of farmers to use the farmland for the farming purpose, that is, to allow the farmers to adopt several forms to circulate the contractual right of land and achieve the corresponding revenue on the premise of stabilizing the long-term property right of farmers to the contracted land. On the other hand, it is to strengthen the protection of rights and interests of farms to use the farmland for the non-farming purposes. In particular, it shall allow the rural construction land for the collective operation to enter the market of construction land, and allow the farmers to participate in the development and operation in a variety of legal ways, thus benefiting from the land appreciation as well as sharing the achievements of industrialization and commercialization.

Specifically speaking, future direction of land reform mainly includes:

**Perfecting Delimitation of Land Property Right** Land right confirmation is almost the premise for all the other land reforms. The first is the clear subject of property right. Preventing the blurred land right of farmers shall be based on the land right confirmation to household of farmers to strengthen the protection to land rights and interests of farmers, especially the land rights and interests for non-farming purposes. It means not only to clearly delimitate the collective ownership of land, but also to clearly delimitate the right of farmers to use or operate all the rural farmland, mountain forest and construction land as well as the ownership of residence of farmers. It shall effectively confirm the land use right of farmers legally through the land registration (namely, cadastral registration) and issuance of the corresponding certificate of land right. The second is to give the full property right, that is, to give the full contractual right of land and full right to use the homestead, in particular, it shall allow the homestead of farmers to enter the land transaction market for the circulation. In the perfection of protection system of land property right, it shall further strengthen the subject position of farmers. In the land circulation and replacement process, it shall also adhere to the principle of "returning and giving the right, and independence of farmers", dilute the administrative color, respect the wishes of farmers and transform the system leaded by government to the system with the fully play of market roles.

**Reform in Land Expropriation System** Regulation by the state to land market has been transformed from the micro regulation to the macro regulation. Land supply, development and interest sharing are more determined by the market. The 18th National Congress of the CPC clearly proposed to reform the land expropriation system and enhance the distribution proportion of farmers in the revenue from land appreciation. The first is to reasonably define the standards for land expropriation compensation. The second is to encourage and promote the compensation and settlement mechanism for land expropriation through diversified ways, ensure the realization of development rights and interests of the ordinary people, and practically protect the persistent survival and development capabilities of farmers. The third is to establish the rational and orderly unified urban and rural land market. The fourth is to give fully play to the subject role of farmers whose land has been expropriated. The fifth is to make the procedures for land expropriation become open and transparent.

**Allowing Collective Construction Land to Enter Market Directly** It is the best breakthrough to change the issue of same land enjoying different right. *Decision* of the Third Plenary Session pointed out that rural collective operating construction land is allowed to enter the market if such land complies with the planning and purposes, and enjoys the equal right and price as the state-owned land. This will involve the significant legal revision. Article 10 under the exiting *Constitution* in China provides that urban land is owned by the state. Future urban land is not completely owned by the state and may be owned by the collective if the collective operating construction land can enter the market and such land is within the scope of urban planning. Therefore, the *Constitution* needs revising. Moreover, Articles 43 under the *Land Administration Law* provides that collective construction of farmers shall not sell or transfer the land to others for the non-farming construction purposes in any way. This article also needs revising since collective operating construction land can enterprise the market according to the spirit in the *Decision* by the Third Plenary Session. Therefore, central government specially emphasizes that the reform in land system affects the overall situation and must be conducted after the careful determination, and the pilot shall be very carefully, prudently and steadily promoted.

**Reform in Homestead System** Future direction of reform in the homestead of farmers shall be on the premise proposed by the related departments of ensuring the residence of farmer to give the farmers the more complete power related to the homestead, positively create the conditions to gradually incorporate such homestead into the unified urban and rural construction land market, prudently and steadily promote the exploration in the realization forms of power and functions of the usufructuary right of homestead and housing property right of farmers. At present, some regions have conducted the experiment of collateral, guarantee and transfer of housing property right of farmers. Under the existing national conditions, transfer of housing property right of farming shall have certain restrictions, some principles and measures proposed in the experiment can be further studies, such as sticking to the bottom line so as to ensure the residence of farmers; defining the scope of collateral circulation; preventing the moral hazards, and beneficiary of reform shall also bear the costs of reform.

**Promoting Orderly Circulation of Farmland** It is the basic requirements for the development scale agriculture and realization of agricultural modernization, and also the requirements for the changing trend in the structure of rural labor force. (1) Encouraging innovative forms of land circulation. (2) Strictly standardizing land circulation behavior. Contractual right of land belongs to the family of farmers, whether to circulate the land, how to determine the price and which form to choose shall be independently decided by the contracted household of farmers, and the revenue from circulation shall be owned by the contracted household of farmers. (3) Strengthening the land circulation management and services. (4) Rationally determining the scale of land operation. Local governments shall study and determine the appropriate standards for the scale operation of lance based on the natural economic conditions, rural transfer of labor force, level of agricultural mechanization and other factors so as to prevent the trends which are alienated from the reality, violate the wishes of farmers and simply pursue the oversized scale operation. (5) Supporting scale production of grain. (6) Strengthening control on purposes of land circulation. It is to strictly adhere to the protection system of farmland and effectively protect the basic farmland, and it is prohibited to carry out the non-farming construction in the name of land circulation. In a word, it is to further promote the separation of contracting and operation rights as well as to achieve the division of ownership, contracting right and operation right on the premise of sticking to the collective ownership of rural land, and provide space for the system innovation of land circulation through stabilizing the contracting right of household of farmers and releasing the operation right of land.

Land, as the production factor, surly flows with the flow of rural personnel. Letting the land factor flow will stimulate the vitality, but the flow shall be standardized and there shall be bottom line for such flow. Therefore, it needs to always take the maintenance, realization and development of rights and interests of farmers as the starting point and foothold to adhere to the three bottom lines, including that public ownership of land cannot be changed, red line of farmland cannot be broken and interests of farmers cannot be damaged, and orderly promote on the basis of the pilot.

## 10.7 Reform of Household Registration System

The Third Plenary Session of the 18th National Congress and working conference of central urbanization in 2013 pointed out to give consideration to the graduates from colleges and universities as well as vocational technical schools, inter-city and inter-town personnel with employment in other places, and agricultural population in the urban and suburban areas with migrated agricultural population as the focus, plan and promote the reform in household registration system and equalization of general public services. Therefore, the task of reform in household registration is to promote the permanent resident population that is capable of steadily taking up an occupation and living in the cities and towns to orderly achieve the citizenization, and the core is to enable the migrated agricultural population to enjoy the equal basic public services and welfare as the residents with household registration in cities and towns.

*State Council, Opinions on Further Promotion of the Reform of Household Registration System* officially issued on July 30, 2014 provided to further adjust the migration policy of household, unify the urban and rural household registration system, comprehensive implement the system of residence permit, accelerate the construction and sharing of basic information database of national population, and steadily promote the compulsory education, employment services, basic pension and medical care, housing security as well as other basic public services of cities and towns to achieve the full coverage of permanent resident population. By 2020, it is to basically establish and comprehensively complete the people-oriented, scientific and efficient, and orderly new system of household registration which is adaptable to the moderately prosperous society, effectively support the social management and public services, and safeguards the civil rights by laws, and strive to achieve the settlement of migrated agricultural population and other permanent resident population of about 100 million in the cities and towns.

Necessity and significance of reform in householder registration is: firstly, there is great gap between China's urbanization rate of resident population and urbanization level with householder registration in the local cities, such gap is caused by the floating population that permanently lives in the cities but does not have urban household registration. Purpose of reform in household registration is to strip the public services and welfare attached to the household registration, and enable the floating population to enjoy the basically same rights and treatment as the local residents in the employment, education, medical care, social security and other basic public services. Secondly, reform in household registration with the "citizenization" of migrated rural workers as the core can play the role of killing three birds with one stone: in the long run, it can enhance the potential growth rate of economic growth in China; improve the consumption elasticity of residents, especially the migrated agricultural population in the permanent resident population in cities; and ensure the long-term social stability, such role may be effective even within a short period of time. Thirdly, from the perspective of deepening reform, reform in the household registration is not only a significant issue of China in the future reform in the economic and social fields, but also the basis for a series of system reforms and innovation in the field of livelihood.

Smooth promotion of reform in household registration needs the coordinated matching and collaborated promotion of reforms in the related system. For example, effectively safeguarding the legitimate rights and interests of migrated rural population and other permanent resident population needs to quickly formulate the matching policies in education, employment, medical care, pension, housing security, rural property right, financial security and other aspects, improve the regulations and implement the fund guarantee.

Reform in household registration shall take the size of population, public resources, fiscal burden and other constraints into account to orderly achieve the citizenization, promoting the system of resident permit and differential regional policies is necessary. However, it must break the existing division of administrative areas, gradually and orderly promote the equalization of permanent resident population in cities and towns in the basic public services and welfare on the primary basis of the actual citizenized affordability in cities, follow the "synchronized nationwide promotion and consideration of regional differences" as well as basic reform ideas and program, and ensure the rational allocation of citizenization costs between the regions and cities.

Purpose of reform in household registration is to achieve the goal of "one household registration for one family" of permanent resident population in cities and towns under the conditions of the urbanization level reaching 70 %, and annual dynamic growth of 10 % in the basic public service and welfare per capita in 2030. Reform in household registration and promotion of urbanization with the orientation of equalize basic public services and welfare is feasible, and the key point of reform is the good cost allocation system. Central government shall assume larger responsibilities, nationwide overall promotion, breaking division of administrative areas and consideration of regional differences cannot simply take the urban size or directional areas as the standards for division.

## References

Corden WM (2007) Those current account imbalances: a skeptical view. World Econ 30:363–382
Huang Qunhui (2013) How to actively develop mixed-ownership economy in New Era. Administration Reform, Dec 2013
Ren Jin (2014) New level of reform in administrative approval system. Outlook Wkly 34

# Chapter 11
# Conclusion

Reforms are undergoing on the way. The conclusion here does not mean to draw a full stop to China's reform. On the contrary, China's reform under the new normal has just started. The central economic work conference at the end of 2014 clearly pointed out that understanding, adapting to and leading the new normal was the major logic of China's economic development at present and in the subsequent period. Reform is precisely the most powerful gripper to lead the new normal.

The so-called "new normal" means that in a relatively long period of time in the future, China's economic development will show the new characteristics significantly different from those in the past (especially the rapid growth over last more than 30 years). The new characteristics are mainly reflected in the following three aspects:

**The First Is the Deceleration and Gear Shifting of Economic Growth** China's economic growth rate has shown the overall continuous trend of slowdown since the global financial crisis, and the growth rate of annual GDP has obviously slowed down from the peak of 14.2 % in 2007 to 7.4 % in 2014. China's economy has changed from the double-digit high-speed growth to the middle and high-speed growth of about 7 %. It is closely related to the periodical changes in the supply pattern of factors. (1) Supply of labor factor. Over the last several years, momentum of continuous large-scale growth in absolute quantity of labor force has changed due to rapid transition in population. Firstly, since 2007, the quantity of newly increased working-age population sharply declined; in 2012, the inflection point appeared in the total working-age population and it was the first appearance of absolute drop. China's structural change in population has also made the trend of population dependency rate appear the reverse. Total dependency rate started to show the turning changes in 2011 and child dependency rate also initially showed the upward indication in 2012, meaning that the positive effect of "demographic dividend" on the growth would be gradually weakened until it disappeared. (2) Supply of capital factor. With the changes in population age structure, especially the worsened aging issue, the high-saving level also has shown the downward trend although



X. Zhang, X. Chang, *The Logic of Economic Reform in China*, China Insights,
DOI 10.1007/978-3-662-47404-4_11

the high-saving model will not greatly change in the short run. (3) Resource environmental constraints. In recent years, rapid growth in energy consumption and sharp increase in the strength of energy consumption have led to the gradually enlarged gap between the demand and supply of resources. Taking petroleum as the example, China became the country of net petroleum import in 1993. External dependence of petroleum has constantly increased over the years and reached 58.1 % in 2013. In the meantime, China's environmental pressure has gradually increased, the emissions of major pollutants have been in the relatively high level in recent years, and carbon dioxide emissions of unit GDP have been nearly twice of the average international level. Driving roles of productivity have not covered the position in a timely manner but even have been weakened in the meantime of the declined driving roles of factor investment due to the changes in productivity acceleration brought by the transformation from manufacturing industry to service industry as well as the reduced kinetic energy of technical progress by relying on the technical introduction and innovation imitation.

**The Second Is the Adjustment in Economic Structure and Transformation in Motivation for Economic Growth** From the appearance point of view, the new normal of China's economic development is the deceleration and gear shifting of economic growth. However, it is the process for the restructuring of economic structure and remodeling of growth motivation in nature. For the transformation of growth motivation at the demand level, it is mainly to solve the excess high-proportion of investment and low-proportion of consumption. The investment rate of more than 40 % starting from 2003 has continued for 11 years. Especially since the large expansion and investment plans in 2009, investment rate has been maintained at the high level of 47–49 % for 5 consecutive years. Compared with the international investment rate, China's investment rate is over 1 time higher than the global average level. This brings the trend of excess investment and results in the gradual deteriorating of investment efficiency. The estimates show that the value of gross fixed capital formation of current period/increased value of GDP increased obviously after the financial crisis from 2.77 in 2007 to 8.36 and 8.17 respectively in 2009 and 2012, and even reached the abnormal large level of 9.04 in 2013. It means that the high-growth investment is not sustainable. However, the final consumption rate, especially the consumption rate of residents, is still about 30 % lower than the world average level although such consumption rate has recovered in recent years. How to further expand the domestic consumption needs, and thereby achieving the stable and continuous motivation for the economic growth in the side of demand is still waiting for the interpreting. For the growth motivation transformation in the supply level, namely the input level of factors, it is to mainly solve the relatively low contribution of technical progress or total factor productivity (TFP) growth to the economic growth. Business accounting of the economic growth over the last more than 30 years shows that contributing share of increase in capital, labor and natural resources, including the environmental consumption and other factor input, to the economic growth is higher than the contributing share of technical progress with enhancement in total factor productivity as the representation to economic growth. The growth mode simply relying on the factor input faces the dual-restrictions on the short supply of factors and decreasing marginal return. Economic growth built on the basis of the intensive input of factors is normally hard to continue, but the interaction among factors or the enhancement in total factor productivity is the true source of the long-term economic growth. This needs to further give play to the role of technological innovation. The overall economy will be able to move to the production possibility frontier or the production possibility frontier will be promoted to move up through improving the old production way and introducing the new production way in the marginal progressive way.

**The Third Is the Exposure and Reduction of Economic Risks** With the downward economic growth in China, a variety of potential risks have gradually "come out in the wash" and become dominant, especially the arduous challenges for de-capacity, de- leveraging and de-bubbling in front of China's economy. (1) De-capacity. Utilization rate of industrial capacity has shown the downward trend since 2012, and capacity utilization rate of industrial enterprises was 78.2 % in the first quarter of 2013 which reached the lowest point since the fourth quarter of 2009, and such rate was still lower than the average level of 80.1 % over the period starting from establishment of utilization investigation of capacity in 2006 although it rose slightly again. International experience shows that the utilization rate of 81–82 % is the dividing line to measure the excess of industrial capacity (or manufacturing industry), and the rate of less than 75 % indicates the relatively serious excess of capacity. At present, industries with the excess capacity include the traditional industries such as steel, nonferrous metals, building materials, chemicals and shipbuilding, and also include the emerging strategic industries such as wind power, photovoltaic and carbon fiber. By the end of 2012, the capacity utilization rates of steel, cement, electrolytic aluminum, flat glass, shipbuilding and other industries were only 72 %, 73.7 %, 71.9 %, 73.1 % and 75 % respectively, obviously lower than the international common level. (2) De-leveraging. China's entire social leverage ratio has shown the relatively obvious upward trend since the financial crisis. The weights of total assets of all the departments (residents, non-financial enterprises, government and financial institutions) in GDP increased from 170 % in 2008 to 232 % in 2013, which means the high leverage rate in the entire society and the inevitable de-leveraging, especially from the perspectives of local government and non-financial enterprises. (3) De-bubbling. "De-bubbling" and "de-leveraging" may form the resonance since there is certain interaction between the prices of real estate and social leverage rate under the pattern of indirect financing as well as the financing model with land and real estate as the major collaterals. In other words, real estate market will have adjustment and value of collaterals will accordingly shrunk once the "de-bubbling" starts, forming impacts on the balance sheet of enterprises, so that debt defaults are likely to appear and banking departments will be subject to relative large losses. It is noteworthy that real estate enterprises are the major borrowing objects of the large number of emerging shadow banks. Trust loans and financial products of non- standard credit assets may usually take the real estate or land as collaterals. Shrinkages in the value of collaterals will lead to the increasing loss ratio of loan institutions (shadow banks) if the debtors default. In addition, local governmental debts are highly related to the real estate industry, and dependence of debt repayment on revenue of land transfer is accordingly very large under the circumstances of the limited cash flow of the loan project. For the local government which severely depends on the revenue from land transfer, the effect of land finance may be weakened with the adjustment in the real estate market, indicating the upward debt repayment pressure of the local government.

The central economic work conference at the end of 2014 further summarized the characteristics of the new normal of China's economy from the following nine aspects: consumption demand, investment demand, export and international payments, production capacity and industrial organization form, relative advantages of production factors, market competition characteristics, resource and environmental constraints, accumulation and reduction of economic risks, resource allocation models and macro-control ways.

In the face of the aforementioned "new normal", how to adapt to it and lead it basically lies in the further deepening of reform in economic system. The new normal will become the low-speed and low-efficiency economic growth if the reform cannot be continuously conducted to provide the new motivation for the economic growth; all the issues will "come out in the wash" at that time and the severe challenges in front of the economic society will be conceivable. Therefore, reform is extremely urgent. The major logic of reform is to follow the major logic of economic development, and the new economic normal sets the basic context of the reform in the next step. Meanwhile, slowdown in economic growth is not the whole new normal, and the new normal also means the revolutionary change of economy towards that with higher form, more complicated division of labor and more rational structure through the stages of evolution. However, such changes may be only achieved through the leading by comprehensively deepening the reform. In other words, only reform may enable us to achieve the glorious vision with the new platform, new mechanism and new realm from the "new normal".

MIX
Papier aus verantwortungsvollen Quellen
Paper from responsible sources
FSC® C105338

If you have any concerns about our products,
you can contact us on
**ProductSafety@springernature.com**

In case Publisher is established outside the EU,
the EU authorized representative is:
**Springer Nature Customer Service Center GmbH**
**Europaplatz 3, 69115 Heidelberg, Germany**

Printed by Libri Plureos GmbH
in Hamburg, Germany